Excellent Organizations

How to Develop & Manage Them Using Theory Z

James Lewis, Jr.

J.L. Wilkerson Publishing Company

New York

Copyright© 1985 by James Lewis, Jr.
All Rights Reserved
Including the right of reproduction in
whole or in part in any form·
Published by
J.L. Wilkerson Publishing Company
New York

Library of Congress Catalog Card No. 83-51208
Lewis, James, Jr.
Excellent Organizations - How To
Develop & Manage Them Using Theory Z
Includes Index

HD
ISBN 0-915253-00-3
Manufactured in The United States of America

To all those human beings who may
have suffered under my leadership.

Contents

Illustrations

Preface

THIS BOOK IS a practical guide to the philosophies and strategies associated with Theory Z organizations; as a consequence the text is focused on institutions that have adopted the principles of Theory Z management with studied deliberation. Some enlightened organizations—presently and historically—have used Theory Z techniques without being aware they were doing so and, in some cases, before Theory Z was formulated. These institutions will be discussed: they certainly deserve the designation of excellent organizations.

In reality, Theory Z is an extention of Theory Y, even though Ouchi may not have intended it to be so. For example, in Theory Y, management is responsible for organizing components of the organization in the interest of economic needs. Theory Z has enlarged these needs to include social needs. The Theory Z organizations of today understand that high quality and productivity can be realized only if they are concerned with and attentive to the whole person and help to fulfill both physiological and psychological needs. In Theory Y a major responsibility of management is creating the opportunity for employees to assume responsibility for achieving organizational goals. Theory Z has expanded the concept of building people to a process in which employees are constantly provided with knowledge, training, and opportunities for growth and development on the job so they may assume the responsibility for achieving organizational goals and do so in a highly competent manner. Finally, in Theory Y, management's chief responsibility is seen to be establishing organizational conditions so that employees can achieve their personal goals while in pursuit of organizational goals; Theory Z extends the effective fulfillment of this responsibility by the various methods and techniques used by management to create a support system composed of caring, trust, and intimacy which are vital to the achievement of both personal and organizational goals.

My major purpose is to provide workable commentary on Theory Z, setting forth the necessary information and procedures to construct a philosophy or guidance system that will govern all the human efforts of an organization.

I cover the nominal group planning process and the program planning processes in ways which will involve a maximum number of the members of the organization (including management and labor) when the guidance system is formulated.

Theory Z management philosophy is readily associated with Japanese organizations; American management specialists have had sufficient time to study the process, implement it in this country, and make a number of positive, productive inferences from their scrutiny. As jury after jury, here and abroad, comes in with new, supportive verdicts on Theory Z, a significant literature has emerged, most of which is theoretical.

I have commented on the better available literature, linking it with my own managerial experience to provide a step-by-step technique for any organization that wishes to transform its management style into the Theory Z philosophy.

Many Americans relate Theory Z strictly to the Japanese, and regard it as warily as they do a new sushi restaurant in the neighborhood, worried, I suspect, that they are suddenly going to find in it the managerial equivalent of raw fish or sea urchin eggs. But Theory Z is neither alien nor incompatible with America, and as you read these words, Theory Z is already as much American as it is Japanese.

A unique feature of this book is the numerous items I cite throughout to illustrate how American organization and managers have successfully implemented various features of Theory Z principles and practices not labeled as such.

William Ouchi, the originator of Theory Z, has demonstrated

at some length in *Theory Z: How American Business Can Meet the Japanese Challenge* that many of the excellent organizations in America use the principles and practices related to Theory Z.

My examination of Theory Z research focuses on the similarities between excellent organizations in America and Japan; I use these commonalities to define some basic assumptions about excellent organizations:

1. Success of an organization is predicated on its people, the manner in which they are treated, and the way they respond to that treatment.

2. Organization charts and job descriptions, the security blankets of many large, foundering companies, may be entirely removed, provided there is more interaction among the employees and they assume more of the responsibilities of running the organization.

3. If today's managers expect to be successful, they must be caring, trusting, and supportive of the institution.

4. An organization pursuing excellence must keep in its aggregate mind the seven Ss: Staff, Skills, Style, and Superordinate goals, all blended with Structure, Systems, and Strategy.

5. In most instances, the best decisions are those decided by consensus.

6. The key to results is teamwork.

7. Employees will improve their performance if managers lessen control over them (by relaxing protocol, deemphasizing time management, instituting an open-door policy, and using employees' mistakes as opportunities for training and developing).

8. Job rotation is an excellent method for upgrading the training and development of employees and for transferring knowledge and skills across the organization.

9. When an employee's performance is below par, one or more managers are usually at fault.

The chief executive officer (CEO) must become the prime mover to pursue organizational excellence. The CEO and top-level managers, working as a team, must become the microfacilitators to effect improvement; they must have a good understanding of the research related to Theory Z and excellent organizations; they must be trained to work effectively as a team by reviewing critically each aspect of the organization and their own management style, then reach a consensus on what must be done to achieve or maintain organizational excellence. The CEO is responsible for initiating training activities and meetings the functions of which are to strengthen the roles of middle managers and supervisors as microfacilitators: a pursuit of excellence in Theory Z must be planned—it cannot be stumbled upon—and it must involve all members of the organization.

The pursuit of excellence must be seen as a training and development process which will bring about changes in behavior and attitudes. To many Old Guard managers and Traditionalists, there is something inherently sinister about the concepts of behavior modification and attitude change; visions of Skinnerian training, mindless obedience, and repressive techniques are frequently mentioned by those who are unwilling to give up their preconceived notions. But note well, the excellence sought by Theory Z in general and the following pages of this book in specific is not mindless or in the slightest bit repressive: it is open, nourishing, and evocative of the best everyone can give.

HOW TO USE THIS BOOK

Read the entire text once to get the flavor. Make special note of the bibliography; read at length from all books and journal articles that evoke a particular interest, then prepare for discussions and Theory Z meetings by reading from the appropriate works cited. (Prior to preparing statements of philosophy, for instance, read *Corporate Cultures: The Rites and Rituals of Corporate Life* by Deal and Kennedy.)

Supplement reading knowledge by attending appropriate conferences and seminars, by visiting excellent organizations, by inviting consultants in to present facets of the Theory Z concept, and by meeting regularly to discuss the literature.

Begin to lay plans for pursuing organizational excellence. Management can start from scratch: begin rebuilding the organization with the preparation of statements of philosophy, implement practices associated with excellence, then evaluate how well these vital pieces were put together. Management can also conduct a critical analysis of the organization: determine its strengths and weaknesses for the purpose of enhancing the former and removing the latter. Add to the organization all the principles and practices that emerge as desirable. Listen to what the employees have to say. Don't be contented with partial success.

Acknowledgments

I AM INDEBTED to M. Scott Meyers, author of *Every Employee a Manager*, who was a visiting professor at MIT when I was a fellow at Harvard University. He influenced my thoughts and ideas in the field of management more than anyone else, which helped me to arrive at this point in my life.

Introduction

Moving Towards Organizational Excellence

AN EXCELLENT ORGANIZATION is characterized by four distinct features:[1]

unity of purpose brought on as a result of the statements of philosophy derived from members of the organization which are inculcated through interaction, indoctrination, training, and style of management;

responsive components which are brought on in terms of the humanistic and egalitarian manner in which managers and employees related to each;

it reacts to the environment using the knowledge and skills learned through the varied practices of the organization;

it interrelates on an individual, team, and organizational level because of problem-solving opportunities, an open system, teamwork, free exchange of information, training and development activities, job rotation, and other related practices.

The Theory Z concept contains all the principles and practices to help organizations pursue a course towards organizational excellence.

Integrated Whole

The first characteristic of an excellent organization is unity of purpose, provided through a strong culture.

We define culture as integrated human behavior that includes thought, speech, action, and artifacts; it involves human beings' capacity for learning and transmitting knowledge to succeeding generations

purpose, identity, and a personality: employees know how things

1

are customarily done. Every organization has a culture; some are strong, and some are weak. In not-so-excellent organizations, things are done in fragmented and often confused manners; employees are loyal to different forces, communication is either stifled or not shared; the personal goals of employees are quite often aimed at "getting to" management, and exacting revenge from it for real or imaginary offenses.

In the not-so-excellent organizations, statements of philosophy exist in theory only; they may or may not be in written form. Management may go through the action of preparing such an important document, but it is *not* actualized because the employees have not been informed of it, or have not discussed and digested its contents. It is also a dead or unrealized document because it is not being practiced by management. Employees are not only unaware how things are done, they don't know what they can expect from management. In essence, the theoretical philosophy perpetuates anything but excellence in an organization.

In excellent organizations, there seems to be an integrated whole; every employee is dancing to the same beat of the drummer, every employee is in harmony with the music of the organization, every employee is being orchestrated by a sensitive manager who is aware of the needs of the members of his or her organization. Because of employee and management efforts to produce an integrated whole, each person knows what can be expected from the other and the organization. Unity of purpose—the very essence of excellent organizations—nurtures self-awareness among employees and other components of the organization. Unity of purpose helps excellent organizations become more today than what they were yesterday. Unity of purpose helps employees focus their energies on defining and fulfilling the purposes, mission, and objectives of the organization, rather than on power issues. As a result, the purpose of these organizations is more adequately distributed through information sharing, consensus decision-making, and problem-solving. Managers are able to build credibility through their ability to use the collective perspective of the organization to manage more humanly, to solve and let problems be solved, to find new ways to improve conditions for employees, and to foster within the work environment a people-building philosophy that improves unity of efforts of everyone within the organization.

Some employees have in excellent organizations been involved in the formulation of the philosophy from the onset; all employees are indoctrinated, sometimes through a strong orientation program and, at other times, through a comprehensive training program for each critical aspect of the philosophy. As a result, shared values are implemented, expectations of behavior are defined, prescribed procedures are illuminated, and the treatment of employees is prescribed for management. In the excellent organization the philosophy is alive and striving, it's preached and practiced every-day by all employees, it serves as a living document which is the basis for the organization to become self-actualized, always in the pursuit of gaining great excellence in achieving its objectives.

Responsive Components

The second characteristic of an excellent organization is its respon-sive components. In not-so-excellent organizations, managers manage through authority. Their performance is reflected in a "superordinate-subordinate" relationship with their employees: they demand actions from their employees without considering them as equal human beings, highlight status differences through the R.H.I.P. policy in which rank has its privilege, prefer to send me-mos rather than to personally confer with employees, complain that they don't have enough time in the day to deal with "human matters," so they will institute time management as a way out; they don't have confidence and respect for their employees. As a result of their misconception about human beings, they run a "tight ship" and give employees very little freedom to perform on the job. Individual components that are managed by this kind of manager are not really responsive to the objectives and goals of the organization. A manager who does not foster a responsive en-vironment is actually bent on restricting employees from acting in a responsive mode for realizing the purposes of the organization.

In excellent organizations, all components or systems respond to each other; the egalitarianism of the managers helps bring this about. Information is freely exchanged. Because managers care, trust, and are intimate with their employees, each is more at ease in performing, enjoys the work, and will most likely produce more. In an excellent organization authority is respected but collabora-tion is one of the major ingredients for success: individuals confer between and among each other, teams relate to and compete with other teams in fulfilling the purposes, mission, and objectives of the organization; managers and employees are engaged in a system where sometimes employees meet with other employees and, at other times, with managers, to solve not only unit, but complex organizational problems. A responsible manager will respond to both employees and the situation by switching from one leadership style to another in order to get maximum results, always respecting the individuality of human beings.

React to the Environment
The third characteristic of an excellent organization is its ability to react to the work environment. In the not-so-excellent organization, management tends to be secure with the external environment. They tend not to recognize that changing times bring on changing conditions and, unless they maintain some sort of reality-orientation, they will continue to remain less than excellent. Organizations that are not responsive to the environment tend to be more reactive than proactive. Consequently, time controls the organization rather than the reverse. Not-so-excellent organizations quite often become mired because their managers fail to realize and respond to the single most important influence in shaping an organization: how it reacts to the ever-changing external environment. History of management studies are replete with examples of once thriving organizations that failed because of their microscopic perception of the external environment

In the excellent organizations, managers are acute to the environment. Individuals, teams, and the organization continuously interchange ideas, programs, activities, information, and energies with other components of the environment in which they serve and depend on. This massive interchange system is a continuous process for planned transactions; through this process, the organization indicates its purposes, mission, and objectives to stakeholders and in turn gathers critical information that may have an important impact on decisions, objectives, and plans. Excellent organizations are strong in reacting to the environment because they prepare for change; they maintain skills and processes to decipher data, to formulate the information into objectives and plans, and preserve unity of purpose while reacting to the environment. As a result, they avoid crisis management.

Interrelating Characteristics by Levels

The fourth characteristic of an excellent organization is the inter-relationship of unity of purpose, responsive components, and reacting to the environment. In the not-so-excellent organization, systems or component interrelationship tends to be a serious problem when individuals do not share information with their peers, teams, or management; teams, if they exist at all, are not together and collaborating with either individuals or management; and the organization lacks articulation, coordination, and cooperation because the components lack interrelationship.

Interrelationship is achieved on an individual level when individual employees like and are aware of themselves as individuals, and appreciate who they are; employees become aware of their basic needs and desires and are able to fulfill them on the job. It occurs because employees are free and willing to interact with other employees by seriously listening, stroking, caring, trusting, being intimate, and sharing goals.

When interrelationship exists on a team level, it is usually because individuals unite in team effort, and become dedicated to meeting the goals as a team. Team members are usually aware of and appreciate each other, and each team is usually interacting with other teams within the organization, sharing common concerns and problems in an effort to realize the mission of the organization.

When such interrelationship is achieved on an organizational level, it is usually because employees and teams are gathering data and interchanging information from inside and outside the organization to solve unit and organizational problems; it is usually because the entire organization is keenly aware of the purposes of the organization; and it is because the organization scans the external environment to determine how it should relate to changing times and conditions.

Action Steps for Pursuing Organizational Excellence

This book provides a how-to-do-it approach for managers and employees (and sometimes other stakeholders) of an organization who wish to reach a level of performance identified as excellent. Here is a summary of these steps:

1.   Use Theory Z as the Basic Philosophy of Management.

Theory Z has evolved as an important concept in management because its elements were present in excellent organizations in both America and Japan. While not a panacea, it is an appropriate management style for developing full commitment to and participation of employees in the various operations of an organization. Section One shows how managers can improve their skills when managing employees. By improving skills, style will also be positively affected.

In addition, this book describes many of the essential aspects of Theory Z that can be used for planning change, training employees, establishing statements of philosophy for governing human behavior, and instituting practices that will provide the fuel for organizations to move towards excellence.

2.   Train Managers to Strengthen Humanistic Competencies.

It can no longer be taken for granted that managers care for, trust, and are intimate with their employees. Managers must be taken from ground zero and provided with the knowledge and practical training to use those humanistic competencies that will help strengthen organizational performance. Section One deals with these competencies. The emphasis for this training is to build an organization in which a "family feeling" is apparent, where employees enjoy working with their peers and managers, where managers are proud of the job they are doing, where an atmosphere of loyalty, caring, respect, and friendship, exudes throughout the organization.

3.   Examine the Statements of Philosophy.

All the components of sound statements of philosophy are discussed in Section Two. Critically review the present statement; compare it with what is desired, then read this section. Rewrite where necessary. Establish an appropriate committee, choose one of the techniques recommended by the author, provide for adequate interaction among committee members before finalizing the statement, and only then do so by consensus. Put vitality in the statements of philosophy by sharing the contents with all employees. Discuss each element at great length. Build a strong program to indoctrinate new employees with each essential aspect of the philosophy and make sure the concepts are clear to all stakeholders throughout the life of the organization.

4. Conduct a Critical Analysis of the Organization.

Initiate a critical analysis, self-profile, or an organizational audit to focus on where changes or improvements should occur. In this way, there will be no need to effect changes where they are not needed. Several techniques are suggested in this book to assist in this analysis.

5. Use Existing Organizational Structure for Change.

When organizations find themselves experiencing difficulties, they often rely heavily–too heavily–on a new organizational chart prepared by management, or the CEO. New job descriptions and procedures for communicating with managers are the result of response to crisis. If a critical analysis reveals that the organization should be changed, then by all means, change it, but first speak to the employees, guarantee them that their jobs are secure, and use a major Theory Z tenet: maximize the number of employees involved in the process.

6. Emphasize Training.

Organizational excellence cannot evolve unless more emphasis is given to training. Theory Z is a people-oriented and people-building approach to effective management; employees must be continuously trained and rotated to varied jobs and functions to combat obsolescence. An adequate budget for training will equal from one to ten percent of the gross income. An adequate training and development program should encompass from 90 to 180 hours yearly depending on the position and function. This figure includes not only in-house training, but also seminars, conferences, and workshops held outside the organization.

7. Implement Consensus Decision Making.

Many excellent organizations have instituted consensus management in an effort to gain improved commitment to decisions. The chapter included in Section Three of this book shows how to train employees and managers in consensus decision-making.

8. Train Teams to Solve Job-Related Problems.

In excellent organizations, teams are the key element for getting things done. Many organizations train individual employees to join teams and solve specific unit problems. A structured process to accomplish is the quality circle, either the pure Japanese model or a modified version. Quality circles are also effective means for solving complex organizational problems.

9. Seek Theory Z Practices That Can Help Improve Conditions For Employees.

Section Three contains a number of Theory Z practices, such as lifetime employment, career path program, performance evaluation and promotion, changes, and team building. Managers attempting to improve conditions for employees should carefully examine each of the practices contained in this section, review its organizational properties statement, and select the practices they can live with.

10. Institute Inspirational Activities.

Consider the varied kinds of hoopla activities mentioned in Section Three of this book. Decide which should be incorporated to demonstrate appreciation for improved employee performance. Recognize and reward employees who help the organization to pursue organizational excellence.

Section One

The Humanistic Competencies of Theory Z

MANAGERS OF EXCELLENT organizations are first and foremost builders of people. They possess certain human competencies that enable them to be admired and respected by their employees. Human competencies tend to be interrelated; one cannot be adequately acquired unless efforts are made to become proficient in another. It is almost impossible for a manager to gain the employee's trust unless he or she nurtures an intimate relationship with them. It is almost impossible for a manager to gain the trust of employees unless a caring relationship is established. It is equally difficult to establish a caring relationship with employees unless some of the decisions involving them show consideration, subtlety, and trust.

1

The Developmental Stages of the Humanistic Competencies

THE MANAGERS OF all organizations interested in implementing Theory Z will go through several stages of development before they have acquired the proper behavioral attitudes to adopt the program. Some managers will proceed through these stages rapidly; others will never reach all stages.

The extent to which Theory Z is fully implemented in an organization is predicated on the flexibility of the managers and the degree to which a comprehensive training program is planned, developed, and established.

Perhaps the most difficult aspect of the Theory Z philosophy is the acceptance associated with the humanistic competencies. The old adage that familiarity breeds contempt is heard—and feared to be true—often in American business philosophies. As a consequence, managers are reluctant to become friendly with employees.

It is difficult to establish a caring relationship in the work environment if there is little or no trust between employees and managers, and between employees and employees. It is also difficult to think intuitively unless managers have extablished an intimate relationship with employees over a protracted time. Many managers will find it difficult to implement all the practices covered in the next four chapters, and, no doubt, some managers will find it extremely painful to engage even half of my recommendations. When I speak of humanistic competencies inherent in Theory Z management, I mean programs, processes, systems, thoughts and actions which have their basis on the nature, dignity, interests, welfare, and ideals of the human beings in the work force.

The main deterrent to accepting the humanistic competencies of Theory Z will be the established beliefs and values that our capitalistic system has nurtured in American managers, beginning in the school systems and supported in the homes and society. The best place to begin is with the developmental growth associated with acquiring these competencies which are building blocks of Theory Z.

DEFINING HUMANISTIC COMPETENCIES OF THEORY Z

Humanistic competencies are behavior and attitudinal skills that relate to the positive feelings of human beings. In Theory Z, they relate to skills that managers must acquire in order to pursue excellence: the broad human traits of caring, trust, intimacy, and intuition.

William Ouchi identified the humanistic competencies of trust, intimacy, and subtlety as strong elements of quality and productivity.[1] He assumes caring is a concomitant. Most Americans, in and off the job, take caring for granted. As a result, most human beings do not practice good caring relationships. In fact, one of the reasons why there is such teamwork, love, and concern for people in Japan, is because the children are taught at an early age in school two important doctrines: 1) to have respect for work; and 2) to get along well with their fellow persons (to care).

DEVELOPMENTAL STAGES OF THE HUMANISTIC COMPETENCIES OF THEORY Z

Attitudinal skills that relate to the humanistic competencies of Theory Z, and the concept as a whole, are connecting, responding, personalizing, and initiating. Each one is explained below using behavioral change activities and resultant attitudinal change expectations.

Level 1–Connecting

At this level, the need is to give managers a variety of opportunities to become linked to and sensitive to Theory Z philosophy and practices.

BEHAVIORAL CHANGE ACTIVITIES

To begin behavioral change, expose managers to a variety of "connecting" activities:

A. **Readings**–There are a number of books and articles on Theory Z excellent organizations and Japanese management. Use them as the basis of a resource center somewhere in an organization. Keep current. The bibliography at the end of this book will be helpful. Require all managers to read selectively. Someone should be designated to conduct a discussion on each of the articles. After a number of articles have been read and discussed, the books on American and Japanese management, cited in the bibliography, should be read and discussed by all managers.

B. **Conduct Awareness Sessions**–Invite experts in to discuss Theory Z in specific terms, provide opportunity for managers to attend outside awareness sessions. All such activities should be followed up with a presentation and discussion with all managers.

C. **Visit Excellent and Theory Z Organizations**–Find opportunities for small groups of managers to spend a short period in excellent and Theory Z organizations and to report the substance of their experience with other managers. Maintain a journal describing the experiences of each group.

D. **Conduct Periodic Discussion Sessions**–Either on a monthly or bi-monthly basis, top management should meet with all managers and discuss the merits of Theory Z. Use appropriate films, slide presentation, or actual data.

ATTITUDINAL CHANGE EXPECTATIONS

Any attitudinal changes during this stage will take place on two sub-levels:

1. Awareness

Managers will become conscious of Theory Z principles and practices; they will begin to recognize characteristics of Japanese management and begin to contrast it with American management.

Awareness indications on this connecting level:

(a) Develop an awareness of the Theory Z concept
(b) Begin to differentiate between Theory Z and other philosophies
(c) Recognize that there may be a better way for managing employees

2. Receptive

Some, maybe all, managers will begin to take serious notice of Theory Z, give it more attention by reading appropriate books or articles on their own volition, discussing it with other managers and, perhaps, with some employees. Receptive indicators on this connecting level are:

    (a) Listens to Theory Z experts with respect

    (b) Accepts differences among various ways of managing employees

3. Attending

This is the highest level of connecting: attending means making physical or psychological contact. Managers not familiar with the Theory Z philosophy will "experience" the process without tension or assessment, while those who are already familiar with the philosophy may or may not experience some tension, because of the presence or absence of conflict with their values and beliefs. Training emphasis is on gaining a keener awareness of what has already been learned about Theory Z.

Attending indicators on this connecting level are as follows:

    (a) Listens carefully to others when they speak about the advantages and disadvantages of Theory Z

    (b) Alertness as to variation in growth toward practicing Theory Z management style

Level 2–Responding

At this level, managers are motivated to the point of gaining more information and insight into the Theory Z philosophy. Responding usually takes place on three levels: complying, willingness, and satisfaction.

BEHAVIORAL CHANGE ACTIVITIES

Provide managers with activities that will enable them to explore and expand their knowledge about Theory Z.

A. Conference–Conduct a conference for managers to more formally introduce them to Theory Z. The chief executive officer makes some introductory remarks about the merits of Theory Z and describes his or her expectations. An expert, such as William Ouchi, speaks to the group of managers about the philosophy underlining Theory Z. At the conference, a number of seminars are offered whereby managers are provided with multiple opportunities to become more familiar with the concept.

B. Seminars–Seminars are awareness sessions, designed to whet the knowledge appetite of managers. They are intended to act as a springboard to get managers to explore the concept in more depth.

ATTITUDINAL CHANGE EXPECTATION

Response usually takes place on three sub-levels:

Complying–managers receive the Theory Z concept, but have not fully accepted the requirements for doing so. In an absence of pressure to respond to the concept, managers may opt to settle for another alternative. Depending on how the concept was introduced to them, they will either respond to it in a congenial manner and give it some time to "thaw out," or begin to internalize some tension and resistance.

Complying indicators on this responding level are:

    (a) Read appropriate articles on Theory Z
    (b) Willingness to attend brief training sessions
    (c) Willingness to participate with other managers on various Theory Z activities

Willingness–At this elevated level, managers are willing to cooperate and read more information about the Theory Z philosophy on their own initiative.

Willingness indicators on this responding level are:

    (a) Voluntarily looks for article and books on Theory Z or excellent organizations
    (b) Engages in conversations about Theory Z philosophy with employees and managers
    (c) Asks for pertinent information about Theory Z requirements at meetings and other events
    (d) Responds with consistent interest to matters pertaining to Theory Z

Satisfaction–At this high level, managers get favorable emotional response from the acquisition of more knowledge about Theory Z. Generally the emotional response is one of satisfaction, pleasure, or zest.

Satisfaction indicators on this responding level are:

    (1) Finds enjoyment in reading about Theory Z
    (b) Responds emotionally to situations that prove the merits of Theory Z
    (c) Takes pleasure in relating the Theory Z concept
    (d) Enjoys going to Theory Z events

Level 3–Personalizing

Managers will begin to demonstrate through actions, words, and deeds an acceptance of the philosophy behind Theory Z, a preference for its practices, and a strong commitment to become a Theory Z manager.

BEHAVIORAL CHANGE ACTIVITIES

Introduce a formal training and development program to all managers; fortify them with the appropriate behavior and attitudes to implement Theory Z. The program should consist of a variety of activities providing much more in-depth knowledge such as:

A. Theory Z Workshop—Incorporate a variety of training activities such as lectures, role playing, slides and filmstrips. Assign homework.

B. Lecture—the presentation of course of instruction by an expert. Usually, managers do not interrupt the instructor, but take notes during presentation. Questions and answers are reserved for the end of the lecture. In a workshop, however, lecture is usually interrupted whenever a manager has a question. This question is used as a springboard to guide more interaction until the point has been fairly well covered.

C. Homework is sometimes presented to managers in order to determine how well they grasped the previous instructions and/or to prepare for subsequent formal instruction. Sometimes, periodic tests are given to managers to determine whether or not all the subject matter has been adequately mastered. If not, the expert will review the materials or cover it in a different mode.

D. Slides, filmstrips, and films are usually used during a workshop to introduce new materials to managers or to summarize what has been covered. Almost any quality training magazine contains listings of organizations that produce visual aids that cover some of the humanistic competencies of Theory Z. It may also be necessary for the organization to produce their own. There are as yet no visual aids that cover all of the particulars of Theory Z. Therefore, if this is a problem, it may have to be solved several weeks in advance of the formal training program.

E. Role playing is an excellent way to introduce the humanistic competencies to the managers. To make this teaching mode more realistic, use employees. A manager can be given the role of demonstrating a caring relationship with an employee, or showing how he or she would display trust among a group of employees. Role playing helps to provide variety in the instructional process and makes learning more fun and enjoyable.

F. Experiential learning should be part of every Theory Z workshop. Place managers in real on-the-job situations. Prior to the learning situation, the managers are given the rationale for the training, the learning objectives, the process, and other relevant information. A time is usually designated. After the learning period is over, each manager returns to the workshop and makes a presentation concerning the learning experience. After the presentation, other managers have an opportunity to query the presenter. The expert will usually add to the learning process by asking questions, searching for more options, and sharing more knowledge with managers. Experiential learning can be applied in teaching managers how to make decisions, thinking intuitively, discussing how the decisions were made, what was the consequences, etc. This learning process should be reserved until the latter stage of this developmental level so that managers have some knowledge and background to call upon in the real on-the-job situation.

G. Behavior modeling is also an excellent teaching tool that can be used in the workshop. It is based on the theory that a manager can adequately acquire the desired behavior by observing and emulating an expert, who describes and demonstrates exemplary behavior. The manager then emulates the behavior with the employees; sometimes, the behavior of the manager is video taped and used for discussion purposes. Feedback is important; unless managers are shown good behavior techniques in a given situation, they may exacerbate existing difficulties.

ATTITUDINAL CHANGE EXPECTATIONS
There are three developmental stages to this level:
    Valuing—at this lowest level of personalizing, managers will be seen to have emotionally accepted the Theory Z concept. A distinguishing characteristic of this developmental level is consistency. Employees and managers will see that the beliefs, attitudes, and actions of these managers will consistently reflect a concern for employees and need to involve them in the decision-making process.

Preference—at the next level of personalizing, managers will value Theory Z beyond the point of being associated with it, and will live its principles and practices.

Commitment—at the highest level of personalizing, managers will become involved in a number of Theory Z activities in order to expand their growth and development. They will "preach" the theory sermon whenever they have social contacts, and will seek new "converts" to the Theory Z philosophy.

BEHAVIORIAL CHANGE ACTIVITIES

Provide comprehensive, on-the-job, and/or outer-job learning activities for managers as a final stage of training before implementing Theory Z throughout the organization. After an organization has adopted Theory Z, training should become a continuous cycle, as indicated in Chapter 11.

A. International learning trips

Some organizations have sent cadres of managers and employees to Japan for several weeks to experience a Theory Z organization at first hand. Most managers and employees who were able to learn abroad found the experience informative and worthwhile. This training and development activity can be prohibitively expensive if large numbers are sent at one time. The technique is best used on high-echelon management such as prospective CEOs, operations managers, or department heads.

B. National learning trip

If cost is a problem, locate already established Theory Z organizations in the United States. Unless a parent organization has already implemented Theory Z, it may be difficult to get volunteer organizations to provide the training. Some organizations in the U.S. that have implemented various aspects of the Theory Z philosophy and practices, either prior to or after the advent of the Theory Z concept are: Proctor and Gamble, Delta Airlines, Hitachi, Hewlett-Packard, Digital Equipment Corp., Honda, Nissan, IBM, and the Tandy Corp.

C. In-house consultants

An excellent training activity used by many American organizations in the early 1980s involved sending a cadre of managers and employees to Japan to receive training in Theory Z and other successful managing practices. Once trained, the cadre becomes in-house trainers for implementing Theory Z and other related activities within the organization.

D. In-house, in-depth training

Hire a professional consulting firm to devise a comprehensive training program for implementing Theory Z. This plan should cover several weeks of training, on-the-job supervision, periodic assessment and improvement sessions, and an audit of the entire program. Hire professional Theory Z consultants not associated with the original consulting firm to provide different insights into how the program is being implemented.

Level 4–Initiating

At this high level of internalization, managers will consistently apply the Theory Z philosophy. At the lowest level of initiating, the quality of conceptualization is being improved. At the next sub-level, managers' unique personal characteristics will be those covered under the principles of Theory Z. And, finally, at the next sub-level of development, managers will establish Theory Z as a total philosophy to be practiced in and off the job.

ATTITUDINAL CHANGE EXPECTATIONS

This is desired behavior and attitude for implementing Theory Z; it is the zenith of development. The more managers who are on this level the better the program.

Conceptualizing:

At this level of initiating, managers will fully conceptualize the Theory Z philosophy to the point of organizing it into a set of activities, values, and beliefs from which actions come.

Some conceptualizing indicators are:

(a) Relates own values and beliefs to the code of conduct expected of Theory Z managers
(b) Judges employees in terms of their behaviors as human beings
(c) Begins to form judgments of the direction in which other human beings should move

Generalizing:

At this level, managers will demonstrate a dominant and consistent set of behavior attitudes, values, and beliefs related to the

Theory Z concept. As such, the Theory Z concept will be perceived as the dominant factor that characterizes the behavior of managers.

Indicators are:

(a) Judges problems in terms of the principles and practices of Theory Z
(b) Has a habit of approaching problems more humanly
(c) Relies increasingly on intuitive thinking to make decisions

Characterization:

This is the zenith of development. Managers will begin to use the philosophy of Theory Z as a code of conduct for guiding their behavior and attitudes on and off the job. In their relationship with employees, they will be perceived as caring, trustworthy, humanistic, etc. At this point, managers will use the Theory Z concept as a philosophy of life.

Some characterization indicators are:

(a) Uses the Theory Z concept as a philosophy of life
(b) Makes decisions on and off the job using the Theory Z philosophy
(c) Develops a Theory Z conscience

SUMMARY

Humanistic competencies are defined as behavior and attitudinal skills that relate to the positive feelings of human beings. The broad humanistic competencies of Theory Z are caring, trust, intimacy and intuition. At level 1, connecting, readings, awareness sessions, visits, and discussion sessions are included to affect or change behavior and attitude. At level 2, responding managers begin to search for more information about Theory Z. At level 3, personalizing, Theory Z workshops, lecture, homework, slides, filmstrips, films, role playing, experiential learning, and behavior modeling are used to affect a change in behavior and attitudes. At the level 4, initiating, international learning trips, national learning trips, in-house consultants and in-house, in-depth training are used to change and modify behavior and attitudes to an acceptable Theory Z level.

2

A Caring Relationship With Employees

A CARING RELATIONSHIP in the Theory Z organizational context is a relationship between a manager and employees, whereby either party is willing to share and/or sacrifice time, money, energy, and other resources, so that both or either parties may grow and develop. One party must be willing to share or sacrifice himself or herself for the benefit of the other. At times, this may be a simple act; at other times, it may be a major task calling for a strong conscious effort and a great deal of sacrificing. A manager should help an employee grow, by assisting him or her to develop full potential, although this potential may not be fully realized. The effective manager must always strive to enable his or her employees to become self-actualized people. As a result, the Type Z manager will begin to bring order to his or her values and activities on and off the job. And after a comprehensive effort and long periods of caring, he or she will begin to realize his or her own purpose in life and manage more effectively, not through autocratic leadership, written edicts, tight controls, but through caring and being cared for.

EXPLAINING THE CARING PROCESS

Our response to another person in need is an examination to determine if responding to the need is compatible with our own goals. If personal goal compatibility exists, a caring act is initiated. As illustrated in Figure 1, when the personal goal is compatible with what is needed to fulfill the need, conscious effort must strongly exist to share or sacrifice either money, time, energy,

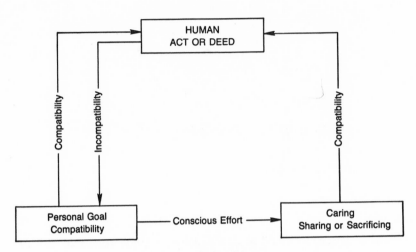

Fig. 1: The Caring Process

or other resources on behalf of the other person. As a result, the recipient of the caring act will continue to grow in some way. However, some acts will produce more change than others. For example, by assisting an employee to change a flat tire, the employee is able to get back on track and continue the growth process. However, it should be indicated that even the changing of a flat tire can be considered as a growth activity in some instances.

Although sharing is a form of caring, sacrificing is a higher form of caring, because the managers must give up something of value in order to satisfy a need or personal goal of employees.

When Delta Airlines experienced a tremendous loss of revenue during 1980 and decided not to lay off any employees, Delta could have recovered from this downfall by laying off hundreds of employees; however, it opted to keep everyone employed, sacrificing high sums of money, demonstrating a high form of caring.

DESCRIBING PREREQUISITES OF CARING

For genuine caring to take place, some prerequisites must exist:[1]

1. Gain Knowledge of Employees

    The manager must have some essential knowledge about the employee:

a. strengths and weaknesses

b. problems and opportunities

c. likes and dislikes

d. interests

e. talents and skills

The effective manager has a thorough knowledge of these important points about his or her employees—knowledge that includes the explicit, as well as the implicit; the direct, as well as the indirect—all related to helping them to grow in the caring relationship.

2. Work at Caring

The successful manager recognizes that it will not be easy to nurture a strong relationship. He or she understands that it must be worked at, that it will require a self-assessment to determine mistakes, and to correct behavior in order to help employees grow.

3. Practice Patience

An effective manager recognizes that to be too time-oriented with employees is to be non-caring. Patience is essential to caring. In this context, patience means more than giving time and space to employees, but by listening to them, being present with them, and being tolerant of them. The Type Z manager understands the need to practice patience, because it is essential for growth and development. Patience not only means being patient with employees, but the manager must also be patient with himself or herself. He or she must use every caring situation as a learning opportunity, to learn more about himself or herself, and employees.

4. Being Honest

Honesty in caring means more than not lying or doing something deceitful to employees. It also means that the manager is honest with himself or herself. This also means that he or she is open to himself or herself and to employees, that he or she sees the employee as he or she really is and not as he or she would like him or her to be, that even when mistakes are made and the facts are unpleasant, they are seriously considered because they help him or her to connect and care for employees. In addition, being honest means that the effective manager from time to time assesses his or her performance to determine if it is either helping or hindering the growth and development of employees, and takes immediate steps to correct it.

5. Trust Employees

   Trust is absolutely essential for caring to take place. This means that the effective manager will trust employees to grow at their own pace and in their own way, that employees will make mistakes and, hopefully, will learn from them, and that this trust will lead to further growth and development. This does not mean that the effective manager will try to dominate and force employees in a certain mold and that employees are not permitted to question either directives or instructions. In addition, the effective manager has the capacity to trust himself or herself, has confidence in his or her judgment, has the ability to learn from mistakes, has the guts to use his or her instincts when making decisions, all capabilities that are intended to help him or her to help employees to grow.

6. Practice Humility

   The effective manager is one who practices humility in the work environment on a continuous basis. He or she is humble and is ready, willing, and able to learn about himself or herself from employees. This means that the manager learns from employees and employees learn from the manager, that no source of information is beneath him or her to get to learn more about his or her employees, including his or her own mistakes, that the effective manager will not abuse his employees with his or her power, that he or she can be with employees without being pretentious and not pretend to be something that he or she is not.

7. Being Courageous

   Being courageous means enabling employees to experiment, to use the trial and error techniques, and to become a champion of a cause. The effective manager recognizes that the more he or she permits employees to go into the unknown, the more courage is required in the caring relationship.

THE TWO KINDS OF CARING

There are two kinds of caring: passive and active.

Passive caring is having empathy for a person, but never expressing the caring in either words or deeds.

When an organization exhibits an active caring attitude toward its employees, the following quotes are the kind of appreciative comments that are frequently made:

"My manager didn't have to do that!"

"Around here you are treated like a person, not a number."

"It makes you feel good that the company does all of these things for us without being forced to do so by the union."

"We don't work here, we have fun here."

"We just wanted to say thanks for the way Delta has treated us."

"I am very happy here because I am an important person in this company."

"I love this company."

Genuine caring involves behavior and attitudes of a person. However, in a person who is a passive carer, the behavior of the person tends to be contained, and only the attitude is present. A passive caring manager tends to listen, and gingerly tries to help an employee with an idea or an assurance. In essence, there tends to be absence of the behavior in a passive carer.

The active carer is one who demonstrates empathy by displaying both behavior and attitude. This kind of manager is a doer and will go to almost any measure to share and/or sacrifice on behalf of an employee.

Genuine active caring basically means two things: 1) that one human is willing to share himself or herself with another and/or 2) that one person is willing to sacrifice either time, resources, energy, and other resources. It is not enough for a person to share himself or herself with another—this is passive caring. In order to put passive caring into action, the manager must be willing to give up something to fulfill the goal/s or to perform some deed on behalf of another human being to become an active career.

Caring also has two dimensions, which this author identifies as ego caring and egoless caring. Ego caring is probably the beginning of the caring process but, as caring becomes more important to a person, he or she will most likely gravitate to a higher level of caring, called egoless caring. Ego caring is exhibited when a person performs something for another person for the purpose of receiving some form of benefit; that is, a good deed is initiated by a person because the expectation is that he or she will receive some reward. The benefit could either be in the form of a recognition, promotion, a reciprocal act, or some other thing of value, now or in the future. When a manager does a deed for an employee, not because he or she expects to recoup something in return, but because it is an established quality which is possessed by him or her, and has become a way of life.

For example, James donates $1,000 to C.A.R.E. because his name will be published in the newspaper and he can claim it as a tax deduction. Mary, on the other hand, donates $100,000 anonymously because she genuinely believes that it is for a worthy cause.

Usually, for egoless caring to exist, the person must have gone through the ego caring stage. However, it is not a certainty that the person's behavior and attitudes would transcend to the egoless caring stage. For this to be realized, there must be a commitment on the part of the person to sacrifice.

UNDERSTANDING SOME CARING PRINCIPLES

One of the most important tasks of management is to create conditions within the job environment whereby employees can develop to their maximum potential. This applies for all employees; not only those who may be liked or disliked by management, but all employees within the organization. Caring in a Type Z organization applies not only to managers to employees, but employees to employees. The following caring principles should be discussed with both managers and employees, and should become the ten commandments of the organization, to be followed by all employees from the chief executive officer to part-time employees.

1. Become a servant to the human race on and off the job.
2. Dependency is not to be avoided, but to be cherished.
3. React to problems and failures not with dismay, but as opportunity for training and development.
4. Accept all employees completely and unconditionally.
5. Be genuinely open to all employees by being willing to fully communicate thoughts, ideas, and feelings.
6. Consider all employees to be perfect, but with limitations.
7. Lead by action, words, deeds, and examples.
8. Create conditions on the job that respect the individuality of all employees.
9. Believe that success will only be realized with employees' experience of success.

10. Firmly believe that the purpose in life for all human beings is to share and sacrifice oneself so that others may realize life's purpose.

Some employees and managers may find it difficult to accept all of these caring principles. In any event, they provide a foundation for treating people as human beings rather than as objects or things, which is so often the case when managers manage their employees and when employees relate to their peers.

ESTABLISHING A CARING RELATIONSHIP

I have used the following steps to teach managers how to connect with an employee, to demonstrate a caring relationship through the communication process, and how to follow up with sensitivity, concern, understanding, and action. The managers have reported good results with the techniques.

1. ATTENDING

Attending means making a conscious effort to be available either to be heard or to be received. Although, initially, managers should take the initiative to connect with the employees (to be heard), at times an employee may be experiencing some difficulty, either on the job or at home. Therefore, the manager should make himself or herself available (to be received) to the employees. This may mean announcing that the office door is always open, managing by walking around or being available at recesses or lunchtime, etc. A point which is being emphasized here, is that a caring behavior cannot take place unless management is available to employees. The following are general guidelines for getting and maintaining the attention of employees when nurturing the caring relationship:

(a) Face the employee directly.
(b) Make and maintain eye contact with the employee.
(c) Slightly bend the torso in the direction of the employee.
(d) Stay within three feet of the employee. Remove all obstacles between manager and the employee.

2. LISTENING

It is almost impossible to really care for employees unless managers make a habit of listening to them. Listening means taking an interest in what is being said without judging or evaluating; it calls for openness and objectiveness. Genuine caring evolves around recognizing the needs of the employees and the subsequent ministering to those needs. This means giving employees the concern, appreciation, and understanding called for in the caring relationship. It is not a matter of what a manager feels like giving, but giving what an employee needs for providing psychological comfort in the fulfillment of a personal need.

No manager can give the kind of caring and concern to employees required in a Type Z organization unless he or she knows them as human beings. No manager can know his or her employees unless they disclose, reveal and unveil themselves. And no manager can initiate meaningful dialogue with employees unless he or she seriously listens. In essence, either singly or collectively, they will most likely be ministering to their own needs, not to those of their employees. Genuine listening is a very difficult human task to perform. It will take conscious effort and hard work to become an effective listener. Whenever a manager is occupied or concerned solely for himself or herself, receptivity is at a low level. As a result, unless a conscious effort is initiated to get in tune with an employee, real listening cannot occur. As a general rule, when an employee comes to a manager, he or she does so because there exists a need to be fulfilled, even though the employee may or may not discuss the reason for the audience.

Some ways to become a successful listener:

A. Stop talking–A manager cannot listen unless he or she takes the first step, and that is, simply, after the connection has been made, stop talking. This chore seems to be very difficult for human beings. Therefore, it will take a conscious effort to control the will to talk.

B. Be silent–Some managers, when listening to employees are silent, but are thinking about something else and, thus, are not connected to the other party. A true listener is one who is quiet and sensitive to what is being said in an active, open, receptive and genuine manner. A true listener is one who is silent inwardly. A true listener does not immediately evaluate or judge what is being said, but acts as a receptical until verbal and non-verbal messages have been received. An effective manager in a Type Z organization is one who has acquired the skill of listening with a high degree of proficiency.

C. Be patient–Employees will need time to reveal themselves at their own pace and in their own manner. When a manager tries to force listening, the connection will collapse, and any conversation will more or less transcend to a meaningless level.

E. Obtain Clarity—The genuine listener does not always remain quiet. At times, the Type Z manager who is a creative listener will have to respond, reflect, express, understand, empathize, and request clarity. Carl Rogers identifies this as reflective listening. During this process, the manager may request more information, or may paraphrase what is being said in order to determine what is inside the employee and to facilitate what the employee wants to communicate.

F. Show Empathy—Employees will more freely open up to a manager if they feel that he or she is sensitive to their thoughts and feelings. This is particularly true if it can be shown that the manager has undergone the same difficulty.

G. Be attentive on two levels—Employees tend to converse on two levels. The first level is identified as the superficial level. On this level, employees will usually voice some petty concerns, interests, desires, and aspirations. It is as if they need a springboard to spring them into the next level. This level will usually identify the real intent of the conversation and the personal goals desired to be achieved by the employee. The effective listener will have to acquire a great deal of skill to decipher when the employee transcends to the official level in the conversation in order to be of assistance to the employee. If a manager does not pursue the employee to move from the superficial level to the official level because of impatience, lack of time or self indulgence, then the real intent of the conversation may never be revealed.

H. Observe nonverbal communication—Employees tend to express about 38 percent with words and 55 percent nonverbally. Therefore, one effective listening technique is for the manager to increase his or her ability to read the nonverbal actions of employees. This is also useful for the manager to improve his or her own body language, thereby eliminating body language which transmits negative clues.

I. Avoid arguing or interrupting behavior—Some managers have a tendency to get overly involved or react emotionally to what is being said by the employee. This will do nothing but stifle the communication process. To avoid falling into this rut, the effective manager will not jump to conclusions, and will help the employee to probe to arrive at the conclusion. It should be emphasized here that one of the tasks of a Theory Z manager during the caring relationship with employees is to enable workers to grow, to take responsibility for their own lives, and to reach their full potential.

3. RESPONDING

Once the manager has effectively listened to the employee, he or she must respond in a way that will enable the employees to accurately and completely convey thoughts, ideas, behavior, attitudes, and feelings. This will shed a great deal of light on the personal goal of the employee and will help facilitate the situation for the manager. One of the most effective techniques for accomplishing this is through probing. This may necessitate the asking of probing questions, projecting questions with silence, pauses, short statements, and requesting information.

4. PERSONALIZING

After a number of responding interactions, the manager should get the employee to personalize his or her difficulty in relation to what has been demonstrated verbally or nonverbally. Again the best method to do this is to use probing questions which will lead the employee to make personal judgment statements in order to arrive at deficient behavior or action that might account for the present situation or difficulty. By using probing questions, the employee will not only personalize the problem, but will get a sense of ownership of the problem.

5. INITIATING

When the employee has sufficiently personalized the situation and gets a sense of ownership for the condition, the time has arrived to complete the caring cycle; do so by getting the employee to identify what he or she can do to initiate activities that will alleviate the problem. Sometimes this may call for simple reasoning; at other times, it may mean involving the parties in heavy problem-solving.

A. Sometimes, the manager may not be able to effect a parallel position to the employee. A suitable alternate position is shoulder-to-shoulder with both parties inclining toward each other.

B. Strokes may be used if done genuinely and with discretion.

C. All employees won't have problems or difficult situations.

Therefore, the connection does not have to be a long one. The connection should last long enough so that the manager and employee get a feel of each other. This means simply that the conversation must be meaningful and during every occasion, each must learn something about the other.

D. Even though an employee acts as though he or she did not see a manager, the latter must take the initiative to make the connection.

E. Finally, once the connection has been made and the manager has determined the need to prolong the conversation to get on the official level of the conversation, all of the guidelines suggested in the first steps should be initiated.

HUMANISTIC QUALITIES THAT DENOTE A CARING BEHAVIOR

The following individual and organizational activities denote either a caring or non-caring behavior; they come from an organization using the nominal group process to identify caring competencies. Some readers may object to certain activities, such as requiring employees to punch a time clock; however, it should be brought out here that any activity that denotes management does not trust employees to some degree, conveys an uncaring posture.

Spending time with an employee who is ill.

Remembering an employee on an important occasion.

Attending a function given by an employee.

Contacting an employee who is absent because of illness.

Greeting an employee with some kind remarks.

Eating with an employee.

Taking an employee out for lunch or dinner.

Presenting an employee with a small gift out of appreciation.

Forwarding a kind note to an employee for completing a task.

Walking around the job greeting employees and inquiring about their health, welfare, etc.

Listening to an employee who has a problem.

Giving money to an employee (as opposed to lending money).

Spending some time with an employee and helping out with a problem.

Introducing an employee to members of the family.

Inviting employee and family over for dinner.

Counseling an employee in need.

Assisting an employee with a task.

Stroking an employee.

ORGANIZATIONAL ACTIVITIES THAT DENOTE A CARING BEHAVIOR

Continuing the compensation of an employee when sick days
have been used.
Implementing a policy of unlimited sick days.
Instituting a flexible schedule (flextime).
Setting up a comprehensive quality-of-working-life program.
Providing subsidized housing for employees.
Providing free lunch for employees.
Granting discount rates to employees.
Instituting an incentive program.
A bonus program.
Enabling employees and family to use recreational facilities
of the organization.
Hiring a member of the family when an employee
has been disabled.
Providing disability and life insurance.
Giving gifts to employees on certain festive occasions.
Organizing cooperative activities for employees and
recognizing winners.
Establishing a wellness program.
Providing transportation for employees.
Instituting an investment program.
Providing free or partially subsidized tuition.
Providing leave-of-absence with pay.
Subsidizing retiring employees to establish a business to
accomodate the organization.

There are a host of ways in which organizations demonstrate that they care for their employees. For example, Merle Norman provides 25 cent lunches, free snacks for breaks, and gasoline at cost for its employees; in 1915 Proctor & Gamble was one of the first few companies to offer its employees life insurance; Quad/Graphics has adapted an employee-owned organization; Celestial Seasonings, Inc. provides a gain-sharing program that pays cash dividends to its employees when it makes a profit; Control Data Corporation provides its employees with a consulting service for starting their own business; Hospital Corporation of America pays its employees for keeping themselves fit; and Leo Burnett Company has a unique way of saying that it cares for its employees by paying them $3,000 for adopting a child.

ACTIVITIES THAT MAY IMPEDE A CARING RELATIONSHIP

Segregated parking areas for managers and employees.
Requiring employees to define their position or status by some
distinguishing feature (color, location, etc.).
Different incentives for employees based on position or status.
Referring to employees by titles.
Segregating employees and managers in the cafeteria by
status or position.
View the work of employees skeptically.
Fail to recognize or reward exemplary performance.
Requiring employees to undergo a lie detector test.
Punishing a group of employees for the misdeed of a few
or of a single person.
Fail to keep employees properly informed.
Penalizing an employee for being wrong or making a mistake.
Reprimanding an employee in the presence of others.
Gossiping about an employee.
Requiring the verification of a sick day with a doctor's note.

IDENTIFYING CARING INDICATORS

During a training session of about seventy employees of a large organization, I asked for some assistance from the group to help define caring in an action-oriented manner in terms of what manager or employees demonstrate when one cares. The following are paraphrases of many of the statements:

1. Doing nothing that will hurt employees either physically or psychologically.
2. Being a good listener and knowing when to speak and how.
3. Being attentive, even when it is difficult to do so.
4. Keeping commitments at all costs.
5. Supporting and appreciating personal differences in employees.
6. Loving employees as managers love themselves.
7. Being concerned about the welfare of others and backing up that concern with actions, words, and deeds.
8. Striving to get to know employees better.
9. Demonstrating interest in employees and knowing what impacts on them.
10. Encouraging an employee to share his or her thoughts and ideas regardless of how painful they may be.
11. Attempting to see situations as the employees see them.

12. Putting the needs of employees before management's needs.
13. Becoming involved in the activities of employees.
14. Being available and keeping promises.
15. Allowing employees to fail without being penalized.
16. Understanding the feelings of employees and enabling them to feel those of managers.
17. Having a desire for employees' happiness.
18. Helping employees to experience success even if it means sacrificing.
19. Showing interest in employees as human beings.
20. Being concerned about both the behavior and feelings of employees.
21. Expressing concern during times of difficulty (death, illness, etc.) and backing it up with some action.
22. Recognizing employees for jobs well done.
23. Creating a compatible environment for employees.
24. Demonstrating sensitivity to individual needs, desires, and personal goals of employees.
25. Being receptive to employees' beliefs even though they may conflict with management.
26. Focusing energy upon "knowing" each employee and being able to anticipate their behavior and attitudes.
27. Documenting and acknowledging employees' achievements and efforts with verbal and non-verbal strokes.

CARING FOR DIFFICULT EMPLOYEES

The supreme test in caring is when a manager can care for difficult employees. A difficult employee is one usually disliked by a high number of employees and managers. They tend to be self-centered and care for no one but themselves. They are quite often insecure about their own limitations and will attempt to shield their weaknesses by projecting their faults onto others. Some guidelines managers should initiate to improve the ability to care for difficult employees:

1. Realize the implications: most American managers do not score high in dealing with difficult employees in a caring manner. When employees fail on the job, many managers are reluctant to share the blame for that failure. They tend to reprimand, scold, write up reports on them, and a host of other punitive measures. This author knows of no situation in which an employee has failed

and the manager was not partially responsible for that failure. The old adage, "the first step towards the solution to a problem is the recognition that one exists," is true in the case of difficult employees. Usually the difficulty exists because conditions on the job have not been created by management to help the difficult employee to grow and develop. This usually occurs because management has either avoided, neglected, or has been unable to solve this human problem.

2. Stop unkind thoughts or behavior toward difficult employees. This will be difficult for some managers, but should indicate the extent to which they will have to work on themselves to perfect their profession as a manager. As long as managers continue to demonstrate hostility, anger, and take punitive measures to deal with difficult employees, they will not grow in their position, and will have lost an ideal opportunity to master their craft in a humane and effective manner.

3. Avoid making critical remarks about the difficult employee; this is not only unprofessional, it is also unkind, and treats the employee with a great deal of disrespect. To some, this will be a difficult problem to overcome because gossiping and speaking unkindly about difficult employees has become a way of life in many organizations. A simple technique used by this author to work on this problem involves identifying difficult employees and saying one kind thing to them on a daily basis. Human beings tend to sense when people think unkindly about them, and are eager to receive genuine kindness through a caring relationship. If a manager is genuinely seeking to improve his or her caring proficiency, the most difficult employee should provide him or her with teaching opportunities to work on himself or herself.

4. Give the difficult employee tasks to accomplish. Many employees become difficult because they have a low self-esteem and have a low image of themselves. This may be due to lack of success, either on or off the job, or simply because they have not experienced too much success, and few people in their lives have ever recognized or rewarded them for what they have done. By calling on the employee to perform some task, and recognizing him or her for the achievement, the manager can help nurture an improved self image and reduce the hostility that is usually associated with difficult employees.

AN ACTION PLAN FOR NURTURING A CARING RELATIONSHIP

Most managers will need to improve their caring relationship with employees if they are serious about establishing a Type Z organization. Here are some guidelines:

1. Identify caring or human competencies that are important to employees. There are probably a number of ways in which this can be accomplished, as indicated below.

   A. Have employees brainstorm the competencies, and rank them in order of priorities.

   B. Use another form of brainstorming, called the nominal group process, and have employees identify and rank competencies.

   C. Organize a committee of either all employees or employees and managers to jointly arrive at caring competencies.

   D. Have a group do the necessary research to compile the list of competencies.

When the competencies are being identified, they should also be given priorities so the manager will know which one should receive the initial attention.

2. Assess management caring proficiency quotient. Once the prioritized list of caring competencies has been completed, construct an assessment instrument containing the competencies that will be administered to each manager. Once the instrument has been scored, each manager should receive the composite score.

3. Prepare an action plan. Based upon the scores received on the instrument, each manager will prepare an action plan to begin fostering a caring relationship with the employees. The action plan should contain the following categories:

   A. Description of the caring competencies and score.

   B. An activity for each competency indicating a description when it is to be initiated, and how often.

   C. A description of how and when the action will be evaluated. After the manager has successfully completed one plan with a set of competencies (No plan should contain more than five competencies to be worked on at one time), develop another and work on it until all the competencies have been mastered. Eventually, there will be no need for the manager to prepare plans because nurturing a caring relationship within the organization should become a way of life for all parties involved; at least this is what is expected and achieved if the manager works on the caring process with serious intent.

SOME INTERESTING FEATURES ABOUT CARING

Caring is not necessarily reciprocal.[2] An employee may not respond to a manager in the same way as the manager behaved. When a genuine caring relationship exists, barriers are broken and caring becomes contagious. As a result, the manager's caring will activate the employee's caring, and the employee's caring helps to activate the manager to care. Each caring helps to strengthen each other.

Although honesty and devotion are desirable in a caring relationship, managers are like other normal human beings, and are subject to have their ups and downs. There will be some days when they may be more caring than others. This fact should be understood, and should not be the reason to be downhearted if they feel that they have not been as caring as they desire.

Since caring is a developmental process, it should have a high level of constancy. Therefore, it can't be nurtured if the manager is never around to become intimate with employees. Management By Walking Around is an excellent process for building and maintaining the caring process.

The process of caring is significantly more important than the end result. The process should be the basis for establishing trust and intimacy which are the tracks to a real, genuine, caring relationship. The caring relationship should be enhanced by considering the present, profiting from the past, and connecting both to the future, where the growth is to be realized.

In caring for employees, the manager should help to actualize himself or herself. By using his or her power of trust, intimacy, and intuitive thinking in the best interest of the employees, self-actualization does take place, but never fully.

SUMMARY

Caring is a process of nurturing a social relationship between a manager and employee, where either party is willing to share and/or sacrifice time, money, energy, or other resources, so that both parties may grow and develop. The caring prerequisites are: 1) Gain knowledge of employees; 2) Work at caring; 3) Practice patience; 4) Be honest; 5) Trust employees; and 6) Practice humility.

There are two kinds of caring: 1) Passive caring means that only an attitude of concern is present in a person; and 2) Active caring involves behavior as well as attitudes. The procedural steps for communicating a caring relationship are: 1) Attending. That is, being available to be heard or received; 2) Listening by taking an active interest in what is being said; 3) Responding in a way that will enable the employees to accurately and completely convey thoughts, ideas, behavior, attitudes, and feelings; 4) Personalizing by getting employees to verbalize his or her difficulty; and 5) Initiating by getting the employee to identify what the manager can do to assist the employee to alleviate the problem. There are basically four steps for caring for difficult employees: 1) Become conscious that most American managers do not score high in dealing with difficult employees in a caring manner; 2) Cease either thinking or doing anything unkind to the difficult employee; 3) Avoid casting critical remarks about the difficult employees; 4) Give the difficult employee tasks to accomplish. There are three specific guidelines that should be followed to maintain a caring relationship with an organization: 1) Identify caring competencies; 2) Assess management caring proficiency; and 3) Prepare an action plan.

3

Trust Between Employees and Managers

EGALITARIANISM IS A key term used to describe the desired relationship for fostering trust in an organization; it implies that all employees, no matter what their status, and no matter what position they hold, should have equal political, social, and economical rights. In an egalitarian setting, all employees should be able to use discretion to perform their jobs without close supervision because they can be trusted. This trust assumes that the personal goals of employees and organizational goals are compatible and that neither the organization, through its managers or activities, nor employees, through their on-the-job behavior, are out to damage the other. When a holistic relationship exists in an organization and egalitarian philosophy is apparent, employees and managers alike will be forced to deal with every individual as a human being. As a result, the work environment will be characterized by honesty, open communication and mutual trust.

ITEM:

The following comments represent signs of trust:

Employees: • "No one tells you how you should perform your job here."
• "You don't have someone telling you every move."
• "I feel more independent, more like my own boss."
• "They give you a lot of responsibility here."
• "Everybody is a manager here."

Managers: • "I believe that every employee knows more about his job than me."
• "If you pick the right people and give them lee-

way to perform they seldom let you down."
- "We operate more as a team than as a boss and employees."
- "I am interested in employees who can take the ball and run with it."
- "We permit our employees to make mistakes, but not the same ones."

This chapter defines trust and its essential properties.

DEFINING TRUST

Trust is at a low level in many organizations because managers are often unaware of the full dimension of this humanistic competency.

Trust, in the Theory Z context, is the anticipation that the behavior of a manager and employee will always be responsive and supportive to the benefit of both parties. There are basically three types of trust:

Disclosure Trust

Disclosure trust is the belief that information shared between a manager and employee will not be used to hurt either party. This type of trust implies that both parties have entered into a psychological state or written agreement to abide by the clandestine principle expected of each other. Disclosure trust deals with values, beliefs, attitudes, and feelings. It can range from a low-risk level when either person merely expresses an opinion, idea, or suggestion, to a high-risk level when either person divulges personal or intimate information either about himself or herself, or someone else. In the work environment, managers should aspire to establish a high disclosure trust level with employees in two specific ways:

1. Become Friendly with Employees.

Initiate a host of intimate activities with employees, as described in the next chapter. These activities enable the manager to share personal information with employees. This aspect of trust is absolutely necessary to facilitate problem-solving, either on an individual or group level.

2. Become Job-Oriented with Employees.

Share information and feelings with employees that are directly related to either jobs, responsibilities, functions, tasks, activities, or issues. Honesty is closely related to disclosure trust, implying that the relationship between the employee and manager is free from lying, stealing, or cheating, and is characterized by trustworthiness, fairness, and sincerity; information exchanged between the two will be used for problem-solving purposes.

Contractual Trust

Contractual trust is the belief that the words, promises, and verbal or written agreements between a manager and employee can be depended upon. This manner of trust implies reliability. Each party can be counted upon to do what is expected or required. Contractual trust is usually developed through conversation, whereby an employee indicates that he or she has the prerequisites to perform a particular job, or will agree to perform a specific act. It tends to be low-risk oriented in that it deals with the behavior of the manager. Whenever a manager indicates something, either through written or verbal statements, employees are constantly observing and evaluating his or her deportment to determine if it is consistent with what was either stated or agreed upon. A manager must always remember that employees are always searching to determine if their behavior supports their words. The higher the consistency, the higher the level of trust. The lower the consistency, the lower the trust relationship between the two parties.

Privacy Trust

Privacy trust is the belief that neither the person, personal information, or wares of either an employee or manager will be violated. This manner of trust implies that a person will not invade the privacy of another person nor harm the other in any manner; it means both parties have a high degree of integrity, honesty, and respect for each other. Privacy trust tends to gravitate from a low-risk orientation in which a manager might search the workplace of an employee, without prior knowledge, to a high-risk orientation whereby a manager keeps a diary of the activities of an employee without prior knowledge.

PREREQUISITES FOR NURTURING TRUST

Trust won't appear merely by wishing it; several prerequisites must be met if it is to be nurtured throughout an organization.

Managers must be the prime movers, but employees must be patient with managers and give them time to change or modify their behavior in order to implement this requirement of Type Z organizations.

1. Reduce external controls by giving employees the opportunity to monitor and correct their own performance.
2. Allow employees to perform tasks, chores, or activities without fear of the outcome.
3. Give more responsibilities to employees.
4. Provide more power and authority for employees to perform their jobs.
5. Provide more freedom for employees to use their own discretion in performing a job.
6. Ask employees to identify trust indicators, then use the results to determine how proficient managers are in this humanistic competency.
7. Keep working at it; trust will not occur overnight. Attitudes, once acquired, are difficult to change, and this will only occur when managers are consistent in their behavior.
8. Personal and organizational goals must be compatible. The actions of the employee and organization are not intended to do damage to either party.

An excellent example of trust and teamwork is shown by Donnelly Mirrors, Inc. in its practice of removing time clocks and organizing its work force into teams of 10 people. Each team member is trusted to keep his or her own production records, and each team member is responsible to the other team members. If a team member is absent from work, another team member takes over the responsibility.

IDENTIFYING TRUST INDICATORS

Here are some trust indicators the author has identified from a number of employees:

1. Following through with assignments.
2. Giving what is promised.
3. Completing a given task on or before a specific timeline.
4. Granting employees the freedom to use discretion in deciding how to perform a task, activity, or job.
5. Giving employees as much information as possible to perform a job.
6. Being truthful (avoiding deception and evasion).
7. Bringing up something for discussion without fear of recrimination.

8. Keeping one's word.
9. Keeping confidences.
10. Completing tasks.
11. Respecting employees' judgments.
12. Depending on employees to complete a task.
13. Treating employees fairly and consistently.
14. Having confidence and faith in employees.
15. Getting loyalty, cooperation, and effort from employees.

CONDITIONS FOR EXPANDING TRUST

In order for mutual trust to be realized between employees and managers, several conditions must be met:

1. Become flexible with employees. Let up on policies and procedures which restrict employees, avoid using employees in jobs not assigned to them, give employees more authority to act without close supervision, and bending the strict adherence to time.

2. Initiate more frequent and longer contact with employees. Make an effort to become more familiar with employees on and off the job through numerous social, personal, and recreational activities. By doing this, managers will transform an unknown and indifferent relationship to one that is close. The closeness will reap, in addition to other benefits, trust. The contacts with employees must be over a long period of time in order to diminish many undesirable practices that were previously nurtured by managers.

3. Provide opportunities which will expand trust. Although managers may become more flexible with employees and meet with them more frequently and for a longer duration, there will be more need for employees to become involved in a number of job-related and personal activities that will reveal evidence of trust.

MAINTENANCE NEEDS AND TRUST

All employees are entitled to a decent living standard and to receive a fair pay for a day's work. Maintenance needs of employees are requisites for trust to exist in any organization. Money, benefits, fair supervision, and a feeling of belonging go hand-in-hand with employee trust and cooperation.

FACTORS THAT IMPEDE TRUST

Although managers may take the necessary steps to expand trust within the organization, some factors may impede their efforts:

1. **Excessive Nonverbal Communication.** One of the requirements for establishing a Type Z organization is the maintenance of an open communication network within the work environment. An inordinate amount of nonverbal communication signals that employees are reluctant to be open with managers, and, therefore, are hiding their real thoughts and emotions. To combat this difficulty, survey employees to detect the communication problems. Each manager should then directly initiate a plan to eradicate the conditions or behavior responsible for the communication problem.

2. **Too Time-Oriented.** Managers who are bent on time management may find it extremely difficult to establish an open organization, where employees feel free to communicate without being restricted by time. When an organization is extremely time-oriented, it is usually because a chief executive officer has a fixation on time management. Consequently, employees fail to communicate their concerns to him or her and managers will also find it difficult to do so. Time management tends to cater to the left hemisphere of the brain, Type Z is clearly a marriage of left and right brain behavior.

3. **Failing to Spend Time With Employees.** Some managers are quick to proclaim that they are too bogged down with administrative matters to meet with employees. There is no way possible to expand trust in an organization unless managers make a conscious effort to conduct periodic long-and short-duration meetings with employees. Failing to do so will impede the progress toward a Type Z organization. All managers aspiring to adopt the Type Z philosophy should develop an action plan for regular meeting with employees in which there are agendas of mutual consequence.

4. **Too Many Low Trusters.** In an organization that has an inordinate number of low trusters, establishing a Type Z organization will probably take more time and more patience. A review of the research should enable the reader to understand the implications and ramifications when a large number of low trusters occupy an organization:[2]

    (1) Low Trusters Are:

        A. More likely to cheat and lie

        B. More likely to behave in an untrustworthy manner

in certain situations, particularly if they feel they will not be caught

C. Not inclined to trust others unless there is clear evidence of trustworthiness

Conversely, organizations with many high trusters tend to flourish.

(2) High Trusters Are:

A. More likable than low trusters

B. Better adjusted psychologically

C. More ethical

D. More attractive to the opposite sex

E. More desirable as a close friend

F. Apt to trust others without evidence of being trustworthy

G. Apt to give people a second chance

H. Less likely to be unhappy, conflicted, or maladjusted

I. More prone to be fooled by distrusting people

IMPROVING TRUST RELATIONSHIPS

Here is an action plan by which managers can work on themselves to improve trust relationships:

1. Determine Employee's Trust Indicators.

Organize a group of employees and use the nominal group process to identify and rank desirable trust indicators. Refer to chapter 6 for a description of this process.

2. Determine Manager's Trust Proficiency.

The human resource unit or the personnel department should establish a committee of three to four employees, and prepare a survey using the ten ranked trust indicators or characteristics realized from the nominal group process. Use a five-point scale to assess the degree to which the manager realizes the indicators.

3. Administer the Survey

Give each employee a copy of the survey and ask him or her to complete it either on or off the job.

4. Assess the Survey Results

The human resource unit should prepare an analysis of the survey results and discuss it with the individual manager.

5. Prepare an Action Plan

After the results of the survey have been discussed with the manager, he or she should prepare an action plan to work first on the indicators that received a rating of "one" and "two," and subsequently the remaining items. The actions should contain the following:

(1) Description of the trust indicator
(2) Description of activities that will foster trust
(3) Statement as to how often it should be initiated
(4) Citation of who should be involved in each activity
(5) Evaluate performance results

The human resource unit should administer the trust survey form to all employees and have them reassess the trust efforts of the manager. Use the results to discuss improvements and areas needing improvement. Revise the action plan.

SUMMARY

Trust is the anticipation that the behavior of a manager and employee will always be responsive and supportive to the benefit of both parties. 1) **Disclosure trust** is the belief that information which is shared between a manager and employee will not be used to hurt either party; 2) **Contractual trust** is the belief that the words, promises, and verbal or written agreements between a manager and employee can be depended upon; and 3) **Privacy trust** is the belief that neither the person, personal information, or wares of either an employee or manager will be violated. The conditions for expanding trust are: 1) Become flexible with employees; 2) Initiate more frequent and longer contacts with employees; and 3) Provide opportunities which will expand trust. Trust is almost impossible to be improved in an organization where maintenance needs go unfulfilled. Factors that impede trust are: 1) Excessive non-verbal communication; 2) Too time oriented; 3) Failing to spend time with employees; and 4) Too many low trusters. One method for improving trust consists of the following steps: 1) Determine employee's trust indicators; 2) Determine manager's trust proficiency; 3) Administer the survey; 4) Assess the survey results; 5) Prepare an action plan; and 6) Evaluate performance results.

4

Intimacy In The Work Environment

As MANAGERS ATTEMPT to develop an excellent organization, one of the most difficult behavioral changes they need to effect will be the intimate relationship with employees. Genuine intimacy cannot occur until other humanistic qualities such as caring and trust have been nurtured over a period of time and a mutual respect has been established between employees and managers. Managers will also be required to reprogram themselves. Old values and beliefs, once held sacrosant, must now give way to contemporary practices that have been proven to be more effective when dealing with employees, not only in numerous Japanese firms, but in many organizations in the United States.

This chapter defines intimacy and describes its requirements.

DEFINING INTIMACY

Intimacy is the process by which managers establish a personal and earnest relationship with employees through the initiation of frequent social contacts, the nurturing of mutual trust, and the maintenance of security and good will. It cannot be acquired unless there are adequate contacts of sufficient duration between employees and managers. Contact is the vehicle for demonstrating a caring relationship and expanding trust. Contact must be personal and social. Some argue that it should also be on an economic level. Perhaps so, but managers do not always have the freedom to respond to economic needs of employees. This is usually solved on an organizational level. On the other hand, managers do have the power and authority to act on an individual or personal level to become actively involved with employees through frequent dialogue sessions.

The Trammell Crow Company is one of the most intimate-oriented organizations in America. Even its president, Trammell Crow, does not have a private office; he shares an open space with his employees. Crow maintains that a major component of a successful business is caring, which will result only if he is available to and associates with his employees.

Intimacy cannot be established unless trust is expanded through frequent associations, and the demonstration of honesty, reliability, and sincerity. When a manager is striving to perfect a caring relationship with employees, these traits will be seen as a routine part of his or her personality, thereby strengthening an intimate relationship with employees.

Intimacy comes when employees are not penalized for being wrong; errors made by employees are used as the basis for further training and development. Managers do not restrict employees, nor do employees have to follow complex protocol to meet with a manager to discuss an issue or problem.

MAINTAINING INTIMACY AND RESPECT

Some managers may be reluctant to become intimate on the job because they fear that employees will lose respect for them. Some employees may try to take advantage of some Theory Z managers, but the following practices will benefit all concerned:

1. Practice Consistent Behavior

Managers who have problems with employees are usually those who are inconsistent with their relationships with them. When a manager is consistent, employees know what is and isn't acceptable behavior, as a result, they will be particularly sensitive to "crossing the border" into unacceptable behavior.

2. Inform Employee of Unacceptable Behavior

By the time a genuine intimate behavior pattern exists between the manager and employees, each will begin to sense when a particular action has annoyed the other. Don't wait to inform an employee that something is unacceptable; discuss it with the employee immediately in a serious mode and state the degree to which you have been affected by the act.

3. Emphasize Management Role

At times, it may be necessary for a manager to describe his or her role to an employee in order to emphasize his "power position." This may be particularly true if the unacceptable behavior has frequently occurred. If this becomes necessary:

A. Decide the type of meeting seating arrangement: should the manager sit adjacent to the employee or across from the employee?

B. Convene a formal meeting with the employee.

C. Begin the conversation in a formal and serious manner and indicate the unacceptable behavior and explain why it was upsetting.

D. Reach an understanding as to the condition that brought on the behavior and how it can be prevented in the future.

E. Use a mere touch, a hand shake, or a hug to demonstrate to the employee that you do not harbor resentment. Thank the employee for the meeting.

F. Follow up the conversation, when appropriate, to thank the employee for making an attempt not to commit the act that brought on the unacceptable behavior.

G. Continue being intimate with the employee. The employee will become a little more guarded with his or her behavior. This is what is expected.

ACQUIRE KNOWLEDGE ABOUT EMPLOYEES. Intimacy requires that managers acquire sufficient information about their employees through personal and social contacts. Through an interchanging process, managers will share information about themselves. The extent to which managers obtain information about their employees will depend largely on how much they are willing to "expose" themselves through the sharing of personal information.

These are some facts that should be in the knowledge reservoir of managers concerning their employees:

1. Name
2. Date of birth
3. Likes and dislikes
4. Names of members of immediate family
5. Educational level

   6. Important dates of employees and family
   7. Hobbies and interests
   8. Strengths and weaknesses
   9. Books read
  10. Happy and unhappy occasions

BECOME FRIENDLY WITH EMPLOYEES

When intimacy has become well established within the organization between managers and their employees, numerous friendship relationships will become apparent, not only between employees and managers, but employees and employees.

BE PRIVATE WITH EMPLOYEES

Intimacy, when fully developed, will involve a very special and private relationship between managers and their employees. Obviously, this can only occur if there is a full understanding and commitment to Type Z principles and practices. The prerequisites for establishing a private relationship between managers and employees are frequent dialogue sessions which are open and honest. As these sessions progress, trust will emerge between the parties and, slowly, employees will begin to divulge the personal side of their lives.

If intimacy is to be found in employees, it must also be present in managers. Don't expect employees to be personal if the managers are not personal; because of the power position of managers, they should take the initiative to become personal with employees.

SOCIALIZING WITH EMPLOYEES

Managers should socialize with employees and should do so with care to avoid spending too much time with any one employee or group. Socializing in Theory Z type companies often begins when managers visit and interact with employees at their work assignment, then graduates to inviting employees to their homes. Other possibilities for social activities that will help foster intimacy:

   1. Visiting employees in the hospital
   2. Eating with employees in the cafeteria
   3. Conducting coffee klatches with employees

4. Helping employees with home chores
5. Getting hands dirty with employees on and off the job
6. Engaging in recreational activities with employees
7. Participating with employees in athletics
8. Having drinks with employees off the job
9. Playing cards with employees
10. Walking around the job area and inquiring about the concerns of employees
11. Inviting employees and their families to dinner
12. Intermingling managers and employees by having organizational-wide meetings, events and other activities
13. Conducting meetings with managers, employees, and suppliers
14. Implementing quality teams employing employees and managers

BE A COMPANION TO EMPLOYEES
Another essential feature of intimacy is companionship, by which I mean a frequent relationship that develops from intimacy. Companionship means basically being present when employees need managers. Sometimes this means being available and taking an active interest in the affairs of employees. At other times it means just being available in the event a need arises that can be shared with managers. At other times, it may mean just being available and listening to what employees have to say. Real companionship will begin to emerge between employees and managers when the two no longer have to be present in order for a spirit of companionship to exist. This is the highest form of companionship, and what every manager should strive to achieve.

Organizations that seem to practive "management by walking around" in order to become intimate with their employees are: Dana, Johnson Wax, Marion Labs, Pitney Bowes, and Viking Freight.

INTIMACY INDICATORS
1. Socializing with employees on and off the job
2. Interacting with employees over a wide range of topics
3. Engaging in recreational activities with employees

4. Allowing employees to effect change to improve the work environment
5. Sharing power and authority with employees
6. Communicating thoughts, ideas, and feelings to employees
7. Caring for employees like one would care for a spouse or children
8. Respecting human feelings
9. Informal chats with employees
10. Traveling a lot, listening a lot, and receiving uninhibited communication from employees
11. Spending money on social and recreational programs for employees
12. Counseling of employees
13. Knowing the hobby, sports, interests, and health condition of employees
14. The large number of helpful suggestions turned in to the organization by employees
15. Showing employees trust, concern, and respect
16. Being responsible for the secure and comfortable lifestyle and welfare of employees and their families
17. Bringing problems directly to top management without going through channels
18. Going out into the field periodically to talk with dealers and meet their spouses
19. The establishment of good will between employees and managers, and the need not to make any special effort to maintain it
20. Managers sharing themselves with employees
21. Managers knowing employees so well that they can usually predict their behavior, and feelings and vice versa

There are a number of ways in which organizations go about establishing intimacy with their employees: CRS Sirrine, Inc. has no enclosed offices; Walt Disney Production managers make it a point to greet all the line employees; managers and employees at E.I. DuPont DeNemours & Company tend to socialize with each other outside the job; H.J. Heinz Company employees are on a first name basis with the managers; and Knight-Rider Newspapers has established a visible management style in which each publisher meets regularly with about two dozen employees and spends an hour and a half listening to them discuss their concerns at a coffee klatch.

22. Employees being able to tell managers openly how they feel about anything without being penalized
23. Employees being able to reveal their weaknesses to managers without fear of adverse effects
24. Being able to make subtle decisions about employees

Suggestions For Effecting Intimacy

It is not easy for managers to become intimate on the job. It takes even greater time and effort to become intimate with someone on a personal basis. For some managers, the task will be too herculean and too painstaking; some may preach intimacy, but will lack the necessary commitment and stamina to bring true intimacy to the job. A select few will become fortified with knowledge about intimacy, then will begin to internalize the necessary humanistic qualities to improve the organization. For this group of managers, the following factors are required:

1. Increase the frequency and duration of contacts with employees.

The amount of time spent with employees by most managers is inadequate. Short visits with an emphasis on the employee's concerns can lead to longer visits with more liklihood of the employee initiating comments that reflect directly on management goals.

2. To expand trust relationships, make commitments to employees.

One successful way to expand trust is to agree on a date and time to carry out a task, chore, or activity (which may be job-related or personal) that will have positive results for the employee—then keep the commitment. In time, the employee will see these acts as sincere expressions of the manager's interest.

3. Maintain all-around contact with employees.

Holistic involvement strengthens the tie between employees and manager over a period of time. Here are suggested "light" and "heavy" contact activities.

LIGHT CONTACT
activities which are generally of a few moments duration, which do not require a great deal of human energy, and are character-

ized by their attitude of thoughtfulness, such as:
—Mail birthday card to employees
—Forward note on important date to employees
—Conduct short, "Hello-how-are-you?" visits to employees
—Visit employees and engage in small talk
—Exchange jokes or humorous observations
—Frequent visits and talks to some employees
—Being present; letting employees know you are available for light
  or heavy contact

HEAVY CONTACT
activities which involve the consumption of larger amounts of time
and energy, such as:
—Sending a handwritten note to an employee on important
  occasions
—Engage in long dialog sessions with employees, covering a wide
  range of topics in some detail
—Engage in serious conversations with employees, taking the
  necessary time and thought to pursue one specific topic to the
  satisfaction of all parties involved
—Invite employees to dinner at your home
—Participate in sports activities with employees
—Have luncheon sessions with employees
—Form car pools with employees
—Visit the homes of employees if they, or members of their fami-
  ly, are seriously ill
—Accept employees' invitations to their homes
—Engage in recreational activities with employees
—Attend funeral services of former employees, send flowers or
  contribute to a designated charity in the name of the organiza-
  tion when an employee, former employee, or close relative dies.
  The main difference between light and heavy contacts is the
expenditure of time, money, energy, and possibly other resources.
Light contact activity, engaged in over a long time span, can
produce the same results as heavy contact.

SUMMARY
Intimacy is the process by which managers establish a personal
and earnest relationship with employees through the initiation of

frequent social contacts, the nurturing of mutual trust, and the maintenance of security and good will. The factors for fostering intimacy are:

1) Acquire knowledge about employees; 2) become friendly with employees; 3) be private with employees; 4) socialize with employees; and 5) be a companion to employees.

Some suggestions for realizing intimacy are: 1) Increase the frequency and duration of contacts with employees; 2) make commitments to employees and expand the trust relationship; and 3) maintain all-around contact with employees.

5

Intuition In Decision Making

THE EFFECTIVE MANAGER has a basic understanding of how the mind works, and strives to increase his or her brain power. In this context, brain power is the ability to use both sides of the brain.

Many American managers have been educated and trained to develop symbolic and analytical skills as opposed to blending these with imagination and iconic skills. As a result, the symbolic and analytical manager tends to place a high value on objective thinking, low value and, quite often, a negative value on subjective thinking that relates to the right side of the brain. Although some job-related decisions can be arrived at in an objective manner, many of them, particularly those dealing with people, must be made subjectively. Harold J. Leavitt, author of *Managerial Psychology*, seems to substantiate this point, by implying that key managerial processes are related more to qualitative, rather than quantitative decisions. In essence, while most managers are trained to become left-sided thinkers, the job environment requires skills related to the right side of the brain.

No wonder some managers will experience great difficulty in acquiring a high degree of proficiency in the humanistic competencies discussed in the first section of this book. These competencies deal primarily with imagination and iconic skills, which are associated with the right side of the brain.

THE OPERATIONS OF THE BRAIN

The human brain is divided into two sections, called the right hemisphere and the left hemisphere. Both are separated by a connector of nerve fibers called **corpus callosum**, which makes it possible for each hemisphere to exchange information. Although both hemispheres receive the sensory impressions and control the movement of the opposite side of the body, each one serves different functions:[1]

LEFT HEMISPHERE

The left hemisphere tends to be more dominant in function; it deals with language and speech, and causes managers to think logically, orderly, rationally, analytically, and in linear and sequential paths. A person who has a dominance or preference for left hemisphere thinking, may be identified either as a linear manager, or left-sided thinker, a left-sided dominant thinker, or an analytical thinker. This type of manager has the following characteristics:

1. Analytical and sequential manners
2. High language skills
3. Problem solver
4. Handles complex problems in sequence of small, logical steps
5. Time-oriented
6. Facts-oriented

Some undesirable terms used by employees at times to describe this manager are:

1. Martinet
2. Dictator
3. Ruthless
4. Calculating
5. Unfeeling
6. Theory X manager

RIGHT HEMISPHERE

The right hemisphere of the brain is usually subordinate to the left hemisphere; it deals primarily with intuition, creativity, holistic and spatial concepts. A person who has dominance or preference for right hemisphere thinking may be identified either as a nonlinear manager, a right-sided thinker, an imaginative thinker, or a right-sided dominant thinker. This type of manager has the following characteristics:

1. Generates ideas and multiple solutions to problems

2. Moves through a problem in a trial and error basis, taking one step at a time, and evaluating results
3. Understands patterns of relations
4. Possesses emotions
5. Controls human action
6. Looks at an entire situation all at once and reacts to it

Some terms used to describe this manager, are as follows:
1. Sensitive manager
2. People-oriented manager
3. Theory Y manager
4. Theory Z manager
5. Imaginative thinker

Intuitive thinking is the process of making a decision about people for some purpose, relating to either ideas, work solutions, methods, and materials. It involves the evaluation of quantitative and qualitative information with more emphasis given to unquantified, introspective, and judgmental data concerning human beings. The decision usually cannot be supported by objective methods or instruments. My position is that intuitive thinking cannot take place unless some left hemispheric thinking has already taken place. I support this contention by citing the fact that the right hemisphere of the brain deals with mass information in parallel, without considering elements or segments. The cooperation involved in the experience bank of the manager is used in some degree to render an intuition judgment. This hypothesis deserves further study.

Following are guidelines for making an intuitive decision.

1. Identify the issue, problem, or situation.

There must be a reason for using intuition to make a decision. Intuitive-oriented decisions always involve one or more persons, and the reason should be known or stated. For example:

> A manager has been requested to select an
> employee to lead a marketing team in the
> development of a strategy for promoting
> a new product.

2. Assess the knowledge requirements.

Before any subjective evaluation takes place, it will be necessary to examine the knowledge requirements in an objective manner. In this case, questions to be considered are: 1) who has the appropriate training, experience, and background to fulfill this position? 2) who may be interested in being selected for this position? 3) who gets along with other employees?

After the manager uses this information to evaluate employees for the leadership position, the next step is:

3. Determine desirable human traits.

The manager identifies the desirable traits for the issue, problem, or situation under consideration. Usually one or two words will suffice:

A. Reliable	D. Instincts
B. Dependable	E. Integrity
C. Aggressiveness	F. Initiative

4. Evaluate employees for the desirable traits.

During this step, the manager will consider all of the employees who were not obviated in step 2, and will select a few finalists who have the vital traits.

5. Make an intuitive decision.

Based on gut feelings, the manager makes an intuitive decision and selects the team leader.

Guidelines 1-5 are not necessarily sequential; all the steps may not be completed by the conscious mind. It will take time, experience, and practice to make effective decisions intuitively.

The guidelines for addressing the problem indicated in item 1 are diagramed for convenient reference.

Step 1		Step 3
		Step 4
Step 2		Step 5
Left Sided Dominant Thinking About the Problem		Right Sided Dominant Thinking About the Problem

Fig. 2: Guidlines for Making an Intuitive Decision

INTUITION INDICATORS

Intuition is:

- Knowing the idiosyncrasies of employees and adjusting work to accomodate these human traits and differences.
- Being able to read the values and beliefs of each employee and using this information to the advantage of the employees and the organization.
- Making some decisions from gut feelings.
- Determining personality compatability and using this information for establishing effective teams.
- Making use of both explicit and implicit information to monitor performance results.
- Indulging in mental keenness.
- Making fine distinctions when rendering a decision.
- Being clever.
- When the reason for making a decision is not readily apparent.
- Making a decision about an employee and knowing that it cannot stand up under objective scrutiny.
- The integration of thinking and feeling.
- Managers' assessment of employees' behavior and attitudes.

ADVANTAGES AND DISADVANTAGES OF USING INTUITION FOR DECISION MAKING

Although more and more managers are beginning to use intuition for decision making, particularly those beginning to practice Theory Z, there are some advantages and disadvantages inherent:

Advantages:

1. It considers deep areas of employees' personality when basing decisions.
2. It is more flexible than most objective approaches for basing decisions.
3. It is, at times, more adequate for basing decisions than quantitative approaches.

Disadvantages:

1. It takes time and experience to learn to think intuitively for making decisions.
2. It cannot stand up against objective scrutiny.
3. It is essentially individualistic, and cannot be easily proven right or wrong.

William Ouchi used the term "subtlety" to describe thinking with feelings. I use the term "intuition" as a synonym for subtlety. The effective manager must not only think intuitively, but must, at times, also be subtle. There are, perhaps, a number of ways in which managers can be subtle. The following are a few of the most common ways to relate to employees in a subtle manner:

1. Tell an appropriate story to get the employee to get an implied meaning.
2. Ask a series of appropriate questions to the employee to get him or her to gradually grasp the gist of the interrogation.
3. Use a non-verbal action to get an employee to realize the intent of the activity.

HOW TO USE INTUITION WHEN MAKING DECISIONS ABOUT EMPLOYEES

One of the most difficult tasks confronting managers who are aspiring to establish a Type Z organization is the accurate evaluation of the traits of employees. Here are some descriptions of common traits of employees that will help a manager to think intuitively when making decisions about them:

Maturity–Maturity means that employees are fully developed to perform a desired act or function.

This definition maintains that the employee must be able to perform the specific act. Therefore, there are situations and activities in which some employees are not mature enough to cope with what is required.

Ambition–Ambition is an energized focus on an objective or goal. The objective may be power, prestige, or wealth. All employees should have some ambition, but a problem exists when employees will do almost anything to get ahead, regardless of who it may hurt. Those employees are overly ambitious, and should be watched and carefully guided and directed.

Values–Basically, values will include employees' aims, ideals, manner of thinking, and principles. When reading values, it is usually best to determine the most dominant, and concentrate on one to help make a decision. Sometimes it may be necessary to focus on two or more values, depending on the complexity of the decision. Following are common personal values managers will have to consider in their decision making:

1. Theoretical value – Employees have a high need to search for knowledge, truth, and facts. Usually, these employees are above average in intelligence, and have a real thirst for knowledge for its own sake.
2. Economic values – Employees having high economic values, tend to be attracted to making the most from things of value. They are practical in saving and spending money, interested in owning property, and are fiscally conservative. However, some employees who have high economic values may be reckless when investing to gain money.
3. Aesthetic values – Employees who value aesthetic things are goal-oriented in appreciating beauty in art, music, literature, etc. These employees tend to be right-sided dominant thinkers, and can almost find beauty in anything.
4. Social values – Employees with high social values tend to be humanitarian and are generous, charitable, helpful, and philanthropic. They enjoy being with people, and usually will stand out within a socio-gram, a term used to describe a process by which individuals in a group identify others in the group they prefer to be with. The team is also used to identify the persons other employees will flock around. Those employees who are the center of attention usually have high social values.
5. Political values – Employees whose aims or goals are power-oriented have a high political value. They enjoy dominating other employees, giving orders, and asserting themselves.
6. Religious values – Employees with high religious values tend to be pious human beings. They are usually very ethical and spiritual.
7. Initiative – Employees who demonstrate initiative, are usually first to perform a feat without being urged. They tend to be goal-oriented, and possess leadership qualities.
8. Aggressive – Employees who are aggressive are usually willing to take direct, and sometimes bold action to perform a feat. However, some employees may be too aggressive, and may create a nuisance for some employees.
9. Beliefs – Some employees have some very strong convictions that certain things are true or real. Because convictions vary with individual employees, astute managers are encouraged

to know those beliefs of their employees, and the extent to which they are strong or weak.

10. Loyalty—Although loyalty is the most desired trait in a Type Z organization, some employees are more faithful then others. A Type Z manager should be able to assess the degree of loyalty of those employees under his or her immediate charge.

11. Integrity—There are some employees in every organization that are sound mentally and emotionally. They are in essence honest, sincere, upright, and possess sound moral principles. These employees have a great deal of integrity, and should be well known by managers. There are countless numbers of traits in employees that can be read with time and experience. Some traits may be more important than others; it most likely depends on the issue, problem, or situation. However, in a given organization, the manager will be able to identify those traits most frequently desired by the organization.

TECHNIQUES FOR USING THE RIGHT SIDE OF THE BRAIN

Some techniques that have been used to help managers to use the right hemisphere of their brain are:

1. Switch off the left side of the brain by tuning out "rational interference." Relax and become responsive to feeling. Useful techniques are daydreaming, doodling, visualizing, becoming totally immersed in the situation, listening to music, sketching.

2. Imagine the problem and situation and draw sketches, diagrams, or pictures to activate the right side of the brain. Pause . . . ponder the images.

3. Think creatively about a solution to the problem, using both sides of the brain. A manager who is eager to develop the creative thinking process, might take several geometry theorems and prove them. Since these exercises require that visual reasoning be translated into logical proofs, repeated exercises using theorems will help develop the creative side of thinking. Try to invent your own right-and left-side games.

USING THE WHOLE BRAIN

A manager who has fully mastered the use of the right hemisphere of the brain will be equipped to use the whole brain in dealing with managerial problems, events, and issues.

1.   Holistic Thinking.

When a manager thinks holistically, he or she is able to see the whole picture as a total view of the situation. In addition, the manager who is a holistic thinker is as concerned about his employees when they are on the job as when they are off the job, in essence integrating the economic and social life of the employees. When this integration exists, the manager is perpetuating a holistic working relationship with employees. To the holistic thinker, key terms are balance, order, harmony and congruency; the values of the organization must be congruent with the values of employees, the personal goals of employees must be integrated with the goals of the organization, the internal environment must be in harmony with the external environment, and short range goals must be designed to meet long range goals. Holistic thinking requires that the manager function to bring forth harmony in the work environment through planning, organizing, leading, and controlling.

2.   Creative Thinking.

Creative thinking may be equated with the imagination, but differs in degree of appropriateness. An imaginative person might not be intuitive, but rather one who fantasizes, which may not be either satisfying, practical, or ethical. On the other hand, the creative thinker is intuitive and imaginative in a satisfying and relevant manner. It is proper to suggest here that the imaginative thinker may engage in meaningless thinking; the creative intuitive thinker always engages in meaningful thinking.

The manager who has mastered right-sided thinking will be able to think creatively and as a result, will be able to make decisions by weighing alternative implications by thinking intuitively, using past experiences and imagination to begin the creative thinking process. There are five basic steps to this process.[2]

A.   Preparation.

This step, associated with the left hemisphere of the brain, involves identifying the situation and assessing the knowledge requirements.

B.   Absorption.

Both sides of the brain are at work; the left side of the brain is absorbed in reading about the problem and thinking about it in a rational manner; the right side of the brain is simultaneously absorbed in visual images, patterns, and symbols.

C. Incubation.

During this stage, the situation or problem is being sifted throughout the right side of the brain which is trying to synthesize a solution. The mode is unconscious.

D. Illumination.

After a search for an idea to solve the problem, the intuitive process triggers illumination. The solution usually emerges spontaneously.

E. Verification.

At this final stage of creativity, the left side of the brain takes over; the intuitive solution is tested for validity and then organized. The synergistic relationship between the left and right sides of the brain has produced creativity. During this process, the right side of the brain produces the idea, while the left side of the brain determines if the idea was sound and logical, making full use of the human mind.

SUMMARY

The brain is divided into two sides called the left hemisphere and right hemisphere. The left hemisphere deals with language, speech, and analytical reasoning. The right hemisphere deals with intuition, creativity, holistic and spatial concepts. Intuitive thinking is the process of making a decision about people for some purpose relating to ideas, work solutions, methods, materials, etc.; it involves the evaluation of both quantitative and qualitative information, but more emphasis is given to unquantified, introspective, and judgmental data. Guidelines for using intuition to make a decision are: 1) Identify the issue, problem, or situation; 2) Assess the knowledge requirements; 3) Determine desirable human traits; 4) Evaluate employees for the desirable traits; and 5) Make an intuitive decision. Using the whole brain involves thinking intuitively, holistically, and creatively. The stages of the creative thinking process are: 1) Preparation; 2) Absorption; 3) Incubation; 4) Illumination; and 5) Verification.

Section Two
The Theory Z Philosophy

THIS SECTION DESCRIBES what some feel may be the "secret weapon" associated with excellent organizations-the philosophy.

The philosophy helps to determine the culture of the organization, to focus the guiding light that governs the human efforts of the organizational activities, and to provide the glue that provides the proper fit for what Pascale and Athos refer to as the soft S's of skills, staff, style, and superordinate goals.

The elements of the statements of philosophy illustrated and discussed in this section are the nature of the organization, organizational thrust, organizational characteristics, and organizational aims.

There are five basic requirements when producing the statements of philosophy: 1) It should be developed involving a cross-section of employees of the organization whenever possible; 2) It should be thoroughly discussed with all employees; 3) It should dictate all actions, words, and deeds for both employees and managers; 4) It should be inculcated continuously throughout the organization; and 5) It should be used as a basis for assessing and improving the organizational culture periodically.

Excellent examples of elements of the statements of philosophy can be obtained from the following companies:
- Socio-economic Purposes-Johnson & Johnson
- Shared Values Statement-Apple Computer, Inc.
- Mission-Marion Laboratories, Inc.
- Organizational Properties-Raychem Corp.
- Organizational goals-ROLM Corp.

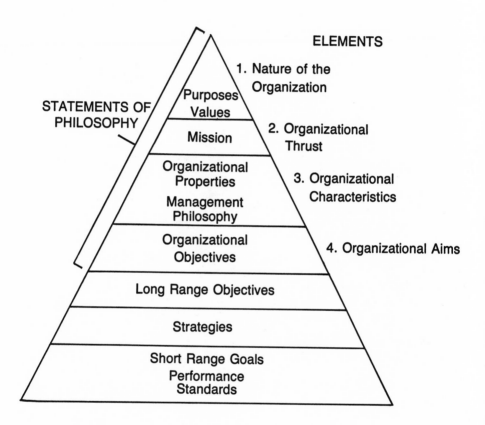

Fig. 3: The Elements of the Statements of Philosophy

6

The Nature of the Organization

THE FIRST ELEMENT of the statements of philosophy identifies the nature of the organization. There are two sections to this element, commonly referred to as the socio-economic purposes and values of the organization. Each of these sections serve different purposes. The statement of purpose describes the socio-economic intent for which the organization exists within a society, and is an integral component of that society. As a result, the purposes for which the organization exists to serve a society should be carefully conceived. Since society is ever changing, the purposes are: basic policy, guiding principles, and basic objectives. The value statement describes fundamental beliefs of what is desirable in an organization, (as well as in personal life of the employees and managers).

Excellent organizations usually have most of the desirable values cherished by the employees. Values, in essence, are the foundations for producing harmony and excellence within the work environment unit. All excellent organizations have values which are the keys that enable them to maintain unity and fulfillment for both employees and managers.

SOCIO-ECONOMIC PURPOSES OF THE ORGANIZATION

Socio-economic purposes are the broad aims of an organization; they are designed to fulfill certain economic and social desires of the people within the organization, and identify how they will function in order to serve the people (consumers) outside the organization. Additionally, they define how the employees should be

71

treated in order to allow them to serve the consumers in a fair and just manner.[1]

Although making a profit is an essential purpose for every business organization, today's excellent organizations serve multiple purposes, involving many segments of a community or society, some of which are:

1. Serve consumers
2. Build people
3. Serve the community
4. Build stronger nation
5. Safeguard the country
6. Enter new fields
7. Practice effective management
8. Observe a code of conduct
9. Contribute to organizational growth
10. Fulfill social responsibilities

METHODS FOR PREPARING THE STATEMENT OF SOCIO-ECONOMIC PURPOSES

Two common methods describe the basic purposes of the organization:

"WE BELIEVE" APPROACH

Each category or statement begins with a "we believe" statement, followed by individual purpose statements, separated by the word "that", as illustrated in the example below:

People

We believe that people are our greatest assets; in order to capitalize on their interests, talents, and skills, the organization should provide for the following:

    a. Involve employees in problem solving
    b. Promote from within
    c. Provide individual and team bonuses
    d. Provide for on-the-job training
    e. Maintain a long-term career path program

Code of Conduct

We believe that all employees should observe a code of conduct which contains

    a. Honesty
    b. Integrity
    c. Fairness in all matters
    d. Loyalty

ROLE STATEMENT APPROACH

This approach is a series of statements which describe the various reasons the organization exists, as illustrated below:

To provide for the personal and professional development of our employees by:

1. Providing equal opportunity for all employees, regardless of age, race, religion, color, sex, or national origin, to develop to their fullest potential.
2. Providing comprehensive long-term career path program for all employees.
3. Providing opportunities for employees to solve problems in their own area of responsibility.
4. Training all employees in a variety of skills.

In order to anticipate our customers' needs for both product and service, we must do the following:

a. Survey their needs on a systematic basis.
b. Insure cost effective and quality sources of supply on a long-term basis.
c. Conduct periodic surveys to determine if they are satisfied with our product and service and, if not, why?
d. Set a price for our products and service at a competitive price.
e. Fill all commitments promptly.

VALUES STATEMENTS

An organization can opt to develop either a CEO values statement and top management values statement and/or a shared values statement. I recommend that the CEO should first develop his or her own values statement; then top management should prepare its own values statement. Use these two values statements as a platform for discussion purposes, then develop an integrated top-management values statement. A committee of a cross-section of employees should prepare its own values statements; use the integrated management values statement and employees values statement as the basis for a lengthy discussion; and reach a consensus over a shared values statement.

DEFINING VALUES

An organization aspiring to become excellent, must begin by clarifying its purposes, mission, and underlying values. This will integrate organizational and employee values. When values are not stated or shared, the organization will find it difficult to unify its components. As a result, each unit usually performs as a separate entity, causing conflicts and disunity among the various segments, and an overall loss to the organization and all it serves.

Values are the broad and fundamental beliefs of a group of human beings, serving to unite them, to integrate their work efforts, to guide their actions, and to channel their energies in a manner that brings fulfillment to themselves and to the organization.

CATEGORIES OF VALUES

There are basically two broad categories of values:[2]

1. Process-Oriented Values.

Process-oriented values are statements describing a desired mode of conduct. They may describe the organization's perception of how employees should be motivated, management style of leadership, and how resources should be used. The following are two examples of process-oriented values:

a. Honesty is required in all endeavors
b. Servants of the people

2. Outcome-oriented Values.

Outcome-oriented values are statements describing a desired end result. They usually identify the beneficiaries of a product or services. Two examples of outcome-oriented values are:

a. High quality and productivity
b. Maximum return on investment

More specifically:

a. Values provide guidelines for governing the behavior of both managers and employees.
b. Values provide a sense of direction for everyone associated with the organization.
c. Values are the basis for guiding managers' decisions and actions.
d. Values affect performance of employees and managers in a positive manner.
e. Values help employees to perform better (because they are influenced by the substance of each statement.)

f. Values communicate to others what they can expect from
the organization.

LEVELS OF VALUES STATEMENTS

There are two levels for writing values statements:

1. The Sublimity Level.

A value statement written on this level is the supreme or highest
value of the organization; no other value takes precedence over
it. An organization with "People Building" as its sublimity value
must direct all its efforts to build its people. An organization's sublimity value can frequently be seen on posters, referred to by
managers, printed on stationery or other pertinent literature of
the organization, and mentioned by employees. To some extent
the sublimity value statement gives priority to the values of the
organization, and helps set the guidelines for the type of culture
the organization desires.

2. The Fundamental Level.

Fundamental level value statements are standard beliefs of the
organization, subordinate to the sublimity value statement. These
values statements are indicators to help realize the sublimity value
of the organization. Fundamental level value can easily become
a sublimity value when changing conditions warrant same. Prior
to the Theory Z movement, one organization I watched had "We
aim to please" as its sublimity value. In pursuit of organizational
excellence, this organization focused on its employees, and
changed the sublimity values statement to "PEOPLE are our
greatest assets." As a result of the change, managers passed the
word to employees and discussed its implications, employees told
their family members and friends, and the organization changed
all of its printed matter to reflect the change in the sublimity value,
setting in motion a shift in the culture of the organization.

THE CEO'S VALUES STATEMENT

The chief executive officer (CEO) should set the tone for the
organization to implement the Theory Z program. The first step
should be the preparation of a CEO's values statement, sometimes
referred to as a belief statement, a written document prepared
by the executive to delineate his or her beliefs of how the organization should be managed, and to be used as parameters for guiding human behavior.

Once the values statement has been prepared, the chief executive officer should arrange to take top managers to a resort for

a weekend to discuss each phase and make any necessary revisions once the statement has been thoroughly gone over with the management team. Some creative CEO's have requested the training division to develop the statement into a visual aid to be used as a springboard for discussion.

The purposes of the CEO's values statement are as follows:

1. To describe how the organization should be managed.
2. To identify the values, beliefs, expectations, and attitudes of the CEO.
3. To use as a basis for synchronizing the values of top management with the CEO.
4. To provide guidance and direction for managing employees of the organization.
5. To forecast where the organization should be heading.
6. To provide a springboard for arriving at a shared values statement.

Two Approaches for Preparing the CEO's Values Statement

Two successful ways to prepare the CEO's values statement have been the terse approach and directional approach.

TERSE APPROACH

This approach is a number of brief statements reflecting the beliefs of the CEO, as illustrated in Figure 3.

1. This will be one of the most important tasks of the CEO, particularly those seeking to implement Theory Z throughout the organization. Allocate sufficient time to be comprehensive yet brief; be prepared to work out of the office if necessary.

2. Ponder values and brief terms. An effective manner to complete this step is to brainstorm as many key descriptive terms as possible. Relate them to The Theory Z philosophy. Here are some examples:

    a. Trust
    b. Care
    c. Respect

3. Group key descriptive terms. When a large number of key descriptive terms have been derived, group them under separate categories and write one or two brief sentences to describe the

values statement. Here are examples of values statements keyed to the terms used in item 2, above:

    a. Trust will be afforded to everyone

    b. Care most for the least

    c. Respect all employees

4. Give the statement to someone for review. Check the contents of each sentence with an assistant to determine whether something has been omitted and/or a sentence needs to be revised.

5. Prepare an audio-visual aid. Assign someone the responsibility of putting the statement into script form; and use either actual photographs or illustrations to make the substance of the statement visual.

DIRECTIONAL APPROACH

Ponder the task at hand and use directional statements to construct values statements. Theory Z Philosophy in general, key success factors, or a combination of both can be the base for orienting the statements. Some directional statements are:

(a.) I believe this organization should . . .

(b.) My perception of this organization is . . .

Following are techniques for preparing CEO's value statements using the directional statement approach:

1. Decide the sub-topics

If Theory Z is the basis for preparing the statement, identify key elements such as the following: caring, trust, life-time employment, career path, etc.

2. Select a directional statement and use it as a base for developing personal values and statements. Write values sentences using the key elements prepared in item 1, such as:

I am under the firm opinion that . . .

(Caring)

a caring relationship should be nurtured between employees and manager.

(Trust)

trust should be expanded throughout the organization

(Life-time employment)

all employees should feel secure in their jobs.

3. Review the statement with an assistant

The CEO should present a copy of the statement to an assistant who will read the essential elements and assess their clarity. Any necessary points should be added, modified, or omitted.

GUIDELINES FOR PREPARING THE CEO'S VALUES STATEMENT

Some general guidelines for preparing the CEO's values statement:

1. Include only belief statements.
2. Review the statement for clarity, effect, and accuracy.
3. Limit each statement to affective (attitudes, values, beliefs) matters. Avoid behavioral or cognitive matters.
4. Use a directional statement to construct values statement, regardless of the approach selected.

DEFINING TOP MANAGEMENT VALUES STATEMENT

Top management values statement is the collective beliefs, feelings, and attitudes of top managers of the organization. Such statements:

1. provide a written document in which top managers reflect their beliefs about how the organization should be managed.
2. provide a document in which top managers reflect their beliefs about how the organization should be managed.
3. provide a base for determining the extent to which management has a positive or negative effect on the job environment.
4. provide one source for assessing the culture of the organization.
5. identify a philosophy of top management that all managers can live by.
6. provide a common platform for the CEO and top management to arrive at an integrated top management values statement.

In 1981, the president of Borg-Warner Corporation requested about 100 of his top managers to help him draft a management value statement. Each manager submitted an individual values statement. After eight months, Borg-Warner produced a brochure describing its management values statement containing five areas: (1) dignity of the individual; (2) responsibility to the common good; (3) endless quest for excellence; (4) continuous renewal; and (5) commonwealth of Borg-Warner and its people.

THE SHARED VALUES STATEMENT

When the CEO's and top management values statements have been produced and merged into an integrated-top-management values statement, a cross-section of employees must be organized to debate and arrive at their own values statement.

Similar to top management, employees should be trained in the use of the nominal group process to reach a consensus over their own values statement. When this has been produced, top management and the committee of employees make further use of the nominal group process to select similar and dissimilar values, debate on the latter, and reach a consensus on a shared values statement.

The shared values statement should identify basic and common beliefs that top management and employees feel are desirable for the organization and personal life. These core shared values then become the guiding light for producing within the organization a strong culture, the backbone of an excellent organization.

Experience gained from observing excellent organizations seems to indicate that when shared values are visible within an organization, managers and employees give emphasis to the strong points in the values statements; managers are able to make better decisions because they are guided by the values, and employees tend to produce more because of the dedication to the values.

A team of about a dozen employees at all levels of the Apple Computers, Inc. spent several months discussing and refining its shared values statement. The statement is divided into eight sections: empathy for customers/users, achievement/aggressiveness, positive social contributions, individual performance, team spirit, quality/excellence, individual reward, and good management. This shared values statement is used as a parameter for determining if a manager can fit into the "Apple culture."

USING THE NOMINAL GROUP PROCESS TO PREPARE
A VALUES STATEMENT

One effective way to arrive at a statement of values—top management or shared value—is to use the nominal group process. Steps for using the process to develop values statements are:

1.   Become familiar with the process. (It is fully explained at the close of this chapter.)

2.   Organize a committee to use the nominal group process to identify and rank values. Even the CEO who decides to personally prepare values statement should establish a committee of top managers to use the nominal group process to arrive at their own statement; synchronize or synthesize the top management values statement with the CEO values statement. An integrated statement can result only after a consensus has been reached on each aspect of the statement. Once the integrated values statement has been formulated, the CEO may desire to go further and involve a cross-section of employees in the preparation of a shared values statement. To do this, organize a cross-section of employees into a committee. Use the nominal group process to generate and rank employee values for a statement. The integrated values statement and the employees' value statement are used as a basis to discuss similar and dissimilar values, and to clarify and improve values for arriving at a shared values statement. There is no set number of values that should be included in the statement. However, each value should be written in from four to six words. There should be a reasonable number of values, so that they will be read and inculcated in the members of the organization.

NOMINAL GROUP PROCESS DEFINED

The nominal group process is a structured method to allow maximum management involvement in making decisions through a controlled interaction process. Nominal in this context means noninteraction in the early stages of the process, where managers are limited in terms of how much interaction is permitted. Later in the process, interaction is vital to clarify issues. (See Step 4 in the procedural steps.)

HOW TO USE THE NOMINAL GROUP PROCESS

The nominal group process can be used effectively with small groups of 9 to 11 managers, medium sized groups of 44 to 55 managers, and large groups of 99 to 110 managers. Larger groups are more likely to experience problems. More problems will also be encountered, depending on whether voting or consensus is used to arrive at decisions. Consensus decision-making is the preferred process for arriving at an agreement on the contents of the management values statement. However, it is more difficult to execute because of the skill required by the facilitator to iron out difficulties, to build teamwork, to solve conflicts, and to nurture the proper environment to make the process work.

ADVANTAGES AND DISADVANTAGES OF THE NOMINAL GROUP PROCESS

Following are some advantages of the nominal group process:

1.   The silent response to the problem and the generation of ideas in a round-robin fashion by the managers, enhance equality among the members and eliminate the domination of the meeting by a single person.

2.   The silent recording round-robin citation of ideas produces more comprehensive ideas.

3.   Arguments and conflicts tend to be limited because the structured process provides managers with equal attention by group members.

One disadvantage of the nominal group process: unless the facilitator has had several occasions to implement the process with different groups, the process may be too difficult to use with large groups.

RESOURCES NEEDED FOR THE NOMINAL GROUP PROCESS

The following procedural steps and resources are needed to implement the process[3]:

MEETING ACCOMODATION

The nominal group process should be conducted in a medium or large room with several small rooms available to accomodate smaller groups. A round table and chairs should be available in each of the smaller rooms.

The furniture in the large room should consist of one or two rectangular tables, situated in the front of the room, and enough comfortable chairs to accomodate all participants.

MATERIALS NEEDED
The following materials will be needed for each group:
1. Flip chart
2. Masking tape
3. Felt-tipped pen
4. Problem description forms
5. Problem ranking cards, or 3" x 5" cards
6. Sheet to record and rank all ideas
7. Action plan

PROCEDURAL STEPS
The nominal group process can be implemented in an hour-and-a-half or less, using the following steps:

1. Introduction to Nominal Group Process
A receptionist presents each person invited to attend the large group meeting a packet consisting of one worksheet, two ranking cards, a pencil with eraser, and a card with each participant's name and room assignment. An example of the worksheet and ranking card are illustrated in Figures 4 and 5 respectively.

When all participants have assembled, the CEO is introduced to the group by the facilitator. The CEO greets the participants by emphasizing the purpose of the meeting, explaining the importance of this meeting to the overall improvement efforts, and thanking the group for participating.

The facilitator explains the nominal group process, elaborates the operation of the process, presents a time for the group to reconvene, and directs the participants to go to their assigned rooms.

2. Implementing the Nominal Group Process
After the smaller groups have convened, the designated group leader requests the group to select a recorder. When the recorder has been selected, the group leader proceeds through the following steps to arrive at the group's prioritized values statement:

A. Reinstructing the Groups on the Process
The group leader reinstructs the group in the Nominal group process and responds to all queries.

B. Respond to Problem Silently
The group leader instructs the recorder to record the problem on the flip chart located in front of the room. A correctly written

statement on the problem is as follows:

"Identify some essential management values"

The group leader will focus on the problem by reciting it, explaining its meaning, and clarifying questions from group members. After the group leader feels that all group members feel secure with the process, he or she requests the group to respond to the problem by writing terse three-to-five word statements on the problem worksheet. After sufficient time (usually 10 to 15 minutes) for written response to the problem, each group member turns in his or her completed worksheet to the recorder.

C.   Citing the Responses

After the completed worksheets have been turned in to the recorder, each response is numbered and recorded on the flip chart by the recorder. Once a sheet is filled, position it on a wall where everyone can clearly see it. During this step, there are no discussions of responses, however, additional responses can be added to the list.

D.   Discussing the Responses

When all of the responses have been listed and posted, each idea is discussed. The purpose of this step is to make certain that each group member has the same understanding of each idea. Individual members can at this time, either defend or promote his or her ideas. After the discussion session, each group member is requested to list the five most important ideas indicated on the flip chart sheets, and to rank the items from 1 to 5 on the ranking cards. The facilitator summarizes the ranking of ideas by:

1.)   assigning the number 5 next to the most important item.

2.)   placing the number 1 next to the least important item.

3.)   continuing to rank the remaining items in descending order.

E.   Tabulating the Ranking Results

Once the ranking of items has been completed, the participants turn in their ranking cards to the recorder. The facilitator dismisses the group for a 10 minute coffee break and tabulates the ranking cards with the assistance from the recorder. To tabulate the result, a tabulation sheet should be used. The horizontal axis contains the ranking order, and the vertical axis contains all listed items. After the five prioritized responses have been determined, they are written on a flip chart sheet and briefly discussed with the group. After the discussion, the group leader requests all participants to reconvene in the medium or large group meeting room.

F. Arriving at the Final Values

When all participants have reconvened as a large group, each group leader presents his or her group's five prioritized responses. Duplicate responses are deleted, additional responses may be added. The group can either discuss individual group's responses or wait until all of the responses have been reported. Once the discussion has been concluded a decision has to be reached as to the number of values to be included in the values statement. When this decision has been made, this figure is used to designate the final number of responses each participant is required to list and rank on his or her remaining ranking card. After this step, items E and F should be reinitiated. Some managers have found it more desirable to consensus instead of listing and ranking to arrive at the final values statement.

Procedural steps and time spans for implementing the nominal group process are:

Activity	*Time*
1. Introduce the process to participants	10 minutes
2. Silent writing of ideas	10 minutes
3. Citing responses in a round-robin fashion	30 minutes
4. Discuss listed ideas	15 minutes
5. Select and rank ideas	10 minutes
6. Tabulate results	5 minutes
7. Discuss ranked ideas	10 minutes
8. Select and rank ideas	5 minutes
9. Tabulate final results	5 minutes

OTHER USES OF THE NOMINAL GROUP PROCESS

The nominal group process can be used to identify and solve a variety of problems:

1. Identify problems besetting a certain group of employees within an organization.

2. Bring together a diverse group of employees to effect change.

3. Gather information and ideas concerning program change, policy change, process changes, people changes, etc.

NOMINAL GROUP PROCESS PROBLEM DESCRIPTION WORKSHEET

Name_____ Date _____

Position _____

Organization _____

Problem Description:

Problem Identification:

1. _____

2. _____

3. _____

4. _____

5. _____

6. _____

7. _____

8. _____

9. _____

10. _____

Fig. 4: Problem Description Worksheet

NOMINAL GROUP PROCESS PROBLEM RANKING CARD

Name _____ Date _____

Position _____

Organization _____

Problem Identification:

		Value	Rank
_____	_____	____	_____
_____	_____	____	_____
_____	_____	____	_____
_____	_____	____	_____
_____	_____	____	_____
_____	_____	____	_____
_____	_____	____	_____
_____	_____	____	_____
_____	_____	____	_____
_____	_____	____	_____

Fig. 5: Problem Ranking Card

HUMAN RESOURCES NEEDED TO IMPLEMENT THE PROCESS

The nominal group process is not difficult to implement once some initial training has been acquired. After each complete cycle of the process, the facilitator will gain more experience, as well as more confidence, in implementing the steps.

Although one facilitator can orchestrate all of the activities of the nominal group process with a great deal of success, particularly if the group is small in size, I recommend two facilitators; usually a coordinating facilitator is responsible for implementing the process, and an assistant facilitator is available to help improve the overall success of the process.

SUMMARY

Socio-economic purposes are the broad aims of an organization that are designed to fulfill certain economics and social desires of people that it is intended to serve. Two common approaches for preparing the socio-economic purposes of an organization are: 1) We believe; and 2) Role statement.

Values are broad and fundamental beliefs that serve to unite a group of humans, integrate their work efforts, guide their actions, and channel their energies in a manner that brings fulfillment to them and to the organization of which they are a part. There are two categories of values: Process-oriented values (statements describing a desirable mode of conduct), and Outcome-oriented values (statements describing a desired end result).

The CEO values statement is a written document prepared by the chief executive officer to delineate some beliefs, aspirations, or desires concerning an organization that are intended to be used as a parameter for governing human behavior. There are two approaches for preparing the CEO values statement: 1) Terse approach and 2) Directional approach. Top management values statement is the collective beliefs, feelings, and attitudes of the top managers of the organization. Value statements can be written on two levels: 1) The sublimity level; and 2) The fundamental level.

A shared values statement identifies basic and common beliefs that both top management and employees feel are desirable about the organization and in personal life. The nominal group process is an ideal method to enable top management and employees to prepare values statements. The nominal group process is a structured method that allows for maximum management involvement in making decisions through a controlled interaction process. The procedural steps for implementing the nominal group process are: 1) Introduction to Nominal Group Process; 2) Implementing the Nominal Group Process; 3) Reinstructing the groups in the process; 4) Citing the responses; 5) Discussing the responses; 6) Tabulating the ranking results; and 7) Arriving at the final results.

7

The Mission of the Organization

THE SECOND ELEMENT of the statements of philosophy identifies the mission of the organization. The mission theorizes the operations of the organization, is usually stated in abstract terms, and endows everyone in the organization with a sense of direction. It is the formula for developing the other elements, preparing plans, and assessing the organization.

Names used to describe the statement of mission are: charter, role, and definition of the organization. Mission is stated in order to mobilize every manager and every employee within the organization into a concerted effort to fulfill its destiny; it also provides a focus whereby management nurtures the appropriate climate to attain cohesiveness and harmony among the human beings who comprise the organization.

A MISSION

A mission is a statement of something desired, and a strong commitment to pursue the vision; it gives guidance, direction, and life to an organization, and is the crucible for forging the principles and practices of Theory Z.

A mission is a statement that can withstand well-reasoned change.

A mission is the basis for developing plans and allocating resources.

A mission is the key for facilitating the identification of strength/opportunities and weakness/problems that must be addressed when planning.

Finally, mission is a statement that provides parameters for governing the actions of all employees within an organization.

PURPOSES OF THE MISSION

The mission statement serves a multitude of purposes, the following of which appear to be the most important:

1. Describes the reason for the existence of the organization.
2. Provides guidelines for the development of strategies and operational plans.
3. Defines the scope or limitations of its endeavors.
4. Provides a basis for making the right kind of decisions.
5. Serves as a vehicle for measuring organizational success.
6. Provides a belief that will foster an organizational climate that will produce quality and productivity.
7. Determines how resources will be allocated.
8. Determines the market segment in which the organization will operate.
9. Determines the size of the organization.
10. Facilitates the task of identifying opportunities and threats that must be addressed.

SATISFYING THE EGALITARIAN REQUIREMENTS OF THEORY Z

William Ouchi has suggested that egalitarianism is a basic feature of a Theory Z organization. I propose that mission statements incorporate features which are associated with how human beings function in an organization. Basically these features would encompass the following:

1. Giving employees broader discretionary powers
2. Operating without close supervision
3. Being free to be creative
4. Trusting each other
5. Being flexible
6. Sharing of power and authority
7. Union and management working together for the common good.

Review the mission statement in terms of these criteria to determine if they directly or indirectly are implied. If not, some discussion and rewriting may be necessary to produce an atmosphere of egalitarianism.

Four Types of Mission Statement

There are at least four common types of mission statement, all of which should be stated at least in terms of services and market. Without designating the market segment, the mission may encompass too wide a scope, which may deplete limited resources and doom the organization.[1]

The four methods for developing the mission statement are:

1. Standard Format

The most common form of mission statement, this usually contains four components:

  a. Begin with the word "To" and specify an act: "To provide . . ."
  b. Identify the product/services: " . . . high quality electronics . . . "
  c. Sometimes it explains "how" the product/services will be provided, such as the following: " . . . at a reasonable cost . . . "
  d. Describes the customer/client market: " . . . within the Apex City."

2. Slogan Technique

This mission statement, used frequently in the past, is seldom used today because it tends to be too broad. It involves the development of a terse statement describing the general thrust of the organization:

> People are our business
> Provide quality services at a reasonable price
> Making things better through training

3. Primary and Secondary Form

This mission statement is seldom used by private organizations, but is used to some extent by public organizations. It involves citing the primary and secondary missions of the organization by using the standard format, as illustrated below:

> The primary mission of the Newton Human Relations Division is to prevent discrimination in all public housing by responding to complaints of citizens in a timely manner. The secondary mission is to provide guidance and direction to all matters pertaining to enhancing human relations.

4. Grand Design

This mission statement is perhaps the most comprehensive of all, and the one recommended by organizations implementing Theory Z. It includes a general statement about the thrust of the organization and specific statements regarding the following:

    a. Stockholders/stakeholders
    b. Customers/clients
    c. Suppliers
    d. Employees
    e. Community
    f. Government

The mission of the Beta Organization is to be a worldwide integrated manufacturer and marketer of electronic products and related equipment, and to be perceived by all stockholders and stakeholders of the corporation as being dedicated to improving their welfare, as well as our own. More specifically, the corporation shall endeavor:

    a. To provide STOCKHOLDERS with the optional investment opportunity, tailored to meet their individual needs without putting the organization in jeopardy.

    b. To provide EMPLOYEES with high quality working life, regardless of their position in the organization, including opportunities for making decisions for solving unit and organization problems.

    c. To provide CUSTOMERS with high quality products and services at a reasonable price.

    d. To be perceived by SUPPLIERS as an organization that is appreciative of their products and services.

    e. To actively support the COMMUNITIES in which the organization does business (nations, states, countries, and cities) in order to improve its citizens' quality of life and to assist in the development of their communities.

    f. To convince the GOVERNMENTS in which the organization operates, to give constructive support to our endeavors.

GUIDELINES FOR DEVELOPING A MISSION

The preparation of a mission statement is probably the second most important task a chief executive officer can perform, the most important being to manage the organization in such a manner that the mission would be fully realized. Important guidelines when the mission statement is being developed:

1. It should be developed by a cross-section of the employees and stakeholders/stockholders of the organization.
2. It should be prepared after a lengthy discussion has taken place.
3. A consensus should be reached concerning its contents.
4. The Theory Z philosophy should be a key factor.
5. Allot enough time to disseminate to employees a copy of the mission statement and to clarify it throughout the organization by discussing each of its key elements.
6. Be prepared to make minor revisions, if warranted.
7. Present the mission statement to the Board for their reactions prior to presenting it to the employees.
8. Whenever possible, use a consultant to facilitate the preparation.

PREPARING THE MISSION STATEMENT

The approach or method for preparing the mission statement depends on the management style and creativity of the chief executive officer. If the CEO is autocratic, he or she will most likely prepare it himself or herself, or get a small group of people to prepare it. A CEO who follows the Theory Z management style may invite a cross-section of employees to participate in the process. Here are some methods for preparing the mission statement:

1. Survey Feedback Approach

Selected managers and employees are assigned to work with a mission committee of two or three organizational development specialists to prepare an appropriate survey form and administer it to key managers (and sometimes employees, dependent on the desire of the CEO). The substance will be used for discussion purposes to arrive at a mission statement using consensus.[2]

The mission committee will usually design questions, analyze and interpret data, verify data, meet with key managers or others as dictated by the CEO to discuss the substance of the survey, then polish the final version of the mission statement.

The survey feedback approach effectiveness rests on several assumptions:

A.   Information that has not been previously shared with employees and is used for discussion purposes can have a positive affect on organizational change.

B.   Sharing information can be instrumental in helping employees to be responsive to change.

C.   Information that is shared in a "what exists" and "what should exist" manner, can stimulate employees to change.

D.   Participating in decision making can lead to increased commitment to change.

E.   Interacting differences through employees can often lead to consensus.

The survey feedback approach is sometimes referred to as "sensing" and can be conducted with the following:

A.   A team

B.   Across various working teams

C.   A cross section of employees

D.   Units, department, division, or throughout the entire organization.

Some of the key elements organizations should consider in order to develop a proper survey form to begin the mission development process are:

A.   What is the business of our organization?

B.   What is or should the be basic purposes of the organization?

C.   What is/are or should be our market?

D.   What is our competitive edge?

E.   What are our shared values or aspirations?

F.   How should we plan to serve:

    1) employees?

    2) customers/clients?

    3) suppliers?

    4) communities?

    5) stockholders/stakeholders?

G.   What are our key success factors?

H.   What should be our strategic thrust or role?

I.   What should be our code of conduct?

J. What is the desirable work climate for this organization?
K. What should be the personal aims or ambitions of top management?
L. What should be the philosophy of the following:
1) management?
2) real estate?
3) merchandising?
4) growth?
M. What should be our ethic standard and business conduct?
N. What should be general objectives of the organization?
1) employees
2) profit
3) customers/clients
4) field of interest
5) growth
6) management
7) citizenship
O. What is and should be our position in the industry?

The above questions are indicated, not as a prescription for preparing a mission statement, but to provide a base for making decisions regarding the content of the survey form. To a large extent, the mission statement will be based on the quality of questions asked, the quality in which they are addressed and answered, and the quality of the conversation and discussion developed from the completed survey forms, the synthesis arrived at over a lengthy interaction, the quality of the written document, and the quality of commitment exerted to fulfill the mission.

The survey form can be administered to either all top managers in the organization, or all managers. The discussion or interaction session should be carried out with a small group of either top managers, or a cross-section of managers and employees. In any event, the mission statement should be written only after a consensus is reached by the group.

2. Key Success Factor Approach

The CEO identifies prime movers of the organization to meet with a selected group of top managers, or a cross-section of managers and employees to identify key success factors of the organization. Key success factors are elements or strengths of an organization that give it an advantage over its competitors.[3] Some key factors I find useful for this purpose:

A. *Personnel* What is the make-up of our people? Are they the best in what they do? Have any of them invented or executed something useful for the firm? Have they developed any patents? How do they compare with our competitors? Can they be depended on to out produce our competitors in the future? How strong is our recruitment program? What is our turnover rate? Do our people have talents and skills our competitors don't have and desire? What is the reputation of our people? Are they among the top 5 present in the field?

B. *Product/s* Is There a high demand for our products? Are our products easily serviceable? What is the reputation of our products? Have we improved our products recently? Is the resale volume of our products high? How durable are our products? Is our distribution system adequate?

C. *Price* Are our prices reasonable and competitive? What kind of financial incentives can we offer our distributors? Do we consistently increase our sales volume each year? Do we get excellent return on our assets? Can we get our products produced cheaper in another country?

D. *Positioning* Can we locate an appropriate country to test our products? What is the track record of our strategic plan? How successful have we been in putting our product on the market?

E. *Programs/Projects* How effective is our training and development program? What are our outstanding programs and projects? Are our programs and projects different than our competitors? How effective have we been in acquiring federal contracts?

F. *Promotion* Do we promote effectively? Do we field test our products before putting them on the market? Do we have a wide assortment of marketing techniques? Is our trade market easily indentifiable by our customers? Do we have a comprehensive and thorough communication network to announce our products? How effective is our marketing division? Has our marketing division won any awards for outstanding marketing strategies?

G. *Production* Do we produce our products in a timely manner? Do we use modern technology to fulfill our production quotas? What are our production capabilities?

These questions and areas are cited merely to present some "food for thought." Each organization should develop its own list of questions to use as a springboard to bring forth the required interaction and thought necessary to create a mission statement.

Where the key success factors have been critically and adequately received, put the major key points into writing and use them as a basis for further discussion, considering many of the questions covered in approach.

After a lengthy interaction has been concluded, prepare a draft of the mission statement, and reach a consensus on its contents.

3. Top Management Approach

The CEO or a small cadre of top managers prepare a mission statement in isolation from other employees, basing their work on an examination of mission statements of other organizations which may or may not be accompanied by a critical review of particulars of the organization. This approach is more common with small organizations, or those closely controlled by an autocratic CEO. Usually, this approach tends to be narrow in scope, and is not supported with the same kind of enthusiasm and commitment as the previous approach.

IMPLEMENTING THEORY Z VIA THE MISSION

The mission statement should be the basis for implanting the principles and practices of Theory Z. The results will be better if the CEO introduces Theory Z philosophy to be associated with its development in the organization. This will necessitate providing appropriate reading articles for the group membership, conducting awareness sessions, sponsoring seminars and a host of other informative activities related to Theory Z. A cogent reason why I suggest that the CEO's values statement be prepared prior to the mission: here is an opportunity to infiltrate the Theory Z philosophy throughout his or her values statement and provide a springboard for interaction and action.

The principles and practices of Theory Z can usually be covered anywhere throughout the mission statement. As an example of how the general statement of the grand design mission statement has been revised to reflect principles and practices of Theory Z:

"The mission of the Beta Organization is to be a worldwide integrated manufacturer and marketer of electronic products and related equipment, and to be perceived by all stockholders and stakeholders of the corporation that we are a people-building organization; although profits are important, people must be adequately trained, provided with information, given opportunities to be involved in the decision-making process, provided with a healthy job environment, and free from job insecurity, or profits will suffer. More specifically, the corporation shall endeavor . . ."

SUMMARY

Socio-economic purposes are broad aims of an organization, designed to fulfill certain economic and social desires of people it is intended to serve. There are two approaches for preparing statement of purposes: "We believe" approach; and Role statement approach.

A mission is a statement that delineates the general purpose of an organization by describing the products/services it desires to provide to customers/clients, and the market segment it intends to serve. Egalitarianism, the basic feature of Theory Z, should be considered when preparing the mission statement. Four common types of mission statements: Standard format; Slogan technique; Primary and secondary form; and The grand design. There are at least three approaches for developing the mission statement: Survey feedback approach; Key success factors approach; and Isolation approach.

8

The Organizational Characteristics

WHEN THE FIRST and second elements of the statements of philosophy have been completed, the CEO should seriously consider describing the organizational characteristics by preparing the third element of the statements of philosophy, commonly referred to as an organizational properties statement and/or management philosophy statement. These statements serve different purposes and can be extremely beneficial to organizations aspiring to adopt the Theory Z concept.

The organizational properties statement actually specifies the characteristics with which managers and employees alike would ideally like the excellent organization to contain. For example, if a young couple is building a house, they would most likely have some ideas about the kind of house they want. They would discuss it with an architect, specifying the number of rooms, types of building materials, the location of windows, etc. The same concept applies with the design of the organizational properties statement. In one organization, lifetime employment may be a desirable element, while in another, it may be absent. Basically, the organizational properties statement actually identifies how or what principles and practices make up the Theory Z organization.

The management philosophy statement describes desirable and expected behavior and attitudes of managers in the pursuit of their job as builders of people. When they can reach a consensus concerning the management philosophy, a common bond has been established between managers and the CEO over the most appropriate way to deal successfully with employees. As a result, this philosophy becomes the basis for nurturing truth and cooperation among all parties involved in the work environment.

THEORY Z ORGANIZATIONAL PROPERTIES DEFINED

Theory Z organizational properties are a set of features that are formulated in order to provide parameters, and to give direction and guidance to management in the operations of the organization. The organizational properties are formulated into a statement form and used as a base for implementing and evaluating the Theory Z concept.

PURPOSES OF THE ORGANIZATIONAL PROPERTIES STATEMENT

There are numerous purposes for preparing the properties statement. Some of the more important ones are:

1. To give top, middle managers and employees an opportunity to discuss and identify what features of Theory Z should be implemented in the organization.
2. To describe the manner in which managers should manage.
3. To identify what the employees can expect in the behavior of managers.
4. To provide a basis for determining if the expectations of the organization were realized and to take appropriate action, if necessary.
5. To facilitate the implementation of Theory Z.
6. To judge manager's behavior and conduct in terms of the Theory Z humanistic competencies.
7. To identify for everyone what is represented as the desirable characteristics for an organization interested in its people.

FORMULATING THE ORGANIZATIONAL PROPERTIES STATEMENT

The formulation of a properties statement can be one of the most exciting steps in implementing the Theory Z concept because it provides managers and employees an opportunity to plan what the ideal Type Z organization should look like when fully developed.

Step 1. Train Managers in Theory Z

Initiate a host of training activities to fortify managers with sufficient knowledge about the Theory Z concept. If employees are to be involved in the properties statement, managers should be used as facilitators to teach the principles and practices of Theory Z during the interaction process that should take place when arriving at the elements.

Step 2.   Familiarizing Employees with the Concept

Conduct awareness sessions and seminars for employees, to give them some base of information for making decisions about the properties statement. During the interaction process, they will become better students of the Theory Z concept, and will be an invaluable assistance to the whole formulation process; they will also become informed Theory Z disciples, spreading the merits of the philosophy. Note: Some CEO's and top managers may seriously object to employees participating in the formulation of the properties statement. There are certainly some pros and cons for employee involvement. Before a final decision is made, managers should discuss the matter, weighing both sides before they render a decision to the CEO.

Step 3.   Declare Constraints

As early as possible, the CEO should announce any constraints concerning the Theory Z program. Usually, the constraints will be an objection to a Theory Z feature such as life-time employment, rotation of job assignments, long-term growth, etc. Each objection, as well as a reason, should be written and discussed with the managers. Some CEO's may find it feasible to listen to constraints from top and middle managers.

Step 4.   Select a Process Facilitator

The CEO should select to facilitate the formulation of the properties a person experienced in group dynamics, conflict resolution and problem-solving processes, such as brainstorming, nominal group process, etc.

Step 5.   Identify a Date and Time

An appropriate date, time, and place should be designated for formulating the properties statement. Usually, a weekend will be needed to complete the properties statement. A comfortable location away from the organization is ideal.

Step 6.   Conduct the Meeting

The facilitator should use either brainstorming or the nominal group process to identify Theory Z properties. I prefer the nominal group process which I find superior to brainstorming: More varieties of properties will be identified, a higher quality of properties will be cited, and a larger number of properties will be selected.

Refer to chapter 6 for an explanation of the nominal group process.

Step 7.   Discuss the Properties Statement with the Board

Before issuing the properties statement to employees, the CEO should arrange a meeting with the Board to discuss each item. Minor changes may or may not be necessary.

Step 8.   Distribute and Discuss the Statement

When the Board has had an opportunity to review the statement, individual managers should disseminate a copy of the properties statement with each employee and clarify each item. If time permits, an audio-visual aid should be made (such as a slide presentation) to illuminate the essential features of the properties statement. Each frame is used as a springboard for interaction. The minimum contents of an audio-visual aid should include:

1.   an introduction.
2.   a description of the properties.
3.   a demonstration of how the statement will be used.
4.   an intimation of what you can expect to realize from the properties statement.

Step 9.   Assess the Organization

Develop assessment instruments to determine the degree to which the properties statement was realized.

One of the vice-presidents of Mead Merchants reported good results from using the nominal group process in planning, developing, and implementing various principles and practices of Theory Z. An expert on the problem-solving process was retained to train managers and employees. According to reports the chief advantage of this process is the reduction by several months of the time needed to implement Theory Z.

ORGANIZING THE PROPERTIES STATEMENT

To ensure that the entire spectrum of the organization is covered, the preparations of the properties should be organized around a list of topics such as: Theory Z, key success factors, and organizational needs.

1.   Theory Z Topics

Select essential features of a Theory Z organization. Identify constraints, separate them from Theory Z features then, briefly define each feature.

EXAMPLE: Topic—stabilize employment—What kind of work environment would offer equity, challenge, and participation in decision making?

Should there be full-time and part-time employees? Should full-time employees receive life-long job security, etc.?

2. Key Success Factors

Use the seven "Ps" previously mentioned in this book, and further define each factor with thought-provoking questions, such as the following:

EXAMPLE: Topic—Personnel—Should there be slow evaluation and promotion? Should we give more emphasis to training and development? Should we establish a formalized career PATH Program? Should we require learning by doing? How should we work toward caring, trust, intimacy, intuition, etc.?

3. Typical Organizational Factors

These organizational factors are elements that characterize any organization. Typical of them are:

A. Products/services
B. Markets and marketing
C. Distribution
D. Product services
E. Production
F. Support Services
G. Organization and management
H. Personnel
I. Finance
J. Environment

Once the typical organizational factors have been identified, develop thought-provoking questions.

EXAMPLE: Organization. How should the organization be designed? What should be its philosophy? How will the organizational performance be assessed, and how often? What should be the central theme of its policies and practices, etc.?

Regardless of the approach used to generate the best of properties, considerable interaction should have taken place to clarify and to get a consensus on each point. The quality of the properties statement will be based on the amount of interaction and how disagreements were settled. In the future, it may be necessary to modify the properties statement. This should be done only after more interaction and reaching a consensus.

GUIDELINES FOR FORMULATING A PROPERTIES STATEMENT

Some useful guidelines when preparing the properties statement are:

1. Involve a maximum number of managers (and employees, if desired) in the description of the properties statement.
2. Prepare a draft of the organizational properties statement for review and approval by the CEO, if he or she was not actually involved in the formulation of the list.
3. Group by topics whenever possible in order to provide good coverage of details.
4. When the properties statement has been completed, it should be evaluated with what presently exists. If major gaps exist, either modify the list or change the organization accordingly.
5. Expect the properties statement to be changed and extended with changing times and conditions.
6. Use a directional statement to ensure that all statements are written in a consistent manner. An example of the directional statement is: The ideal organization exists when . . .

DEFINING THE MANAGEMENT PHILOSOPHY

Management philosophy is a statement that describes desired behavior and attitudes for managing people. It is used as a basis for dictating the expectations of managers. The contents of the management philosophy will, most likely, vary from one organization to another, and will contain such items as:

1. A description of some functions of top management,
2. A description of the lattitude given to operating units,
3. An outline of restrictions and constraints imposed on management,
4. Specific requirements of managers,
5. A description of expectations of managers,
6. A description of desirable principles and practices of managers.

There are numerous approaches for preparing the management philosophy; three are described and illustrated below:

1. The End Approach.

Use a directional statement to identify some specific requirements of top management, operating units, and/or managers.

A. Responsibilities of Top Management.

Top Management at will:

a. set projected gross income.
b. approve all strategic plans.
c. allocate resources.
d. mutually agree to objectives and goals.

B. Description of the Lattitude Given Managers

All sub-units will be provided with the freedom and responsibilities to:

a. manage their own units.
b. develop long-range objectives and strategies.
c. operate their units consistent with the statements of philosophy.

2. The Style Approach

Develop a number of statements to identify a prescribed approach for managing people. Each statement is lead or captioned by a description of the desired management style.

Two examples:

Management by walking around. All managers are expected to get out of their office frequently and walk through their unit, talking, listening, and assisting employees.

Decision by consensus. In order to ensure a strong commitment to carrying out plans, employees who are going to be affected by the change, must be involved in the development of them.

3. The Direction Approach

Cite a number of general statements which indicate the direction of the organization. Sometimes, a directional statement may be used as a springboard to arrive at each statement.

The Alpha Organization strives to provide:

• a work environment based on caring, trust, and intimacy.
• a process that will allow for the untapped talents, skills, and interests of employees to be put to use in solving unit problems.
• decision making, using consensus.

An effective way to formulate the management philosophy is to decide on the approach to be used, and on the specific content to be contained in the statement; then use the nominal group process to generate points to be included in the management statement.

THE MANAGEMENT PHILOSOPHY FORMULATING PROCESS

One organization that experienced a great deal of success in nurturing teamwork among managers, used the following process to formulate a management philosophy statement. Variations are effective so long as they do not inhibit interaction and agreement on the major components.

1. Assess Management Effectiveness.

Assign top management (or a cross-section of managers) the task of implementing the survey feedback approach or nominal group process to collect enough input to be used as a basis for extracting through debate pertinent information. Address the questions of what managers do well, what they do poorly, what needs to be improved, and how the improvement is best made. A facilitator should be included in these meetings to ensure that all views are heard, that managers have been able to vent their emotions, that no one person dominates the meeting, that CEO's potential to improve management effectiveness is identified, and that the group reaches a consensus on a synthesized version of the management philosophy statement.

The CEO should attend these meetings, and should be careful not to dominate the meeting nor present his or her version of the model manager.

2. Confer with Other Managers.

Individual managers of the first group, should be assigned to meet with small cadre of other managers of the organization in order to thoroughly debate each sentence in the management philosophy statement. Certain elements of the statement may need further clarification, depending on the discretion with other managers.

3. Prepare Audio-Visual Aid.

Illuminate each aspect of the management philosophy statement. This aid should be professionally executed to denote the importance of the statement, as well as to help make sure essential points are clearly understood.

4. Meet with Employees.

Managers and/or supervisors, using audio-visual aids and a printed document of the management philosophy statement, explain the extent of the statement and all of its contents.

Managers must be mindful that all employees are constantly observing and evaluating their behavior to determine if it is consistently supportive of the philosophy of management. When the actions of managers are in tune with the philosophy, trust will be at a high level. Therefore, one facet of the guidance system, the management philosophy becomes one basis for nurturing trust within the organization.

SUMMARY

An organizational properties statement is a set of features with Theory Z characteristics; they are formulated in order to provide parameters, and to give direction and guidance to management in the operations of the organization. To formulate the Theory Z organizational properties statement: 1) Train managers in Theory Z; 2) Familiarize employees with the concept; 3) Declare constraints; 4) Select a process facilitator; 5) Identify a date and time; 6) Conduct the meeting; 7) Discuss the properties statement with the Board; 8) Distribute and discuss the statement; and 9) Assess the organization.

Some topics for organizing the list of properties are: 1) Theory Z topics; 2) Key success factors; and 3) Typical organizations factors. The management philosophy statement describes desired behavior and attitudes for managing people. There are at least two approaches for preparing the management philosophy statement: 1) The end approach; and 2) The style approach. One process for formulating the management philosophy consists of: 1) Assessing management effectiveness; 2) Conferring with managers; 3) Prepare audio-visual aids; and 4) Meet with employees.

9

Organizational Aims Formulated

THE FOURTH AND final element of the statements of philosophy identifies the aims of the organization. These aims are usually formulated on what is commonly referred to as a statement of organizational objectives, which usually evolve as an organization grows and prospers.

The impetus for formulating organizational objectives may come about as the result of the CEO's exposure to awareness sessions, seminars, and other managers although it may emerge from outside stakeholders such as ecology experts, minority groups, consumer groups, or from pending legislation. As the result of four recent best selling books in the area of management, thousands of managers are beginning to consider modifying their philosophy, organizational style, and managerial practices, to improve quality and productivity. The first step will involve a critical review of the basic purposes, mission, values of management and employees, and organizational objectives.

The previous chapter dealt with the first three components of the philosophy. This chapter defines organizational objectives and cites some of its purposes.

ORGANIZATIONAL OBJECTIVES DEFINED

The terms, objectives and goals, have been used interchangeably by planning practitioners and authors for years. Unless these terms are specifically defined, some readers may mistake objectives for goals, and vice versa. In addition, some objectives and goals are defined in measurable terms, while others are defined in general or abstract terms. In order to avoid these problems, I use the term organizational objectives to define broad, general, and long-term descriptive statements of purpose of an organization that provides definitive direction for management and employees, and that serves as an instrument for interpreting human efforts. When these organizational objectives have been finalized, they are formulated into a written document, called a statement. Organizational objectives serve a number of purposes as indicated below:

- They provide parameters for human action.
- They are the basis upon which relationships are developed between the organization and employees, customers, stockholders, community, and suppliers.
- They are guidelines at the top of the organizational level and at unit levels of the organizations.
- They are closely related to sub-objectives.
- They are the basis for giving direction, channeling energy, and setting limits.
- They are standards to evaluate an organization's growth and progress.
- They are intentions, aims, and purposes of an organization.

THE MINIMAL ELEMENTS OF AN ORGANIZATIONAL OBJECTIVES STATEMENT

Unless the organizational objectives statement identifies some minimum elements, such as the people and purpose of the organization, a code of conduct, and the market, it will fail to meet the essential requirements of an organizational objectives statement.

1. People

The statement of an organization striving to implement Theory Z should begin with people-oriented organizational objectives such as:

To enter into a holistic relationship with emloyees.

To provide lifetime employment for all permanent employees.

To treat and use people well in the environment.

2. Purpose

The statement of organizational objectives must include the rationale for the organization—what its business is. Although this does not mean the delineation of specific products or services, there should be evidence of output such as:

To build people.

To attain twenty-five percent of the foreign market.

To identify and pursue acquisitions overseas.

3. Code of Conduct

The statement should also describe the manner in which the organization will carry out its business and is usually reflective of attitudes, beliefs, and some values, some of which are:

To maintain the highest level of honesty and integrity with customers.

To offer customers products which present high quality.

To adhere to the Golden Rule.

4. Market

The statement should also include a general description of the market to be served, expressed by type of customers/clients, geographical location, ranking and other nonspecifics such as these examples:

To improve its position in the far eastern market through judgement.

To confine operations to the United States.

To be among the three major organizations satisfying the security needs of the United States and NATO countries in land, sea, and air.

5. Profit Requirement

The statement of organizational objectives should also contain what the organization expects to realize in profits and returns on investments.

Examples of organizational objectives involving profits are:

To achieve continuous growth, sufficient enough to attract and hold stockholders.

To secure stockholder investment in the parent organization through prudent and fiscal conservative management.

To achieve a rate of growth which will maximize strengths and minimize weaknesses.

TECHNIQUES FOR DEVELOPING ORGANIZATIONAL OBJECTIVES

Four common techniques for developing organizational objectives are:

1. Topic approach.

Managers identify a number of sub-divisions of the purposes and aims of the organization and define each, which is then discussed at length, after which one or more organizational objectives are formulated. In addition to those indicated previously, some other topics for formulating organizational objectives are:

Growth
Product and product leadership
Resources
Productivity
Innovation
Social Responsibility
Organizational structure
Customers
Field of interest
People
Management
Citizenship.

2. Key Result Areas Approach.

Key result areas are focal points where performance and results directly and vitally affect the survival and growth of the organization. Some examples of key result areas are:

1. Productivity
2. Financial resources
3. Physical resources
4. Innovation
5. Social responsibility
6. Human Organization
7. Marketing
8. Profit requirements.

3. Key Success Factors Approach.

The key success factors of the organization is another approach for guiding the development of organizational objectives. This is accomplished by identifying the key factors for success in an organization. Some examples of key success factors are:

1. Design
2. Product range/variety

3. Servicing
4. Sales force
5. Production Equipment
6. Distribution network.

4. Scenario Approach.

A scenario in this context is a description of what the organization might look like in the future. The strength of the scenario is based on what the organization does rather than what happens to it. Thus scenarios are qualitative predictions about the organization at some future time. To construct a scenario involves reviewing past performance, trends and patterns, etc., and determining major aspirations.

Usually a scenario will cover:

1. Introduction—some brief comments on the uses of scenarios.
2. Organizational Aspirations—general statements concerning the aims and aspirations of the organization. The subject for each objective can be devised from either the first, second, or third approach mentioned earlier.
3. Constraints—identify constraints that limit the aspirations.

The organization should limit its activities in the United States.

METHODS FOR WRITING ORGANIZATIONAL OBJECTIVES

Two common methods for writing organizational objectives are:

1. The Action-Oriented Approach.

State the action required to help realize the basic purpose and mission of the organization. Begin with an action verb preceded by the word "to", and indicate a desired level of performance.

An example of an organizational objective using the action-oriented approach:

To make certain that products are supported by prompt and efficient service.

2. Rationale Approach.

Give a brief statement about the reason for the objectives; indicate a desired result. Begin with a rationale statement followed by a desired condition.

As an example: PEOPLE BUILDING. We are in business

to build people. We should provide employees with an opportunity to learn a variety of skills.

FORMULATING ORGANIZATIONAL OBJECTIVES

The Theory Z concept diminishes the difficulties sometimes associated with formulation of organizational objectives. Some underlying assumptions about setting organizational objectives are:

1.   Organizational objectives, the nucleus of every Theory Z organization, provide the basis for unity of effort, efficiency of operation, and effectiveness in realizing its purpose.

2.   The organization does not perform in a stable environment. The external environment is always in a state of change. Management must be willing to respond to those changes that will have a negative impact on the purpose of the organization.

3.   As many as possible of the persons who have a stake in the operation of the organization should be involved in the objective setting process.

ORGANIZATIONAL OBJECTIVES CRITERIA

In order for organizational objectives to be useful, they must meet certain criteria:

1. Validity

Organizational objectives must be valid for the organization, the achievement must support the basic purpose and reason of the organization. An objective that does not point the organization in the direction for fulfilling its reason for being serves no useful purpose.

2. Feasible

Organizational objectives should be achievable. They should be neither unrealistic, unchangeable, or unpractical. Feasible objectives are set in terms of what exists today and what is most likely to exist in the future.

3. Acceptable

Organizational objectives are achievable when they are acceptable to the people in the organization; objectives not in tune with the value system of managers or employees may never be realized.

4. Flexible

Organizational objectives should change with changing times and conditions; they should be flexible and changed in the event of unforeseen circumstances.

5. Understandable

Organizational objectives should be understood by all employees and managers who are going to be affected by them. An organizational objective such as "To foster an egalitarian relationship with employees" may have no significance to either managers or employees if the term "egalitarian" is not understood.

6. Commitment

Organizational objectives should be supported by a strong commitment. The ideal way to get this kind of support is allowing workers and managers to participate in formulating and reaching a consensus over them.

7. Linkage

Organizational objectives should be linked to the basic purpose and mission of the organization. Sub-level objectives should be linked to organizational objectives right on down the line. When proper linkage exists between and among objectives and sub-level objectives, a set-up will exist to ensure continuity of human action.

CONDUCTING AN ORGANIZATIONAL AUDIT

When the statements of philosophy have been completed and have been in practice for five years or more, the CEO will need to determine how well the philosophy is being implemented. The audit will reveal where the organization is in terms of practicing its philosophy at present. If there is a large gap between the statements of philosophy and what is practiced by its managers and employees, then the organization is said to have a weak culture. It is assumed that the philosophy incorporates many of the principles and practices of excellent organizations. If, on the other hand, the gap is small between the philosophy and the practices of the organization, it is said to have a strong culture. Every excellent organization is reported to have a strong culture that unites the people to pursue the purposes and mission of the organization.

THE IMPORTANCE OF AN ORGANIZATIONAL AUDIT

Every organization should conduct a periodic audit to determine the health of its culture. This is similar to a physical examination of a person, which should be conducted from time to time to determine if all of the essential parts of the body is functioning properly. An organizational audit will reveal which aspects of the statements of philosophy need attention so that appropriate attention can be given them by management. An organizational audit serves three purposes:

1. To determine the presence and extent of the cultural gaps.
2. To determine how the organization applies its management philosophy to make use of its resources.
3. To assess whether or not positive changes have taken place in the organizational culture.

TECHNIQUES FOR CONDUCTING AN ORGANIZATIONAL AUDIT

Here are some techniques for conducting the organizational audit:

1. Assess the Key Success Factors

Use the nominal group process. Select a committee of managers or a cross-section of members of the organization to identify things that the organization does not do well, and what can be done to improve the organization. Once this information is generated and ranked, a small committee develops the information into an organization profile which then becomes the basis for interaction with other managers and employees. The profile may be changed, as determined by the discussion with other members of the organization, and is the foundation for producing an action plan for improving the health or culture of the organization.

2. Retain an Organizational Development Specialist

Hire one or more outside organizational development specialists to use the survey feedback approach. Collect data on the health of the organization, use it to discuss with members of the organization, then finalize a document that becomes an action plan to improve the culture of the organization.

3. Retain a Diagnostic Review Consultant

A diagnostic review is an in-depth, self-study of an organization.[1] It is a very comprehensive and intensive study of all facets of the organization. An outside consultant, usually experienced with this technique, is hired to facilitate the process. Because of its thoroughness, considerable time must be devoted to this process by management. The consultant establishes a process by which he or she gets management to answer some basic questions about the organization, such as:

(a) Where are we presently?
(b) Where do we want to go?

(c)   What are our strengths?

(d)   What are our weaknesses?

(e)   Where must we improve?

(f)   How should we improve?

The diagnostic review and self-study demands that management, and sometimes employees, be actively involved in the process. The end result will produce a comprehensive and in-depth professional analysis, a written document containing diagnosis and recommendations for change, and a process for improving the skills and practices of managers. The statements of philosophy and the Theory Z concept should be the foundation for detecting problems of the organization and guidelines for changes.

4.   Prepare an Organizational Profile

Using a cadre of managers and a facilitator, conduct a study to obtain a profile of the organization.

(a)   Prepare questions to be included in the profile which are to be used for the study.

i)   Determine profile categories. These categories can be arrived at using key success factor, key result analysis, typical areas of an organization, etc.

ii)   Indicate a starting point for the analysis. The starting point could be ten years ago, before a major event such as a war, or the present.

iii)   Describe what the organization has done well.

iv)   Describe what the organization has not done well.

v)   Indicate what can be done today to improve the organization.

vi)   Indicate what the organization can do in the future to improve.

(b)   Once a consensus has been reached over the questions, situate them in a survey form and submit them to the appropriate managers for response. Summarize the substance of the survey; use it as the basis for discussing with managers. A great deal of interaction must take place at this stage in order to get managers to convey their true feelings about the critical comments on the survey. When the summary has been fully digested by the managers, prepare an action plan to effect changes in the organization.

(c)   When the action plan has been developed, prepare an audio-visual aid to vividly display the contents of the profile; use it for interaction among managers and employees.

SUMMARY

Organizational objectives are broad, general, and long term descriptive statements of purpose of an organization that provide definite direction for management and employees, and serve as an "umbrella" for integrating human efforts of all units into a total collective effort. Minimal elements of an organizational objective statement are: 1) People; 2) Purpose; 3) Code of conduct; 4) Market; and 5) Profit requirements. The approaches for developing organizational objectives are: 1) Topic approach; 2) Key results area approach; 3) Key success factors; and 4) Scenario approach. The two basic approaches for writing organizational objectives are: 1) Action-oriented approach and 2) Rationale approach. The underlying criteria for formulating organizational objectives are: 1) Validity; 2) Feasible; 3) Acceptable;   4) Flexible;   5) Understandable; 6) Commitment; and 7) Linkage. Techniques for conducting an organizational audit are: 1) Assess the key success factors; 2) Retain an organizational development specialist; 3) Retain a diagnostic review consultant; and 4) Prepare an organizational profile.

10

How To Build A Strong Organizational Culture

MERELY PREPARING A comprehensive statements of philosophy will not produce an excellent organization; the statements of philosophy must come alive. All employees must be given a copy of the philosophy, each aspect must be thoroughly discussed and digested, and all elements must be practiced by managers and employees. A living philosophy is one that has been inculcated throughout the organization, thus giving it a soul.

A prevailing problem in far too many organizations in this country is the stagnation that takes place when a philosophy has been formulated. Usually, the principles and guidelines that have been evolved, sometimes with adequate employee involvement and deliberation, and sometimes without, are not shared with employees. As a result, it is as if no philosophy exists and managers and employees alike go about performing their jobs with no set of macro-principles and guidelines. To inculcate the philosophy of an organization, its CEO and management must plan and execute a formal program to make this essential step to excellence a reality.

TECHNIQUES FOR BUILDING A STRONG ORGANIZATIONAL CULTURE

The inculcation of the philosophy is intended to build a strong organizational culture. The emphasis of this chapter is to use training as a key technique. Here are useful techniques for building a strong organizational culture:

1. Managers Performing As Role Models.

The behavior and attitudes of management. If the words, actions, and deeds of managers are consistent with the norms and values of the organization, a strong culture will result; if not, a weak culture will be evident. Role modeling can also be demonstrated through written documents, as well as through the use of audio-visual aids provided by the training department. I have also found it useful to have managers present skits in which they assume roles to demonstrate various aspects and stages of the philosophy.

2. Recognizing Philosphy Compliance.

Recognize managers who are observed exemplifying an element of the philosophy. Send a note of praise to an employee who is seen practicing a desired value or norm; if the deed has a significant impact on the reaction of other employees, give that person a bonus, a raise, time off, etc. In some organizations, employees or teams that exemplify the desired elements of the philosophy are given a gift certificate which can be exchanged for merchandise at a store, membership in a health spa, a number of Mondays or Fridays off (thus creating a long week-end), or free lunches, served by managers.

3. Communicating the Philosophy.

Prepare a philosophy manual and use it as a tool during employee orientation. Such a manual contains all of the essential elements of the statements of the organization's philosophy. Each element is segmented; sometimes questions follow each element to test the employees' understanding of that aspect of the philosophy. This manual is invaluable when implementing the varied training activities associated with orientation and career path growth. Some organizations have produced newsletters to help spread the gospel of the philosophy, others have produced "white papers" and essays, and distributed and discussed these with the employees.

4. Implementing Long-Range Training Activities.

A number of organizations have a long-range training program, designed to cover all of the elements of the philosophy. This training program usually is conducted over two-to-three years, and involves regular monthly training sessions lasting for twenty-to-thirty minutes. Most of the substance of this chapter is devoted to the kinds of training activities that can be implemented for this purpose, one of which is becoming increasingly popular: someone from top management reads a book that is consistent with the desired values and norms of the organization, and holds meetings to discuss its contents.

5. **Subtle Techniques Designed to Help Inculcate the Philosophy.** Some Theory Z companies use tests and layers of interviews to screen prospective employees. If personality and character are compatible with organization values and norms, the candidate is hired. Another subtle form for inculcating the philosophy involves adapting certain practices and organization design that are consistent with the philosophy. Some common practices of excellent organizations may involve an open door policy, no lay-off plan, promotion from within, career development path, etc. Perhaps the most subtle technique for inculcating the philosophy is physically designing the facilities to embrace the values and norms of the organization. In an egalitarian organization, there would be no reserved parking spaces and, in an open organization, offices would be replaced by open work stations.

INCULCATING THE PHILOSOPHY

Inculcating the philosophy of an organization is the process of impressing upon employees the importance of certain macro-principles and guidelines or expected behavior, attitudes, and parameters for the successful operation of the organization. As a result, these macro-principles and guidelines are frequently repeated throughout the organization by numerous and varied activities. When the philosophy has been fully inculcated throughout the organization, a strong organizational culture has been produced and, as a result, employees are aware of its principles and working within the guidelines. Thus, the organization is achieving an essential step in the pursuit of excellence.

The purposes of an inculcation are:
1. to build and nurture a strong culture to be passed down from one generation of employees to another.
2. to transmit values of the organization.
3. to define philosophical weak spots in order to initiate corrective actions.

4. to enable individual parts of the organization to come together to fulfill their intended purposes.
5. to enable all employees to have similar beliefs.
6. to foster shared understanding of what is really important to the organization and its activities.
7. to promote managerial continuity throughout the organization.

MANAGEMENT ROLE IN THE INCULCATION PROCESS

Every manager has two basic training functions: inculcate the philosophy of the organization, and train employees in the basic skills to perform their jobs. In excellent organizations, both functions take place continuously throughout the tenure of employees. In other organizations, the inculcation of the philosophy through training and other means is virtually nil, while some training in the basic skills is provided to some employees on a short-term basis.

The inculcation of the philosphy usually takes place before skill training, and is expanded through formal and informal means. Employees hired directly after graduation from high school or college are less likely to have to be "decontaminated" and then indoctrinated in terms of the principles, practices, and guidelines of the organization. Top management is responsible for the formulation of the statements of philosophy in collaboration with a cross-section of employees. Another mission of top management is to develop appropriate policies and procedures which inculcate the philosophy, then make certain periodic analyses are conducted to determine the extent to which the philosophy has been implemented, and take any appropriate corrective action. Top management is also responsible for bringing attention to various elements of the philosophy through their actions, words, and deeds.

Middle management is responsible for the execution of the policies and procedures regarding the inculcation of the philosophy. To this end, all middle managers will spearhead the formal and informal activities to inculcate the philosophy. This means that they will conduct numerous appropriate training activities, involve employees in assessing the extent to which they are adhering to the philosophy, and to recommend changes and corrective actions to top management.

PROCEDURE FOR INCULCATING THE PHILOSOPHY

The inculcation of the philosophy of an organization must proceed through six steps: (illustrated in Figure 6)

Step 1. Preparation of the Statements of Philosophy.

Top management determines what elements of the statements of the philosophy should be incorporated in its organizational philosophy. Some common elements contained in the philosophy are:

a. Socio-economic purposes
b. CEO values, top management values, and/or shared values
c. Mission
d. Organizational objectives

After deciding which elements to include in the philosophy, top management determines how many committees should be involved in the formulation of the philosophy, the make-up of each committee, and a schedule for completing each phase of the philosophy. The following is an example of the number of members and the composition of committees designated to dwell on specific elements of the philosophy of one organization:

ELEMENTS	NO. OF MEMBERS	COMPOSITION
Socio-Economic Purposes	5	CEO and four senior managers
Values:		
1) CEO	2	CEO and administrative assistant
2) Top Management	11	Senior Managers
3) Employees	11	Cross section of employees, representing sex, race, and divisions
4) Shared values	11	One senior manager, four middle managers, and six employees
5) Mission	11	Two board members, CEO, and eight senior managers

6) Management Philosophy	11	CEO, five senior managers, and five middle managers
7) Organizational Properties	11	CEO, three senior managers, three middle managers, and four employees
8) Organizational Objectives	5	CEO and four senior managers

New Skill Training

When appropriate skills have been acquired to perform the varied functions necessary to accomplish a job over a period of time, the employee is then rotated and receives training in new skills in order to perform in the new assignment. A number of different training methods are used to facilitate the expected changed or modified behavior.

Problem-Solving Training

When a problem arises on the job, sometimes problem-solving training is instituted; the employees go through brainstorming or some other problem-solving techniques to achieve a breakthrough on a unit or team problem. Quality circle training usually involves the following training periodically for the positions indicated:

(a) Circle Members-One hour per week over a period of three to four months
(b) Circle Leaders-Eighteen to twenty-four hours over three days
(c) Facilitator-Thirty to forty hours over five days

TRAINING STRANDS

A training strand is a series of interrelated knowledge and/or skills to be taught or to be learned; without the knowledge or skills in the strand, a specific activity cannot be performed.

Employee Training Strand
(a) Multiple functions
(b) Team work
(c) Quality circles
(d) Problem-solving
(e) Communications

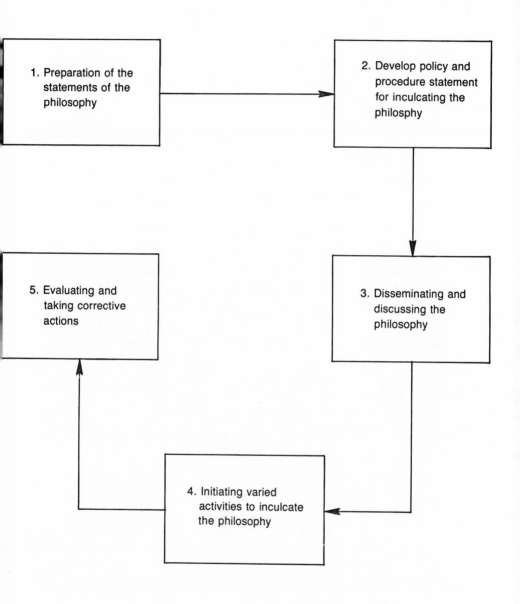

Fig. 6: Procedural Steps for Inculcating the Philosophy

Manager Training Strand
(a) Multiple functions
(b) Team work
(c) Quality circles
(d) Quality controls
(e) Problem-solving
(f) Group dynamics
(g) Conflict resolution
(h) Participative management
(i) Interpersonal skills
(j) Principles and practices of Theory Z
(k) Motivation
(l) Strategic and operational planning

CONVERTING RESPONSIBILITIES INTO FUNCTIONS

Examine the differences between Japanese and American management styles in the use of organizational charts and job descriptions. Neither instrument is frequently used in Japanese organizations; if team work is going to prevail in an organization striving to implement Theory Z, a strong case could be made for the use of an organizational chart to depict responsibilities. The job description has been a job instrument that is, at most, used about four to six times a year. Frequently it can be found in back of a drawer with an accumulation of dust.

No committee should exceed eleven members; research indicates that when membership on a committee exceeds eleven, its effectiveness tends to diminish.

Once the committees have been organized and ready to proceed, assign a facilitator to each:

1. to ensure the meeting operates smoothly.
2. to read and discuss the charge of the committee.
3. to disseminate appropriate information and working materials to committee members.
4. to ensure adequate interaction has taken place before an action is made final.
5. to help the committee to reach a consensus on all items.
6. to make certain personal feelings and concerns of each committee member have been accommodated.
7. to assist the sub-committee to finalize the finished document.
8. to report the progress of the committee to the CEO.

9. to assist committee members during difficult times.
When the facilitators have submitted their committee's finished
document to the CEO, he or she should then:

1. review each document carefully to determine if there are
any items which are contrary to his or her personal beliefs, or in
opposition to organizational policies and procedures. If there are,
the CEO should be prepared to discuss them with the facilitator,
and a decision will have to be made as to whether or not a special
meeting has to be conducted with the committee to hear the concerns of the CEO and to resolve the issue.

2. determine how each element is to be arranged in the
philosophy. For example, the CEO may decide to position the
shared values statement after the mission statement instead of before it.

3. arrange a meeting between the CEO and the facilitators,
during which each facilitator makes a presentation of the activities and events leading up to the committee's finished documents.
Issues, events, and concerns are brought up and resolved. Although
minor changes in the finished documents can be made, substan-
tive changes must be brought back to the original committee for
consensus resolution. When the CEO has carefully positioned all
of the statements (finished documents) of the philosophy, a copy
of the finished document should be presented to each facilitator.

Step 2.   Develop a policy and procedure statement for inculcating the philosophy. Top management makes basic decisions
relating to how the statements of philosophy should be inculcated.

a.   How should management be introduced to the philosophy?

1)   Should the CEO and top management go away on a
retreat to introduce the philosophy to management?

2)   Should facilitators introduce their individual elements of
the philosophy to management at prescheduled meetings in a
location within the organization?

3)   Should CEO conduct special meetings with top management to introduce the philosophy?

4)   Has top management been actively involved in all elements of the philosophy so that additional meetings are not
necessary?

5)   What is the best way to get maximum interaction from
management?

    6) How much time should be devoted to the introduction?

b. How should employees be introduced to the philosophy?

    1) Should facilitators or managers introduce the philosophy?

    2) What is the best way to get maximum interaction from employees?

    3) What role should the CEO and top management play in the introduction?

    4) How much time should be devoted to the introduction; when and where will it take place?

c. Should audio-visual aids be used to introduce the philosophy?

    1) Who should prepare the aids?

    2) How much should be budgeted?

    3) How much planning and development time should be allocated to the preparation of aids?

d. What activities should be used to inculcate the philosophy?

    1) Should an organization song be written and by whom? How often should it be sung and on what occasions?

    2) Should an organizational creed be prepared, and by whom? How often should it be recited and on what occasions?

    3) How and when should management focus on the philosophy?

    4) What training activities should be initiated to inculcate the philosophy?

    5) How much time should be devoted to training activities and when should the activities take place?

    6) How should employee feedback be used to strengthen the inculcation of the philosophy?

e. What process should be used to evaluate the extent to which the philosophy has been inculcated?

    1) Should an outsider or an insider be used to evaluate the inculcation of the philosophy?

    2) How much should be budgeted for the evaluation?

    3) How much time should be devoted to the evaluation?

    4) How should corrective actions be taken?

When all pertinent questions have been considered, organize a team of senior and middle management to prepare a comprehensive policy and procedure statement on the inculcation of the philosophy. From time to time, it may be necessary to revise this statement.

Step 3.   Disseminating and discussing the philosophy
Once guidelines have been developed to inculcate the philosophy, copies of the philosophy must be distributed to all employees and discussed. Middle managers are responsible for introducing the philosophy and initiating the various activities to inculcate the philosophy in their various units. Facilitators and the audio-visual aids are useful for adding spice to the introductory sessions.

Step 4.   Initiating varied acitivites to inculcate the philosophy
Use a variety of activities to inculcate the organization philosophy. These should be well-designed and planned prior to their execution. In some instances, it will be top management's responsibility to determine frequency use, such as how often should the organizational song be sung. Some common activities to inculcate the philosophy:

ORGANIZATIONAL CREED. Organize a committee of employees and charge them with the responsibility for producing an organization creed. Once the creed is acceptable to management, decide how the creed will be used. Some ways in which creeds are used in excellent organizations:

1.   Place a border around the creed, print, and distribute sufficient copies for all employees.

2.   Post the creed in various conspicuous locations throughout the organization.

3.   Require all employees at a specific time to recite the creed on a daily basis.

An example of organizational creed:

> Improved quality and productivity can only be attained through the combined efforts and cooperation of each employee of the organization. Therefore, each of us shall always keep this point in mind as we continually pursue excellence for ourselves and our organization.

Use the statements of philosophy as a guide when developing a creed to ensure that important aspects of the philosophy are included.

ORGANIZATION SONG. A useful practice for inculcating aspects of the philosophy throughout the organization is to solicit employees to write an organization song, using the statements of philosophy as a guide for the lyrics. The individual or team producing the most appropriate song is given some type of award and/or recognition. The criteria for selecting the song should be based on the most number of points covered by the philosophy that are contained in the lyrics, and the tune.

When the song has been selected it is disseminated to all employees. The supervisor of each team is instructed to lead the team in practicing the song each day for a week before the organization assembles as a whole to sing the song either on a daily basis at a particular time, or on selected events and activities.

ORGANIZATION SLOGAN. Although the mission is usually used as a base to define the organization slogan, any element of the statements of philosophy can be used for this purpose. Some examples of slogans are as follows:

"Excellence in Execution"
"Think Before Acting"
"Caring Means Everything"

To inculcate the slogan: print signs which effectively display the slogan, post throughout the organization; refer to slogan when management meets with employees; use the slogan on stationery and other important documents.

EMPLOYEE ORIENTATION. Some excellent organizations have begun the inculcation of the philosophy during the orientation process when new employees are first hired. Although the substance is brief, all elements of the philosophy are covered.

Items appearing on the agenda of the orientation might resemble the following:

Agenda

What are the purposes of our organization?	(socio-economical purposes)
What do we value in the organization	(shared values)
What services or products do we provide, and what is our market?	(mission)
What can you expect from our managers?	(management philosophy)

What kind of organization
do you work for?   (organizational properties)

What can you expect from
your organization?   (organizational objectives)

TRAINING ACTIVITIES. Design each training activity to be completed within fifteen to twenty minutes. Depending on the amount
of interaction generated, you may need two or more sessions.
Some activities will require the manager to prepare questionnaires
or other instruments for discussing specifics of the philosophy.
Some trainig activities for inculcating the philosophy:[1]

Activity—Self-indoctrination.   Request each member of a
team to become familiar with an essential point of one of the elements of the philosophy, then give a ten to fifteen minute per-
suasive presentation. Presenter must persuade the team membership that a particular detail of the philosophy has been realized.
Team members msut be convinced not only by words from the
presenter, but alo by the deeds and actions of the manager. The
manager is responsible for conducting an interesting and thought-
provoking meeting.

Activity-Using sentence stems.   After the manager explains
an element of the statements of philosophy, he or she requests
an employee to think about what has been presented. The employee is then asked to use any one of the following sentence stems
to share with team members his or her personal feelings about
the element:

> "I believe the mission is..."
> "I don't believe that our mission is...because..."
> "Our managers don't practice what they preach
> because..."
> "I believe that...is a desirable organizational
> property because..."

Activity—Responding to vignettes.   The manager introduces this activity by initiating a discussion about an element
of the philosophy. Employees are then presented with a specific
situation or vignette which calls for some appropriate action. Each
employee is requested to write a brief description of what he or
she would do in that situation. Employees then divide into miniteams of three to discuss their proposal and to determine which

of the three decisions is considered the best. After ten to fifteen minutes, all employees reconvene as a team to discuss the decisions and to reach a consensus on the most desirable course of action. The situation used by the manager should be based on an actual condition existing in the organization.

An example of an appropriate vignette concerning the mission:

"Because you work in the controller's office, you are personally aware that the organization has never contributed anything to the community. This bothers you because the mission statement says, 'To actively support the community in which the organization does business (nations, states, countries, and cities) in order to improve its citizens quality of life and to assist in the development of their communities.' Recently you learned that the organization does business in South Africa. What should you do regarding this matter?"

The manager can capitalize on this activity by referring the best proposal to top management for consideration, or can have top management present their point of view regarding this matter and, at the conclusion, have the team repeat this activity involving each member.

Activity—Sharing the philosophy. An effective way for a manager to get team members to focus on the philosophy is to have them identify or cite situations in which someone was abiding by any one or more elements of the philosophy. The manager convenes the team and asks members to share with the team an incident in which he or she has observed either an employee or manager abiding by an element of the philosophy. Some team members may have some difficulty remembering such incidents. If so, the manager can provide the team with such questions as the following:

"Did your supervisor lead you this morning in stating the organization's creed? What are important points in the creed? What element of the philosophy is involved?"

Activity—Guess what elements. The manager identifies and explains each element of the statements of the philosophy. An excerpt from one of the elements is recited to the team. Individual team members are requested to identify the element. Sometimes the list of the elements are posted so that the individuals can refer to them before responding. When a correct response is given, positive recognition is given and the respondent is asked to elaborate on it. When an incorrect answer is given, the manager will ask the team if the response was correct and seek another individual to give an answer.

Activity—Response questions.   The manager provides employees with a worksheet containing a series of belief statements about an element of the philosophy. Team members complete the worksheet on an individual basis, after which they are divided into three-member teams, to share and discuss their individual responses as:

SA = Strongly agree
AS = Agree somewhat
DS = Disagree somewhat
SD = Strongly disagree

Some examples of appropriate response questions:

1. People are our greatest asset. **SA   AS   DS   SD**
2. The organization fosters initiative and creativity by allowing individuals freedom in the performance of their jobs. **SA   AS   DS   SD**
3. Employees are genuinely involved in the decision-making process. **SA   AS   DS   SD**
4. Most managers trust their employees. **SA   AS   DS   SD**
5. Criticism is viewed as a training opportunity. **SA   AS   DS   SD**
6. Most team decisions are reached by consensus. **SA   AS   DS   SD**

Activity—Employee management assessment.   The manager sits on a chair in the center of a circle composed of team members. Each individual team member gets a chance to cite five ways in which that manager abides by the philosophy of the organization.

Team members are asked to identify how the manager abided by the philospohy and, after the entire team has recited, individuals are asked to cite five ways in which the manager has not abided by the philosophy. One team member is selected to act as a recorder, indicating the substance of the recitations, which is given to the manager at the conclusion of the activity.

This activity is not for the weak of heart, and should not be used by managers who are timid or do not wish to improve his or her performance.

TRAINING REQUIREMENTS FOR INCULCATING THE PHILOSOPHY

Schedule training for inculcating the philosophy in short durations, spread over two or three years. Each training session, with the exception of the orientation, should last from fifteen to twenty minutes and can be conducted once a week, bi-weekly, or monthly. Here is a time schedule used by one organization to initiate the various training sessions to inculcate the philosophy.

Philosophy Inculcation Training Time Requirements

	Duration	No. of Sessions	Total time
Orientation	2 hours	1	2 hours
Socio-economical purposes	15 minutes	8	2 hours
Values:			
CEO	10 minutes	6	1 hour
Top management	10 minutes	9	1½ hours
Shared	10 minutes	12	2 hours
Mission	15 minutes	8	2 hours
Organizational properties	10 minutes	6	1 hour
Management philosophy	10 minutes	9	1½ hours
Organizational Objectives	10 minutes	6	1 hour
Creed	1 minute	Daily	
Song	1 minute	Daily	

Step 5.   Evaluating and taking corrective actions

Because of the short duration of each training activity, it will take from two to three years to complete the inculcation of the philosophy. At the close of the training activities, a formal method must be employed to evaluate the extent to which the philosophy is a reality within the organization. Regardless of whether an insider or outside professional consultant is retained to complete the evaluation, each element of the statements of the philosophy must be used as the base for the evaluation. This document should be used to prepare instruments and interviewing questionnaires. The evaluation should encompass the following positions:

A. CEO
B. Senior management
C. Middle management
D. Employees

Once the individual assessments have been completed, all of the above positions should be combined to arrive at an organizational composite report. The consultant should meet and discuss the substance of the first draft of the report with the various groups to make any necessary adjustments before the report is made final.

When the evaluation has been completed, the next stage of the inculcation of the philosophy consists of taking corrective actions, which should take place on the organizational and individual levels. Strategic long range plans should be developed to improve the organization over a three-year period. Some plans may vary from division to division. Individual managers should be required to develop improvement plans to accommodate the recommendations stated in the evaluation report.

ASSESSING THE ORGANIZATIONAL CULTURE

Every organization, excellent as well as not-so-excellent ones, should initiate a formal and comprehensive program to periodically assess the degree to which cultural gaps exist in the organization, then take appropriate steps to close these gaps. One effective method is the development of an organizational culture improvement plan (illustrated in figure 7).

1. Identify desired organizational culture values and norms

If a statements of philosophy exists, extract the specific norms and values that will be used to assess the extent to which the desired culture exists. If a philosophy is not available in written form, management may decide to perform the next step first and, after learning what presently exists, to prepare the statements of philosophy or specific norms and values statements.

2. Describe present organizational culture norms and values

Conduct an audit using an outside consultant or management-employee committee, which can critically review the following areas in order to determine the present norms and values of the organization:

1. Performance standards and practices

ORGANIZATIONAL CULTURE IMPROVEMENT PLAN

ORGANIZATION_____ DATE_____

NAME OF PREPARER_____ PAGE_____ OF_____

Desired Cultural Norms and Values	Existing Cultural Norms and Values	Cultural Gaps	Improvement Strategy

Fig. 7: Organizational Culture Improvement Plan

2. Communication flow
3. Goals and objectives
4. Strategies
5. Teampersonship
6. Leadership styles and practices
7. Customers/clients services
8. Training and development
9. Performance evaluation practices
10. Peer relationship
11. Innovation practices
12. Organizational pride
13. Productivity and quality of service
14. Relationship with stockholder/stakeholders and community.

Once these areas have been reviewed, specific statements of present organizational norms and values can be produced to identify the unwritten philosophy of the organization. If Step One has not been completed, management must now determine what it considers to be acceptable or desired cultural norms and values and write them in the first column of the plan. An effective technique to prepare the desired norms and values should involve an assessment of what presently exists, related to what should exist. To collect information pertaining to existing cultural norms and values, audit the organizational culture by sending employees a questionnaire and/or interviewing them to determine their impressions of the organization.

3. Describe organizational cultural gaps

When desired cultural norms and values have been matched with existing cultural norms and values, cultural gaps, if any exist, may be identified and described with rigorous analysis and intuitive judgement. Once the gaps have been determined, rank them in order of importance to focus on those which need priority consideration.

4. Identify improvement strategies

Based on the ranked cultural gaps, consider the previous techniques discussed in this chapter when examining improvement strategies. Because these strategies are methods for improving the culture and inculcating the philosophy, both long- and short-range strategies should be identified and cited. To improve the culture, place major long-range emphasis on role modeling and training.

5. Develop action plan

Designating someone or some department to head development of an organizational action plan for implementing the improvement strategies. The human resorce department or training department are good prospects for this charge. The action plan should include a design.

6. Periodically assess the culture

Audit the organization every three to five years. Some Theory Z practitioners feel the audit should be done every ten years; but external environments change so rapidly that an organization waiting ten years to assess its culture may find itself in need of major surgery to eradicate obsolescence.

Assessing the organizational culture can be an enjoyable and fruitful process, especially if all employees become involved in the process. The more people who become meaningfully involved, the more valid the results, and the more likely cultural gaps will be closed and the organization will be persuing excellence.

SUMMARY

The techniques for building a strong organizational culture involve: 1) managers performing as role models; 2) recognizing philosophy compliance; 3) communicating the philosophy; 4) Implementing long-range training activities; and 5) using subtle techniques.

Inculcating the philosophy of an organization is the process of impressing upon employees the importance of certain macro-principles and guidelines or expected behavior, attitudes and parameters for the successful operations of the organization. Top management is responsible for setting policies and procedures for inculcating the philosophy, while middle management is responsible for the execution of those policies and procedures. The procedural steps for inculcating the philosophy are: 1) preparation of the statements of the philosophy; 2) develop a policy and procedure statement for inculcating the philsophy; 3) disseminating and discussing the philosophy; 4) initiating varied activities to inculcate the philosophy; and 5) evaluating and taking corrective actions. Activities that are useful for inculcating the philosophy are: 1) organization creed; 2) organization song; 3) organization slogan; 4) employee orientation; and 5) training activities. Some of the training activities that have been found effective in inculcating the philosophy are: 1) self-endoctrination; 2) using sentence stems; 3) responding to vignettes; 4) sharing the philosophy; 5) guess what elements; 6) response questions; and 7) employee management assessment. To assess the organizational culture will require six steps: 1) identifying desired organizational cultural norms and values; 2) describing present organizational culture norms and values; 3) citing organizational cultural gaps; 4) identifying improvement strategies; 5) developing an action plan; and 6) periodic assessment of the culture.

Part Three

The Practices of Theory Z

THIS SECTION IDENTIFIES a number of Theory Z practices that can help to achieve the socio-economic purposes of the organization and positively effect its mission. These practices are intended to give employees the opportunities to become involved in the decision-making process, the freedom to act responsibly in the pursuit of their jobs, the process for improving their skills and competencies, the techniques for fostering team work in the environment, and procedures for solving problems related to their units. In addition, these practices provide the organization with the techniques for solving complex organizational problems, the procedure for recognizing and inspiring employees, the technique for ensuring loyalty from employees, the basis for training employees in a multitude of functions and skills, and the process for improving the performance evaluation and promotion practices.

11

Training

IT IS IMPOSSIBLE to implement Theory Z unless the organization establishes a comprehensive program which must begin with the chief executive officer becoming highly committed to training by words, actions, and deeds, then extends to cover training all personnel in multiple skills.

This may be more easily said than done. Although excellent organizations do provide comprehensive training for their employees, other organizations provide little training if any. Most excellent organizations train all of their personnel, other organizations train only certain employees. Excellent organizations extend the training process throughout the tenure of the employee, while other organizations train their employees sporadically and for short durations. Supervisors of excellent organizations are responsible for on-the-job training, while other supervisors are, at times, not competent to provide on-the-job training. Managers of excellent organizations understand the importance of building people through massive training; other managers either don't understand the value of training or are derelict in fulfilling its function. Excellent organizations have little to risk because they know their employees will remain with them; many other organizations are reluctant to risk the money necessary to implement a comprehensive training program because many of them do not provide a desirable enough job climate to retain their employees for any considerable length of time. And, finally, managers of excellent organizations understand that when they train their employees, they are investing in people; other managers understand only the expediencies of unsensitive philosophies, short-term goals, and non-productive crisis management.

TRAINING DEFINED

Training is an organized activity designed to improve an employee's performance on the job and his or her worth to the organization. Although training in a Theory Z organization usually occurs in teams, with the supervisor and/or team members training an employee to perform a particular function, there are other forms of training activities such as lectures, seminars, published materials, and consultations with experts.

THE PURPOSE OF TRAINING

The primary purpose of any training program should be to change or modify the behavior of employees in order to improve his or her knowledge, skills, and attitudes on the job.

Excellent organizations currently offering what I consider to be the best training programs are:

- Citicorp
- Control Data Corp.
- Dana Corp.
- General Electric
- IBM
- Proctor & Gamble

Skills

An employee hired by a Theory Z organization will be required to perform a variety of functions, but will often have only minimal skills to do so, making it incumbent on the organization to provide enough training to enable the employee to do a particular job well. Job rotation is one of the most effective ways to help employees master the variety of skills that will be required of them; it should continue throughout the employee's tenure.

Attitude

Although it is uncommon in non-Theory Z organizations to include attitudes as well as skills in their training programs, it is absolutely necessary for the Theory Z organization to do so. Attitude training reflects the expectations and philosophies expected of all employees. To a large extent, the leadership style and behavior of the supervisor and manager will affect the attitudes of the employee. Attitude training in a Type Z organization is essential on a unit basis and an organization perspective, where employees will receive attitude training to help them reach:

1. an understanding and appreciation of the philosophy of the organization.
2. obedience to the code of conduct of the organization.
3. assessment of the climate of the organization.
4. an evaluation of the leadership style of the supervisor and manager.

Attitude training is best performed through the role model behavior of the supervisor and manager. The single most important factor in attitude training is how the supervisor treats his or her employees; a supervisor who seems insensitive to the needs of his or her employees exhibits negative attitudes and feelings on the job. If the supervisor is people-sensitive, then the attitudes of the employee will be positive. Change the undesirable behavior of a supervior and there will be a resultant attitudinal change in employees.

Attitudes are difficult to change, and will usually take a great deal of time. In some instances, the damage created by the supervisor may have been so injurious to the climate of the work environment, that it may be necessary to position the supervisor elsewhere in the organization where he or she will be more effective.

Knowledge

It can no longer be taken for granted that an employee, even though a college graduate, will have the knowledge to carry out a function. Knowledge training provides the employee with the necessary information to function. This may mean work in writing, reading, and counting; it may mean that additional specialized knowledge will have to be acquired to perform a function.

An organization that is striving to adopt the Theory Z philosophy decided to send a group of its managers to Japan to receive formal training in the art of Japanese management. Because all of their managers were unfamiliar with the Japanese culture, several formal awareness sessions were held to expose the managers to knowledge training, showing them what to expect while in Japan.

The Benefits of Training

The implementation of a comprehensive training program carries with it a number of benefits for the organization, unit, employee, and manager.

1. For the Type Z organization:
   a) a minimum of employee turnover
   b) improved quality and productivity
   c) more effective long-range planning
   d) increased potential for meeting future needs
2. For the unit:
   a) better cooperation among team members
   b) competent work force
   c) better morale
   d) improved use of team members' skills
   e) more goal-oriented team members
   f) joint problem-solving
   g) increased respect and dignity
3. For the individual employee:
   a) multiple opportunities to increase capabilities and skills to perform a variety of jobs and functions
   b) greater work satisfaction
   c) opportunities for personal growth
   d) more unity with team members
4. For the manager:
   a) a more stable work team
   b) improved self-esteem and greater personal satisfaction
   c) increased team morale and productivity
   d) more effective leadership
   e) fewer problems, solved easier

Comparative Analysis of Theory Z Training Programs

There are distinct differences between training in a Theory A and Z training program:

Theory A Training	Theory Z Training
The supervisors depend more on a training specialist to facilitate training.	The supervisor's role is viewed as a facilitator of training.

Managers are trained primarily to perform administrative functions.

Managers are usually trained to perform technical as well as administrative functions.

Much of the training is accomplished by attendance in a classroom setting.

Much of the training is accomplished by actual performance.

Employee is responsible for his own training and development.

Organization is responsible for the training and development of employees.

The job is matched to the employee.

The employee is matched to the job.

Skills, attitudes, and knowledge training usually last for a short period of time.

Skills, attitudes, and knowledge training usually last throughout the tenure of the employee.

Attitude training tends to be viewed on a short-term basis.

Attitude training is a crucial part of the orientation, and is emphasized throughout the tenure of the employee.

Attitude training is merely reserved for certain positions such as salespersons and persons exposed to the public.

Attitude training is required of every employee.

Attitude training is usually focused on how the organization is acceptable to the public.

Attitude training is usually focused on how the organization is acceptable to the employee, public, and other stakeholders.

Orientation tends to last less than a day.

Orientation tends to last for several weeks.

TRAINING ACTIVITIES

Although on-the-job training is heavily implemented in a Theory Z organization, other training activities may be more effective and appropriate:[1]

1. In-house Workshops: employees meet at a prearranged date and time to receive additional training in order to improve their skills to perform a given job.

2. Quality Circle Meetings: Employees meet one hour a week to identify and select job-related problems, collect and analyze data, evolve and implement the solution to a problem.

3. Employee Development Meetings: Employees or teams schedule a meeting on a regular basis to discuss facts about the team's charge. This meeting usually deals with operational concerns, time lines, etc.

4. Consultant's Training Programs: Bring in an outside consultant or expert to train team members in an area in which the organization may not have trained teachers.

5. Consultant Advisory Session: Bring in a consultant, either from within or outside the organization, to share information with team members through counseling, analysis, and alternative courses of action.

6. Outside Meeting and Conferences: Employees, either individually or collectively, participate in conferences and workshops sponsored by professional associations and management groups. The International Association of Quality Circles sponsors a national conference on quality circles each year. Several quality circles attend these meetings and conduct phases of the quality circle process to participants.

7. Distribution of Published Materials: Make books, selected articles, journals, abstracts, tapes, video-cassettes, and other forms of audio-visual aids available to employees.

In the Type Z organization, the burden for training rests with the organization. Many supplement their training activities by providing time and money for off-the-job employee training such as outside mini-course and seminars, college or university degree and certificate programs, advanced training at colleges and universities, program instruction, correspondence schools, and computer-assisted instruction.

PHASES OF THEORY Z ORGANIZATIONAL TRAINING

In the Type Z organization, training is experienced by all employees in four different phases:

Induction Training

Employees are orientated to what is expected of them on the job and given some minimal skills to perform a rather simple function as a member of a team. This training usually lasts for several weeks.

Job Skill Training

After the induction training, the employee receives some minimal skills to perform a function and is then given added practical training to perform other jobs. Sometimes, the supervisor or a co-employee acts as a mentor to the employee until a great deal of proficiency has been achieved. At other times, it merely consists of counseling and peer coaching.

An alternative to eliminating the organizational chart and job description is the use of a responsibility chart and function statement. Each major sub-division becomes responsible for fulfilling certain responsibilities to help the organization realize its purpose and mission. The function statement is used by each unit to highlight all of the functions it is charged to perform.

Responsibility Chart

Each major unit of an organization is established to fulfill a specific purpose in the overall mission. The purpose must be broken down into general statements of what the unit has to do to accomplish its purpose. The responsibility chart indicates the various units and sub-units of the organization and cites their responsibilities. Statements of responsibility do not change drastically unless there are some major changes in the organization or unless a legislation requires some organizational adjustment. When preparing statements of responsibility, it should be tersely written—a broad statement free from unnecessary terms—and should be all-encompassing. Some examples of correctly and incorrectly expressed statements of responsibility:

Incorrect: Maintaining quality of product

Correct: Quality of product
Incorrect: Developing personnel
Correct: Personnel

Function Statement

A function statement is a broad descriptive statement indicating what a unit has to accomplish to meet its responsibilities. Although functions tend to remain stable, they are more prone to change than responsibilities, because team members may have added another function to the unit list to cover a new solution to a problem, to reflect a technological advancement, etc. The function statement must be prepared in broad, general terms. The key point here is to provide enough organized ambiguity in order to induce sub-divisions and units to communicate with each other. Experiences have illustrated that one of the chief reasons why communication is such a prevailing problem among organizations in the United States is that "everything" is put into writing and, as a result, talking is not really necessary. This may not be entirely true, but it certainly provides one basis for many of the problems besetting Type A organizations.

The team, not the individual employee, is responsible for performing the functions of the unit. Therefore, a substantial amount of the training should be exposed around making the team function more effectively. The individual employee, essential to the effectiveness of the team, will most likely need custom training activities to improve his or her worth to the team and also to himself or herself.

In a Type A Organization, specific activities for fulfilling each of the functions would be the next list of items to be worked out. Since team work is the order for performing work in the Type Z organization, any activities to be delineated should be the training activities necessary for building teams and improving their function.

Fig. 8 illustrates the interrelationship among units of a marketing division. The chief responsibility of the division is marketing. This responsibility is divided into three sub-responsibilities, each assumed by a unit.

Please note: The name of the unit identifies its chief responsibility. Each unit is obligated to fulfill certain functions. Some of these functions overlap into another unit or two. Nothing also exists to give any other guidance and directions to the units; therefore, it is encumbered upon the supervisor and teams to communicate among themselves and other units to perform a function. This organized ambiguity could induce overlapping and redundancy. However, effective coordination among the managers, supervisors, and teams obviates this potential; forced communication also nurtures a caring relationship and intimacy among the people working in the division. In addition, Peters and Waterman indicate in *In Search of Excellence* that redundancy is not uncommon in excellent organizations.

FACILITATING THE TRAINING PROCESS

Theory Z organization supervisors act as the facilitators of training in addition to their other responsibilities. They:

1. request assistance from the personnel department to meet with the team to explore with them broad training needs.
2. meet with the training assistant to determine what procedures should be used to define the contents of the training and the method of presentation.
3. assist the training specialist to draft the training manual.
4. assist the training specialist to present the draft to team members for their feedback.
5. collect copies of the draft and review the various suggestions in order to prepare an improved training manual.
6. help the training specialist to prepare and implement the training schedule.
7. assist in the training program.

When a formal training program is not necessary, the supervisor may do the following to train individual employees or the team as a whole:

1. provide mini-workshops to explain a function or activity.
2. initiate think sessions to assist the team to solve a problem.
3. call on specialists or experts to tutor a team member or team.
4. initiate a mentorship program for an employee experiencing some on-the-job problems.
5. call on management to present a seminar or workshop.
6. make arrangements for the team to participate in an exchange program.

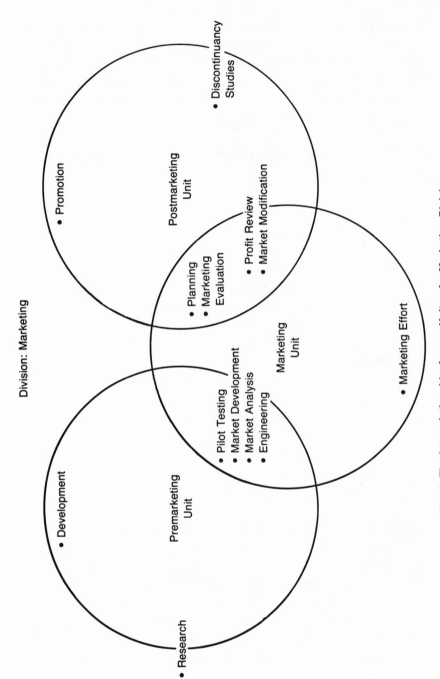

Division: Marketing

Fig. 8: The Interrelationship Among Units of a Marketing Division

SUMMARY

Training is an organized activity designed to improve employee on-the-job performance and overall worth to the organization. The primary purpose of training is to change or modify behavior. The three psychological domains of training are: 1) skills; 2) knowledge; and 3) attitudes. Appropriate training activities that Type Z organizations have found useful are: 1) in-house work; 2) on-the-job training; 3) quality circle meetings; 4) employee development meetings; 5) consultants training programs; 6) consultant advisory services; 7) outside meetings and conferences; and 8) distribution of published materials. The four phases of Theory Z organization training are: 1) induction training; 2) job skill training; 3) new skill training; and 4) problem-solving training. A training strand is a continuum of training activities that are designed to prepare an employee to perform one or more specific functions. A responsibility chart is a substitution for an organizational chart that illustrates organizational units and sub-units and their responsibilities. A statement of function is a substitution for a job description chart that indicates the activities that the unit or sub-units must perform in order to fulfill the responsibility.

12

The Lifetime Employment Policy

EMPLOYEES WHO FEEL secure in their personal and professional lives tend to trust their employers more, are more likely to be loyal to their employers, and are in general more stable than persons with no security. This basic factor is a major reason why the concept of lifetime employment made such an important impact in many of the large organizations in Japan and excellent American firms.

Although an American firm in 1906 may have been the first organization to establish a lifetime employment policy, the practice, to this day, has not gained wide use in the United States; in Japan, approximately 35 percent of the work force is secure from unemployment. There are several reasons for this major philosophical gap. Uppermost among them is the focus many American organizations have on profits, while Japanese organizations tend to be more concerned with the people who help produce those profits.

LIFETIME EMPLOYMENT EXPLAINED

In lifetime or "no-layoff" employment, an organization hires permanent employees and guarantees them a job until retirement age. Japanese organizations usually hire employees once a year, right from junior or senior high schools and colleges. In America, employees are usually hired on an ad hoc basis. Lifetime employees will not lose their jobs unless they have been convicted of a major criminal offense. In the United States, organizations such as IBM, Delta Airlines, and Hewlett Packard, adopting the no-layoff policy, guarantee employees a job for life unless something extraordinary occurs. Many public school systems, colleges and universities, state and federal jobs, permanent employees have a form of lifetime employment based on a tenure system. Under the tenure system, if any employee has satisfactorily served the organization for a period of time, he or she is granted tenure, meaning lifetime employment. However, declining enrollment, budgetary problems, etc., may account for tenured employees being laid off.

The following are some advantages and disadvantages of lifetime employment policy:

Advantages of Lifetime Employment
1. It can produce a stable work force.
2. It is a sound, long term investment for organizations desiring to build a strong coordinated workforce.
3. It promotes pride and a strong commitment to the organization.
4. It increases employees' efficiency during periods of crisis by reducing their anxieties and fears.
5. It helps to prevent employees from joining or forming unions.
6. It's an excellent practice for making specialists into generalists.
7. It helps to shape managers' attitudes and perceptions in the direction of a sound long-term organizational health.
8. It provides no incentive for catering to a group of sycophants.
9. It creates a more harmonious work climate that is conducive to high productivity and quality.

Disadvantages of Lifetime Employment
1. It can be a very expensive practice that could eventually debilitate an organization.
2. Some employees are not happy about being transferred to menial jobs when they are moved to another job on a temporary basis.
3. It can be an excuse used by management not to deal with serious performance problems, because they may feel that nothing much can be done to improve a poor performer with lifetime tenure.

4. It is a practice that should not be adopted by newly created, unstable, or seasonal organizations.

PREPARING A LIFETIME EMPLOYMENT POLICY

Before preparing a lifetime employment policy, contact one or more of the following companies for a copy of their lifetime plan, and carefully examine the language and intent:

- Hewlett-Packard
- Exxon
- IBM
- Johnson Wax
- Advanced Micro Devices
- Digital Equipment
- Proctor & Gamble
- Linnton Plywood

When an organization has decided to adopt a lifetime employment policy, the general guidelines should be explained in a policy statement.

The policy section of the statement usually contains a general comment describing the establishment of a lifetime employment program, beginning with a reason for the policy and a description of it.

1. The Board of Directors recognizes the importance of maintaining a stabilized work force. As a result, a lifetime employment program will be established for all permanent employees.

2. The Board of Directors, stakeholders, and top management, recognizes the need to provide job security for all employees.

The purpose section of the statement describes the various reasons for implementing a lifetime employment program.

1. To stabilize the work force by guaranteeing employees jobs for life.

2. To promote pride among employees, and solicit their commitment to the purpose and mission of the organization.

3. To discourage employees from joining or forming a union.

4. To reduce anxiety and fear of unemployment during crisis.

5. To protect the organization's investment in the training of its employees by retaining the work force.

The procedures section of the statement describes steps used to establish the lifetime employment policy.

1. All classifications of employees will be recruited once a year,

one month prior to the public school and college graduation ceremonies.

2.   Careful screening of applicants will be undertaken to secure an outstanding cadre of recruits in order to involve them in a comprehensive written and oral examination. The emphasis of these assessments will be to determine if the recruits have the humanistic qualities desired of all employees

3.   All applicants will be hired to fulfill a variety of roles dictated by the needs of the organization.

4.   No employee will be laid off unless:

    a.   the employee has performed poorly over a period of three years, after several attempts have been made to improve.

    b.   the employee has been convicted of a felony.

    c.   the employee has shared confidential and sensitive information with a competitor or a foreign country.

    d.   the employee has been disloyal.

LIFETIME EMPLOYMENT IN JAPAN

The Japanese version of lifetime employment rests on three conditions: 1)   Bonus plan; 2)   Permanent and temporary employees; and 3)   Satellite work areas.   An organization desiring to adopt a lifetime employment policy should understand each of the above conditions before it decides on how it should institute its own model.

1.   **Bonus Plan** – Japanese workers receive a salary and a bonus. This bonus is usually given semi-annually and sometimes is as high as fifty percent of the employee's salary, depending on overall performance of the organization. This practice will allow an organization to reduce the bonus and leave intact the base salary during slow growth or a crisis.

2.   **Permanent and Temporary Employees** – Japanese firms instituting lifetime employment retain permanent and temporary employees. In crisis, or if business slows, the temporary crew is reduced or laid off.

3. Satellite Work Areas–Most employees who are employed on a lifetime basis are required to retire at the age of 55. Some top managers stay beyond age 55; when these and other key employees do retire, they can often be provided with a part-time job if they wish it, moving to one of the satellite work areas associated with the organization. Satellite work areas are usually small organizations established by one or more retirees of a large corporation in order to provide it with an essential service or product.

Flexibility is built into the entire system in the event of slow growth or a problematic economy. Any lifetime employment adopted by American organizations must, out of necessity, be able to accommodate uncertainties.

A version of a United States model with three major components is illustrated and contrasted with the Japanese model in Fig. 9.

1. Permanent and Temporary Employees. The Japanese used two categories of employees with some success. American organizations wishing to adopt a lifetime employment policy should seriously consider replicating this three-step practice.

Step 1–Determine the minimum number of employees that could be retained without having a negative impact on the organization. Use this figure to establish the permanent or core employee quotient.

Step 2–Recruit only young employees right out of high schools, commercial schools, and colleges for the permanent employee ranks.

Step 3–Include items 1 and 2 in the policy statement adopting lifetime employment.

2. Base Salary Plan. Establish a base salary plan with either of two techniques:

A. Prepare a policy statement and indicate what percentage of the employees' salary will constitute their base salary, which is defined as the minimum wage an employee will receive in the event of an economic crisis. It is computed in this manner:

Present Salary	$25,000
Base salary percentage	70%
Base salary	$17,500

Somewhere in the policy statement, the issue of the remaining 30% should be addressed. It can be identified as an earning base and as long as the organization is realizing growth, the earning base will remain in effect. If earnings decline significantly because of an economic down turn, then the earning base may be reduced or even eliminated.

−or−

B. Include in the policy statement that no salary will be reduced, or that the salary will not be reduced below a certain percentage during hard times.

3. Personnel Investment Fund. Establish an organizational investment fund; set aside a certain percentage of net profit to reduce any financial strain brought on by the lifetime employment policy and a decline in business. This fund can be used either to keep on a greater percentage of temporary employees or maintain the earning base salary.

4. Built-in Flexibility. Built-in flexibility by contracting certain jobs and services to outside firms, such as maintenance and custodial services, security, etc. With this flexibility an organization can pass these jobs and services to in-house personnel during economic difficulties, therefore defraying the cost of keeping surplus employees. When rotating employees to different jobs, establish a time limitation for all jobs so that no one will remain in one position longer than the allotted period.

HIRING EMPLOYEES FOR A TYPE Z ORGANIZATION

Many American organizations will have some serious objections to adopting a lifetime employment policy. Even if they do not wish to guarantee job security, they will do well to consider the hiring process used by excellent organizations.

Typical of American organizations, the hiring process is usually not drawn out, but is accomplished after applicants submit their resumes to the personnel office. These resumes are screened to determine which applicants have the proper education, background, and experience to accommodate the position. A reference check is made. The surviving applicants are interviewed, usually by the personnel department or by a small group of employees. The top three applicants meet with the supervisor or manager who will interview them and make a choice.

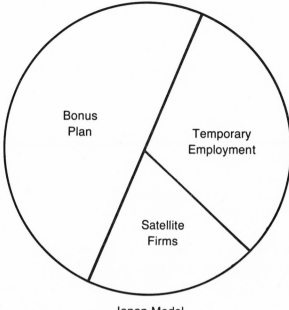

Japan Model

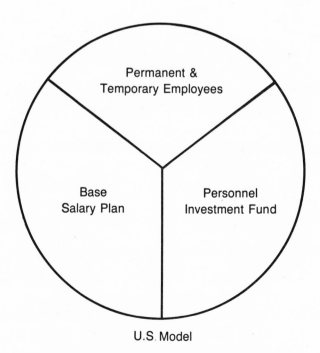

U.S. Model

Fig. 9: Japan and U.S. Employment Models

In the Theory Z organizations, the process for hiring a lifetime employee is completed after a long period of assessment, tough examinations and several layers of employees' interviews, and with the final group reaching a consensus on the choices.

1. Recruitment

Once a year, a team of recruiters are sent to the major universities, junior and senior high schools to recruit employees before they have been contaminated by other organizations. Applicants indicate on their applications or resumes their career path choice.

2. Screening

All applications or resumes are carefully screened by the personnel department. Selected applicants are usually invited to an orientation, which consists of a tour of the organization and information about its operations, principles, and practices.

3. Written and Oral Examinations

A battery of assessment instruments are administered to the applicants over a period of several days, possibly even weeks. These assessment instruments usually have very little to do with the competence of an applicant to perform a particular skill or job. Under the heading of systematic personal qualification system, the applicant is evaluated for a job with the organization based on three criteria: 1) Educational background; 2) Character; 3) Family background.

Even if other aspects of Theory Z are objectionable to some American managers, the careful screening and the long period of assessment of applicant should not be one of those areas. The essential differences in hiring applicants in Theory A and Z organizations are illustrated below:

Theory A	Theory Z
Employees are hired for a particular job or position.	Employees are hired for the organization.
Selection process usually lasts for 1 to 2 days.	Selection process usually lasts for days or week.
Written examination is seldom required or if required involves assessment of applicants' competence in a particular skill or job.	Written examination is usually required to assess the applicant's personality, ability to adjust to the organization, aggressiveness, and character.

Interviewing is usually confined to two levels.	Interviewing is usually confined to several levels.
References are sometimes not checked.	References are always checked.
Applicants' ages vary	Applicants are usually young, right out of junior and senior high school or college.
Selection of finalists is usually decided by one person.	Selection of finalists is decided by a team using the consensus decision-making process

JAPANESE HIRING PRACTICES

No aspect of the Theory Z concept is independent; each practice is dependent to some degree on the others. Lifetime employment is heavily dependent on the calibre of employees hired. If a high number of poor employees are retained, the organization will be hampered with incompetent personnel who may eventually doom its operations.

The main emphasis when hiring employees in Japanese organizations, illustrated in Figure 10, is the assessment of human traits and characteristics. Written and oral tests are administered in order to attract employees who are able to get along with their fellow employees, who are able to care, to trust, and to become intimate with others on the job. Notice that at the hub of the circle is loyalty which, to the Japanese, is the most important trait to be possessed by every employee. The outer circle depicts trust, caring, and intimacy, those very humanistic competencies managers are responsible for nurturing among employees in the work environment. Obviously, these competencies help to establish the kind of loyalty the organization is seeking. The illustration also indicates that, initially, the Japanese organizations require minimal entry-level skills. What they are interested in, in addition to those skills mentioned previously, is employees' education and grades record. To the Japanese, job competence will come as a result of their continuous comprehensive training opportunities and job rotation requirements. Figure 11 illustrates the es-

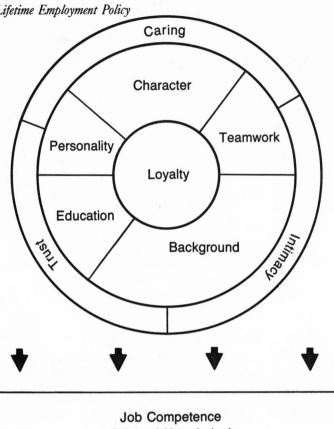

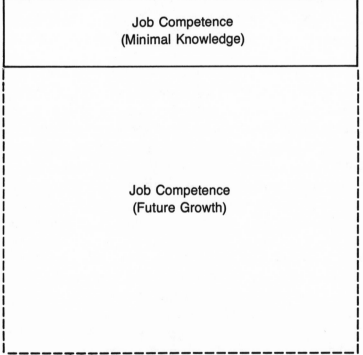

Fig. 10: Japanese Hiring Practices

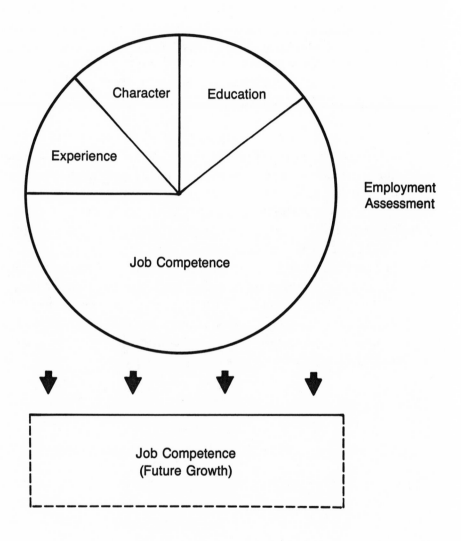

Fig. 11: American Hiring Practices

sential differences between the Japanese and American hiring focus. The American hiring tends to focus on job competence instead of human traits and characteristics. Notice how much weight is given to job competence and how little is given to future job competence—almost the complete opposite of the Japanese model. Obviously, this accounts for one of the benefits of the Japanese model that gives them a lead over some American models in terms of improved productivity and quality.

SUMMARY

Lifetime or no-layoff employment, means that an organization hires permanent employees and guarantees them a job until retirement age. The conditions that make lifetime employment work in Japan are: 1) bonus plan; 2) permanent and temporary employees; and 3) satellite work areas. One lifetime employment model that can be adopted by American organizations is: 1) permanent and temporary employees; 2) base salary plan; 3) personnel investment fund; and 4) built in flexibility. Japanese hiring emphasis is on human characteristics and traits with little attention given to job competence. On the other hand, American hiring emphasis is on job competence with some attention given to human characteristics and traits.

13

The Career Path Program

ONE IMPORTANT FACTOR in the success of Type Z organizations is the ability to select, train, develop, utilize and retain employees who have many skills. This has been a reality in excellent organizations primarily because they have created well-organized and well-administered career path planning programs. An organization desiring to establish a career path program must focus primarily on the direct value the program has to the organization as a whole. If excellent employees are hired on the basis of their potential value to the organization, then the functions critical to the success and prosperity of the organization will most likely be performed more competently.

The career path program should also hold equally important the needs of the employees who compose the organization and the rights of the organization to accommodate its needs; there must be proper opportunities for employees to secure training in many and varied skills. The program should also respect the rights of the individual employee to fulfill his or her own career needs and desires. When this occurs, the employee will not be placed in a function where he or she does not possess minimum competence to succeed; the employee will have some idea what each step up the ladder means in long-term career and promotion opportunities.

CAREER PATH PROGRAM DEFINED

A career path program is a succession of preidentified on-the-job learning experiences involving a variety of multiple functions scheduled on a long-term basis that are geared to improving the employee's skills and his or her worth to the organization.

Here are some assumptions that underly the career path program in a Theory Z organization:

1. It must serve the needs of the employees and the organization.
2. An inventory of current organizational resources must be conducted and a ten-year career planning program must be devised.
3. It must begin with the hiring of new employees and must continue throughout the tenure of the employee.
4. Formal performance evaluation should be infrequently conducted while informal performance reviews should be frequently conducted.
5. Job rotation should come only after a successful formal evaluation.

THE IMPETUS FOR CAREER DEVELOPMENT IN THEORY Z ORGANIZATION

The significant purposes of a career development program in the Theory Z organization are:

1. to transfer certain competencies or skills to other areas of the organization.
2. to make the job more interesting for the employees.
3. to accommodate long-range personnel needs of the organization.
4. to enable employees to think with a macro-perspective as opposed to a micro-perspective.

CONTRASTS BETWEEN CAREER PATH PROGRAMS IN TYPE A AND Z ORGANIZATIONS

There are some distinct differences between career path programs in Type A and Z organizations:

Type A Career Path Programs	Type Z Career Path Programs
Career development activities tend to be voluntary.	Career development activities are essential part of every employee's job and are required.

Specialists tend to dominate.	Generalists tend to dominate.
Job rotation or reassignment usually last from a few months to a year.	Job rotation or reassignment usually last for two or more years.
Onus for career development is placed on the individual employee.	Onus for career development is assumed as an organizational responsibility.
External training and continuing education is a feature of the career development plan.	Internal training and continuing education is offered by the organization.
Requires determining what vacancies are likely to occur at a given time and training employees to fulfill those positions.	Requires providing every employee with an opportunity to acquire varied skills for long-term growth.

Some excellent organizations I have observed to have effective career path programs are:

- IBM
- Quad/Graphics
- Tandy Industries
- Proctor & Gamble
- Citicorp

A CAREER PATH PLANNING PROCESS

Career path planning is similar to any other planning effort; it begins when preparation of a career path strategic plans are required. During this process, a forecast of the future is conducted, some long-range assumptions are determined, career strategies are constructed, and long-range objectives are developed.

Career path operational plans are developed, which become the critical parameters for determining the path to be followed in order to reach long-range career path objectives. When the career path strategic plan and operational plan are being prepared, the needs of the employees and organization must be considered. Vacancies should be projected based on retirements, health problems, and promotions. New technology must be considered as something to be transferred to other divisions or units and teams of the organization.

Once strategic and operational career path plans have been completed, the latter is used as a basis for producing individual employee career path plans. Because the supervisor and/or manager is intimately familiar with the career path operational plan, he or she should assist in the preparation of the individual employee career path plan. This plan usually covers the same period as other plans. In fact, the individual employee career path plan should be seen as one strand of several that comprise the career path operational plan. A copy of such a plan is illustrated in Figure 12. Based on the individual employee performance evaluation and team performance evaluation, adjustments for the inclusion or deduction of information in the individual employee career path plan may have to be made involving functions, time span, etc. The formal performance evaluations should be the basis for initiating the rotation of jobs and/or functions. Within a reasonable period, the career path program should be evaluated in terms of fulfilling its purposes, meeting its long range objectives, accommodating planning assumptions, and meeting individual employee's needs and those of the entire organization.

There are countless numbers of career path program models. The one indicated in Figure 12 covers the most important elements explained above. Those organizations adopting the Theory Z philosophy should review their career path programs with the details covered in this chapter and, if necessary, adjustments should be made. The main point to employees here is that the career path program must begin with a strategic planning thrust and end with the evaluation of the total program based on what is covered in both the strategic and operational plans.

PREPARING THE EMPLOYEE CAREER PATH PROGRAM

The success of the strategic career path program of an organization depends heavily on the cumulative results of the career path plans of all the employees. Fig. 13 and Fig. 13a illustrate a format that contains most of the essential components of an effective employee career path program.

The first section contains information on the employee, such as name, position, unit, supervisor, date the plan was compiled, period the plan covers, and team assignment.

The employee-needs section contains career development needs and desires identified by the employee. The organization-needs section contains a statement showing what organization needs are being accommodated by this plan. The current assignment and date section describes the present assignment of the employee and the date in which he or she was rotated to this assignment. The next assignment and date section describes where the employee will be rotated to permit more training and development; and the date in which the rotation will be initiated.

The training and development-needs section contains a description of needs of the employee determined either by the employee, his or her team members, the supervisor, or management. Rotation action plan contains provisions for describing, over a period of five or ten years, the employee's new assignments, functions, locations, names of supervisors, training period in hours, and the dates the rotation will take place.

Procedural Steps for Implementing the Theory Z Career Path Program

The career path program in a Theory Z organization should be seen as a comprehensive process requiring careful planning and execution. Here is a description of an effective procedure used by one Theory Z organization; organizations with established career path programs need only compare the procedure they are already using to this example to evaluate their own career path program.

1 – Select a person to head a career path unit in the personnel department.
2 – Determine if the career path program is going to be voluntary, compulsory, or both.
3 – Prepare organizational policy to establish parameters for putting the career path program into effect.
4 – Get approval for the policy from top management.

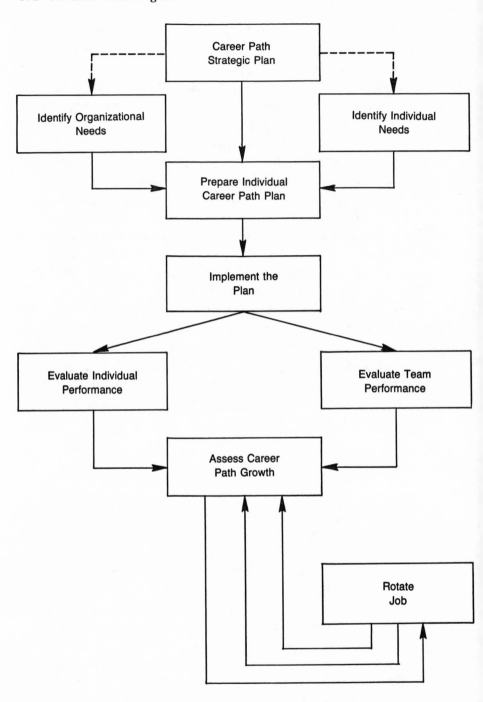

Fig. 12: Career Path Schematic Planning Process

5 – Prepare a ten year career path strategic plan which contains:
  a. forecasted environment condition.
  b. forecasted organizational needs.
  c. a summary of employee needs.
  d. a long-term budget.
  e. career path training activities agenda.
  f. a description of how performance evaluation and training will be incorporated in the plan.
6 – Prepare career path plan for employees.
  a. meet with employees to discuss their career path plans.
  b. prepare plan.
  c. mutually agree-on plan.
  d. implement career path plan.
7 – Evaluate career path program.
8 – Report results to top management.

Advantages and Disadvantages of a Theory Z Career Path Program

Here are some advantages of a Theory Z career path program:
1. employees will become competent in a variety of specialties.
2. an organization is able to achieve coordination across functions.
3. employees will be more productive and more satisfied with their jobs.
4. organization is committed to developing the skills of their employees.
5. more broad, mutually beneficial goals and objectives are set by employees.

Some of the disadvantages are:
1. the organization will not have detailed knowledge of its needs, personnel, and problems.
2. it takes an employee a longer training period to become completely valuable to the organization.

Defining Job Rotation

Job rotation is a formal plan for assigning employees to different functions or training activities across different functions.

There are basically two methods of job rotation:
1. Short-Range Job Rotation

EMPLOYEE CAREER PATH PLAN

Name _____   Date _____

Position _____   Period _____

Unit _____   Team _____

Supervisor _____   Page _____ of _____

Training and Development Needs:

Rotation Action Plan:

Assignment	Function	Location	Supervisor	Training Time	Date

Comments:

Fig. 13a: Employee Career Path Plan

EMPLOYEE CAREER PATH PLAN

Name _____   Date _____

Position _____   Period _____

Unit _____   Team _____

Supervisor _____   Page _____ of _____

Employee Needs:

Organizational Needs:

Current Assignment: Date:

Next Assignment: Date:

Fig. 13: Employee Career Path Program

Assign the employee to a function for a short period of time to familiarize him or her with the function. Some short-range job rotation methods:

a. "Assistant to" position. Assign a young employee as an assistant to a higher-level manager for a short period of time; this will provide the employee with a broader view of the organization, and is useful for training top-level managers to take over higher managerial positions.

b. Special Assignments. Assign the employee to a special assignment for a certain period of time. This method has been used quite successfully in Theory Z organizations when young managers are assigned to "technical functions" and management desires to inform the manager that he or she is not forgotten; it also puts them in a position to work with a high-level manager. This relationship usually ends up in the form of a "mentorship training program."

c. Project Assignment. Sometimes, employees are assigned to perform a particular function in a project. The essential difference between a special assignment and project assignment is that the former is of brief duration; project assignment lasts until the job is completed. This method is similar to the special assignment, and serves a useful purpose in the total rotation program. Some managers strongly object to being transferred or rotated to different jobs or functions. This usually occurs because certain personalities are attracted to certain jobs. As a result, they become "fixed" on a particular job. However, if more excellent organizations begin to establish career path programs that require numerous job rotations and indicate this requirement early in the career of the employee, he or she will eventually become acclimated to this condition. Before Mr. Opel became president and chairman of IBM he was rotated to 19 different functions. What an ideal requirement for a president of an organization.

2. Long-Range Job Rotation.

Rotate the employee to multiple functions over a period of five to ten years. In America, the time span is usually within a five-year period. In Japan, the time span is more like ten years. During each rotational assignment in a Theory Z organization, the employee becomes an integral part of a team or a unit to receive an in-depth knowledge and experience about a particular function.

The following are types of long-range job rotation methods:

a.   Expanded Responsibility–Assign the employee additional responsibilities that provide the kinds of experience indicated in the career path plan. Instead of the employee merely becoming involved in "performing" the job or function, the employee is also involved in the planning and controlling aspects of the job or function. This technique is usually identified as job enrichment or vertical enlargement of the job.

b.   Multiple Job Assignment–Assign the employee a wide variety of job assignments which may cross other divisions or departments. In a Theory Z organization, the employee is usually assigned to a job or function for two or three years, and then is rotated to another job or function.

DIFFERENCES BETWEEN BECOMING A SPECIALIST AND GENERALIST

Theory A organizations tend to produce specialists while Theory Z organizations produce generalists:

Specialist	Generalist
Employees are less productive and less satisfied with their jobs.	Employees are more productive and more satisfied with their jobs.
Oriented toward short-term goals.	Oriented toward more layered goals.
Organization is less committed to developing skills of their employees.	Organization is more committed to developing the skills of their employees.
Organization has the capacity to organize its employees into a coordinated workforce.	Organization has a stronger capacity and does organize its employees into a coordinated and integrated workforce.
Lower job mobility.	Higher job mobility.
Employees are not intimately integrated with one another.	Employees are integrated with one another because of multi-skill orientation.

High employee turnover.   Low employee turnover.

SUMMARY

A career path program is a succession of preidentified on-the-job learning experiences involving a variety of multiple functions scheduled on a long-term basis that are geared to improving the employee's skills and worth to the organization. Procedures for implementing the Theory Z career path program are: 1)   Select a person to head a career path unit in the personnel department; 2)   Determine if the career path program is going to be voluntary, compulsory, or both; 3)   Prepare organizational policy to establish parameters for operationalizing the career path program; 4)   Get approval for the policy from top management; 5)   Prepare a ten-year career path strategic plan; 6)   Prepare career path plans for employees; 7)   Evaluate career path programs; and 8)   Report results to top management. Job rotation is a formal plan for assigning employees to different functions, or to a variety of training activities across different functions. There are two methods of job rotation: 1)   Short-range job rotation; and 2)   Long-range job rotation.

14

Performance Review and Promotion

THE PERFORMANCE EVALUATION of employees has long been a problem for almost all types of organizations. Japanese organizations have, to some degree, improved the assessment of personnel by relying more on informal performance review sessions, group assessment of individual employee's performance, reducing the pace of formal evaluations, and relying more on intuition and subtlety in making decisions about the performance of people within the organization. The central theme of the performance evaluation process of Theory Z organizations is teamwork and team performance.

Any evaluation process must be based on how well the individual employee helps the team meet its goals and standards. As a result, good human relations tend to be of prime importance when reviewing the performance of the employees, the supervisor, the team, and the manager.

Although I do not recommend that American managers adopt the Japanese performance evaluation process intact, I suggest that by applying some creativity, modifying the techniques to accommodate the needs of the organization, and continuing to use existing strong elements, a performance evaluation process with Theory Z overtones can be produced that may be far greater than what presently exists.

PERFORMANCE EVALUATION DEFINED

Performance evaluation is a critical assessment of work performed by a person; it is conducted in a formal or informal manner by either an individual or group. In a Theory Z organization, the evaluation process measures performance in achieving goals and standards, and performance as a team member.

SOME ASSUMPTIONS UNDERLYING THEORY Z PERFORMANCE EVALUATION PROCESS

Performance review of a Type Z organization should be based on some fundamental assumptions which are often ignored by many Type A organizations:

1. People are the most important resource of an organization.
2. Performance review, coaching, counseling, and directing are a day-to-day responsibility of supervisors.
3. If an employee fails to improve, the supervisor is usually at fault.
4. Management is the process of getting things done through and with people.
5. Individual employee performance ratings should be based initially on how well the employee helps the team to reach desired results.
6. The behavior and attitude of the supervisor can either hamper or enhance the performance of employees.
7. Job rotation should be determined by the present performance level of employees and the needs of the employees and organization.
8. Performance review is one of the criteria for determining training and development needs.
9. Employees are more important to the organization than the supervisor.

Many managers will find some or all of these assumptions difficult to accept; this is to be expected. The Theory Z concept often will conflict with the way many Americans were brought up as well as threaten the value system inculcated through the schools, churches, society, home, etc. If supervisors truly understand that they are employed in the organization to serve employees to improve their job knowledge, skills, etc., then they should have little trouble in accepting the assumptions indicated above.

THE THEORY Z PERFORMANCE EVALUATION SYSTEM

Unlike some performance evaluation systems that are used by

some organizations, the model used by Theory Z organizations are interrelated to the various guidance systems mentioned in chapter 13, as illustrated in Fig. 14.

Strategic Planning Activities

The performance review system must, out of necessity, begin with the strategic planning process which determines what kinds of objectives and goals are compatible with the purposes, mission, organizational properties, strengths, and resources of the organization.

Before goals are set, the strategic planning process should answer "why does the organization exist?" and "what is the organization?" When these questions have been answered properly, then it is appropriate to ask, "where is the organization going?" and "how will the organization get there?" When these questions have been answered, the organization will have completed an analysis of its competitors and the environment to determine how resources will be used to maximize strengths and minimize weaknesses.

Operational Planning Activities

After strategic planning activities have been completed, divisions, departments, and units are required to prepare the annual operational plans to help realize the multiyear strategic plans. Therefore, using the strategic plans as a parameter, short-range goals, standard and activity must be constructed to help make the long-range aspirations of the organization a reality. Strategic plans are usually prepared to cover a span of five to ten years.

Unit Activities

Each unit within an organization serves to fulfill a certain function to help realize the organizational mission. As a result, unit objectives and goals must be set along with performance standards. In the Theory Z organization, organization teams set goals and standards and are judged by their ability to fulfill the purpose that they serve. The central focus for achieving goals is teams. Therefore, the performance of the team must be reviewed to determine the extent they serve their purpose. Because the team as a whole is being evaluated, each team member contributes to the performance of the whole. What should be assessed in the performance

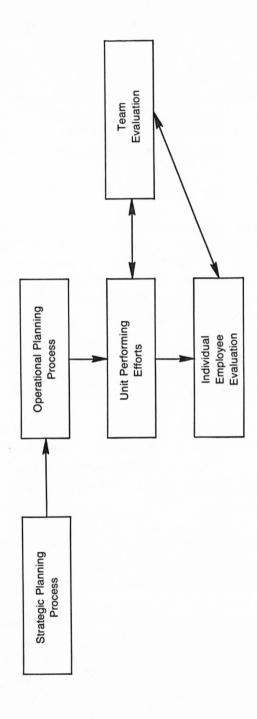

Fig. 14: Theory Z Performance Review System

of the team is the evidence of synergy. The individual performance of the team is greater than its parts.

Team Evaluation

Informal and formal performance evaluation sessions require a process. Because teams are responsible for contributing to the performance efforts of excellent organizations, it is essential that some basis be established to provide the team with constant feedback as to whether its performance has been satisfactory.

Individual Employee Evaluation

Individual employees who make up the team member's performance should also receive frequent informal and formal performance evaluation. This does two things: 1)   On-the-job improvement actions can be initiated while learning by doing; 2)   The supervisor's performance can also be evaluated in terms of how well he or she is assisting individual employees to become a harmonious member of the team.

COMPONENTS OF THE THEORY Z
PERFORMANCE EVALUATION PROCESS

The performance review system in a Theory Z organization will usually involve, as illustrated in Figure 15, a team review, supervisor's review, and sometimes a top management review.

Team Review

Because teamwork is an important feature of Theory Z organizations, members of a team usually conduct the first performance review session. Team review is informal; team members cite strengths and weaknesses of the employee. Each item is discussed in detail. In fact, the team review usually evolves into a training and development session with the employee understanding how a particular task was done right or wrong and how it could have been improved. The employee is asked to identify his or her other needs and concerns. This usually consists of the employee identifying what a member of the team can do to help group a particular activity or task.

It seems appropriate here to indicate what George Odiorne, the father of Management By Objectives, maintains should be the focus of the employee when indicating his or her needs and concerns during the performance review. That is "what can the supervisor do, stop doing, or do differently to help the employer to perform?" This statement quite comprehensively gets to all of the points the employee should consider when giving feedback to supervisor for improving performance.

Supervisor's Review

Employees should meet periodically with supervisors to review performance. If the employee works with a number of supervisors, each one should meet with the employee. The supervisor usually identifies strong and weak performance areas for the employee, and comments on how well the employee gets along with his or her coworkers. At the close of the review, the employee is asked to indicate any needs from the supervisor that will improve performance. These needs may be direct or indirect.

Although the Japanese have been cited for conducting formal evaluations of employees only after about five-to-ten years, I feel this approach should not be practiced in the United States. Informal performance reviews should be frequent. However, whenever an employee is slated to be rotated to either a different task or function, it should only occur when there has been a formal performance review and the performance has been determined to be satisfactory. At that time, the review should be stated in writing, placed in the personnel file, and used as one of the basis for determining job rotation.

Management Review

Sometimes, as an act to get to know the employee better, as well as to protect the employee from any unfairness, a manager may be the final person to review the performance evaluation. He or she will review the statement for both what the team members and supervisors had to report on the performance of the employee, as well as what the latter has stated in terms of what assistance is required from peers and supervisors. Figures 15 and 15a illustrate two performance review models. In the first model, the employees receive a peer evaluation after two months on the assignment. Obviously, it is assumed that the performance of the employee for a particular assignment has been satisfactory. The personnel department working closely with the supervisor, identifies the new assignment and makes appropriate adjustments in the files of the employee. This model or procedure becomes the rotation practice of the organization for those employees who are being trained to acquire multi-skills to accomodate the needs of the organization.

In the second model, the employees' performance is reviewed, not only by the team members, but by a number of managers. The performance review session is accomplished by top management. There are a number of ways or models that can be creatively developed, consisting of the three basic elements of the performance review session mentioned previously. The one used by a given organization should be determined by the strengths of team members and supervisors, how often the performance should be reviewed, the needs of employees and organization, and the time span between assignment rotation.

PHASES OF THE PERFORMANCE EVALUATION

Managers usually think of the performance review as a one-phase process consisting merely of the supervisor reviewing the performance of the employee and presenting an assessment. In Theory Z organizations, the performance review consists of four processes:

1. The Day-to-Day Review Phase. The supervisor reviews the progress of the employee daily, providing on-the-job coaching, guidance, and direction. Usually, the supervisor is located centrally to observe the efforts of the team members in the event that they may require guidance as a group or as individuals.

2. Problem-Solving Review Phase. Team members analyze and solve problems with team and individual employees, providing feedback for correcting performance and taking corrective actions.

3. Periodic Formal Review Phase. The supervisor, peers, and/or manager formally review the performance of a team or individual, providing two-way feedback, recording the assessment, and taking corrective action.

4. Management Formal Review Phase. This phase is infrequent, but may be a review of the employee's performance by management, particularly if a manager feels some concern, notes some cause to believe there may be a discrepancy between his

or her own perception of an employee's or team's performance and the review turned in by a supervisor. This phase comes from a meeting between the employee(s), supervisor, and manager to confer over the discrepancy and to resolve it.

COMPARATIVE ANALYSIS OF THE PERFORMANCE EVALUATION OF TYPE A AND Z ORGANIZATIONS

There are some similarities between the performance review process of Type A and Z organizations, but some differences should be highlighted:

PERFORMANCE REVIEW PROCESS

Type A Organization	Type Z Organization
If employee's performance is below par, he or she is at fault.	If employee's performance is below par, the supervisor is usually at fault.
An error in performing a job or task is sometimes cause for a reprimand	An error in performance is cause for using that situation as a training and development opportunity.
Group assessment of individual employees is uncommon.	Group or team assessment of individual employees is common.
Team performance review is uncommon.	Team performance review is frequent and common.
Rotation on the job does occur, but is usually within common areas.	Rotation on the job is common and is usually in different areas or assignments.
Employee's needs and concerns are seldom explored during the performance review process.	Employee's needs and concerns are frequently explored during the performance review process.
Performance review is usually conducted in a hostile environment.	Performance review is usually conducted in a helpful and congenial environment

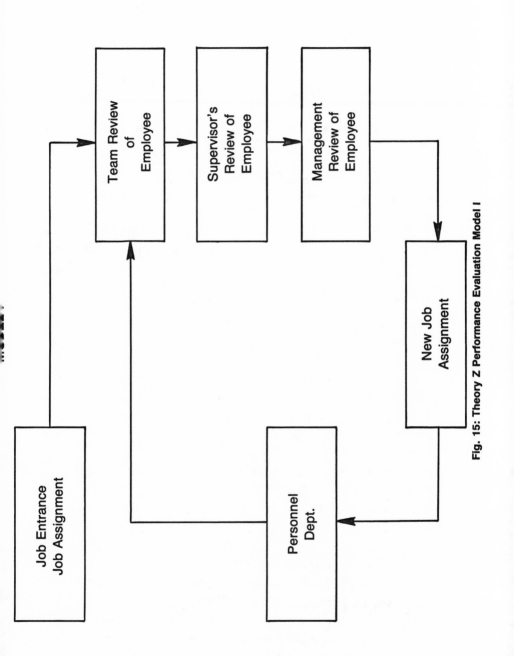

Fig. 15: Theory Z Performance Evaluation Model I

Supervisor is seldom positioned in a location to offer day-to-day performance review, counseling, and coaching to employees.	Supervisor is usually positioned in a location where he or she can observe the action of teams and individual employees to review performance, determine needs, and give assistance.
Excessive paperwork may be a problem.	Paperwork is seldom a problem.
Supervisors are assessed as to what results were achieved.	Supervisors are assessed on the basis of how well they get along with their employees and the achievement of expected results.

TWO PERFORMANCE EVALUATION REPORT FORMATS

There are many ways to conduct the performance evaluation process. The two models illustrated in Figures 15 and 15a were based on common points covered in this chapter.

One performance evaluation format that is suggested in *The One-Minute Manager*, is rather simple and easy to adopt by a Theory Z Organization. I identify it as goal-setting;[1] it involves goals and performance standards.

1. Goal

A goal is a written statement which describes a specific and measurable result to be achieved within a given period, usually one year. Begin with an action verb preceded by the word "to", indicate the desired result, state the time span for accomplishing the goal.

2. Performance Standards

Performance standards are statements of conditions that will exist when a goal has been satisfactorily achieved. Begin by indicating all of the essential elements needed to achieve the goal; describe each essential element with the statement, "this goal will be satisfactorily achieved when...;" make certain each statement has been both quantified and qualified.

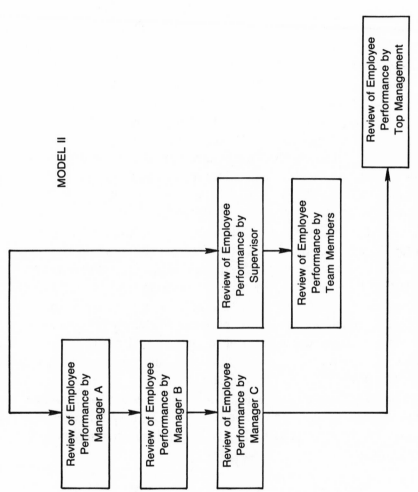

MODEL II

Fig. 15a: Theory Z Performance Evaluation Model II

3.   Performance Outcome

Performance outcome is a description of the termination of planned human effort that has been exerted to reach a goal. The term "planned" is emphasized because performance results are measured as "on plan," "below plan," and "above plan." Each stated result must be accompanied by a description of the actual outcome.

An example of a completed goal-setting evaluation report is illustrated in Fig. 16.

Another format (see Fig. 17) for implementing the Theory Z performance evaluation process has five sections:

1.   Description–includes the name of the employee, team assignment, supervisor's name, the next assignment, date, and the period covered by the evaluation report.

2.   Strength–consists of brief statements describing the strong points of the employee while performing as a member of the team.

3.   Weakness–consists of brief statements which identify areas where the employee needs improvement.

4.   Personal Concern–completed by the employee, who reports three things about the supervisor: 1)   what the supervisor *can do* to assist the employee to perform; 2)   what the supervisor *can do differently* to assist the employee to perform; and 3)   what the supervisor *can stop doing* to assist the employee to perform.

5.   Personal Needs–the employee will identify any personal needs required of the supervisor to assist him or her to perform. This may include making the job assignment more challenging, additional job knowledge requirements, etc.

The supervisor should react to numbers 4 and 5 as an indication that additional training and development may be necessary for the employee, not as finding fault with his or her supervisory assistance.

REQUIREMENTS OF AN EFFECTIVE THEORY Z
PERFORMANCE EVALUATION PROCESS

For a Theory Z performance evaluation process to be effective, managers should analyze the organization's present evaluation program against the following criteria:

1.   Focus on the people-building philosophy

Everything in the performance evaluation process should improve the values, beliefs, and skills of every employee of the organization.

2. Review employee performance by evaluation teams

Frequently throughout the performance of an employee, one or more team members will provide specific guidance, direction, assistance, and encouragement. Not only is this an excellent means of team bonding, it is a form of learning by doing that provides a sound basis for assessing how well an employee is doing on the job, for taking any necessary corrective action, and for determining future career paths.

3. Conduct more informal and less formal performance reviews

Theory Z performance evaluation frequently uses informal methods for reviewing individual employee and team performance. As a result, employees are more at ease with the performance review, eager to participate in it, tend to become highly motivated workers, and increase their on-the-job performance. Formal evaluations do little to improve performance because it is usually

PERFORMANCE EVALUATION

Name_____ Date _____

Unit _____

Supervisor _____

_____
Goal:

_____
Performance Standards:

_____
Performance Outcome:

☐ On plan   ☐ Above plan   ☐ Below plan

Fig. 16: Goal-Setting Performance Evaluation Format

done away from the job, tends to be dominated by the supervisor, and often is not done to provide job improvement, but rather to review someone's perception about the performance of another person.

4. Conduct team performance reviews

Since teams are set up throughout the Type Z organization to do the work necessary to realize the purpose of the organization, their effectiveness should be assessed in order to determine strengths, weaknesses, problems, and needs. Team performance reviews also provide splendid opportunities for determining effectiveness of supervisors, whose chief responsibility is to organize employees into effective teams.

STEPS FOR INSTALLING THE
THEORY Z PERFORMANCE EVALUATION PROGRAM

The following procedural steps should be incorporated in Theory Z performance evaluation program:

1. Explain the nature and philosophy of the evaluation program and show how it is different from the present process.
2. Employees must be patient and realize that when promotions are made, considerable weight will be given to longevity.
3. Distribute planning premises to all units and divisions. Require managers to disseminate appropriate information to teams in need of supporting goals, performance standards and activities.
4. Have each team set goals and performance standards compatible to their functions and charges.
5. Decide on the Theory Z performance evaluation model by indicating the frequency of formal and informal performance reviews, and who will conduct them.
6. Dovetail the formal performance evaluation process with the career development program.
7. Institute the performance review program.

SLOWING DOWN PROMOTIONS

To emphasize the importance of long-term performance to employees, not only is there a slowing down of the formal performance evaluations of employees, but the slowing down of promotions. American organizations usually do the opposite of what the Japanese do; formal performance evaluations are made two or four times a year, promotions might come within a few months on the job. When these two practices are closely scrutinized, the evidence indicates that the performance evaluation process tends to be ineffective or dysfunctional, and those who receive quick promotions usually have been employeed in less than five jobs within a period of two years. This practice has become such a problem that at least one author is proclaiming that "loyalty" cannot be obtained from American employees, the most that can be expected is "respect." American managers have practiced frequent

EMPLOYEE PERFORMANCE REVIEW

Name _____ Date _____

Team _____ Period _____

Supervisor _____

Next   Assignment _____

Strengths:

Weaknesses:

Personal Concerns:

Personal Needs:

Fig. 17: Theory Z Performance Evaluation Format

formal performance evaluations and quick promotions for years without much success on a long-term basis.

It is high time that some attention be given to the Theory Z concept of slowing down the pace of performance evaluations and promotions, but in order to get employees to accept this focus, the following requirements must be met:

1. Employees must feel their presence in the organization is important.
2. Employees must understand that on the long-term basis, they will be highly compensated for their patience and loyalty to the organization.
3. Employees must have a long-term sense of job security.
4. Employees must be continuously informed of the prospect of receiving greater income and promotions in the future.
5. Employees must be put into situations in which older employees provide feedback on the prospect of being promoted.
6. Employees who are relatively new in the organization, must participate in certain work projects that involve other units and divisions.

SUMMARY

Performance evaluation is a critical assessment of work performed by a person; it is conducted formally or informally by either an individual or group. The Theory Z performance evaluation system is interrelated to strategic planning, operational planning, and unit performance efforts. As a result, performance evaluations must be conducted for teams and individuals. The components of the Theory Z performance evaluation process are: 1)   Team review; 2)   Supervisor's review; 3)   Top management review. The phases of the performance evaluation process are: 1)   The day-to-day review; 2)   Problem-solving review; 3)   Periodic formal review; and 4)   Management formal review. The requirements of the Theory Z performance evaluation process are: 1)   Focus on People-building philosophy; 2)   Review employee performance by team members; 3)   Conduct more informal and less formal performance reviews; and 4)   Conduct team evaluations.

15

Decisions By Consensus

THE CONSENSUS MOVEMENT began in this country some thirty to forty years ago, but, because the process involves a lengthy time to arrive at a decision, it was soon abandoned for either the autocratic rule or majority vote.

When the Japanese began using consensus with success as that country sought world dominance in quality and productivity, American managers noted that while the Japanese took a long time to reach a decision, they implemented it quickly and with an unusually strong commitment to the task. On the other hand, most American organizations were experiencing some serious problems. Although decision-making was quite rapid in contrast to the Japanese, implementng the decision was rather slow, and often the end result was different than the original intent. As a result, a large number of organizations have begun to use consensus as a viable alternative to other forms of decision making process, particularly those organizations implementing Theory Z.

DEFINING CONSENSUS
Consensus is a decision-making process where members of a team (group) cooperatively arrive at a mutually acceptable decision which all members will agree to support.

More specifically, consensus means:

1. every member of the team may not be completely satisfied with the decision, but it is the best that can be reached at the time and under the present circumstances.

2. each team member has consented to the decision.

3.   a single team member with a strong objection to a decision has a right to block the decision.

4.   the team must continue searching for an acceptable decision if a decision is blocked.

5.   the focus is on being attentive to each team member's ideas, and taking all the members' reservations and concerns into consideration in an attempt to reach an acceptable team decision.

6.   a team member who relinquishes the right to block a team's decision, has in effect agreed to abide by the decision of the team.

An administration team has been established at Electro Scientific Industries, Inc. composed of those in charge of each division. Instead of voting on decisions or leaving the decision to one manager, the team attempts to make all decisions using consensus.

SOME BASIC ASSUMPTIONS UNDERLYING CONSENSUS

Inherent in the use of consensus decision making are two basic assumptions about the confidence in human beings and groups:

1.   For every problem, there is the best decision for a particular time and under the circumstances upon which all members can unite, if enough time is spent in the discussion.

2.   The aim of the team is to develop a sense of cooperation and belonging.

3.   Every team member participates and shares in the decision.

CONDITIONS FOR USING CONSENSUS

Some conditions or prerequisites must be understood to make the process work:

1.   Top management must clearly indicate when it is appropriate and inappropriate to use consensus as a decision-making process.

2.   Team members must be trained to implement the consensus decision making process.

3.   The supervisor should be trained as a facilitator of the process and in other areas, such as conflict resolution, team building, motivation, and group dynamics.

4.   A manual on consensus decision making should be developed and made available to all team members for future referral.

5.   Everybody who will be affected by the decision should be involved in the process.

6. Everyone should be involved in consensus decision making beginning with the chief executive officer and his or her team, and ending with part-time employees.

7. There must be a common bond uniting the team, such as similar areas of responsibility, linked goals, etc.

8. Each team member must accept the belief that everyone has something to offer the team, that conflict can be healthy, and that any problem can be solved if enough time is spent in discussing it.

ADVANTAGES OF CONSENSUS

In most situations, consensus is the preferred decision-making process, particularly because of the education and sophistication of today's employees; they desire, and occasionally demand to be included in the process of making decisions that will affect their lives. Many excellent organizations recognize the vast reservoir of untapped talents and skills among their employees and provide opprtunities to engage them in consensus decision-making opportunities.

There are some pleasant advantages to making decisions by consensus:[1]

1. It fosters a win-win philosophy as opposed to majority rule in which an individual or side loses.

2. It is a process of synthesizing and integrating ideas rather than selecting one idea over another.

3. Its thrust is to persuade rather than coerce.

4. It provides a setting in which everyone contributes something to the discussion.

5. It provides adequate time for team members to hash ideas over, rather than rushing into a vote.

6. It nurtures a precept that the integrity of the team is more important than a single issue.

7. It helps the team to function as a group rather than focusing on a team member's idea which leads to compromise.

8. It requires honesty, open communication, and a free exchange of ideas.

9. Every team member gets a piece of the action.

10. It enhances the probability that the decision will be implemented with little or no change.

11. It fosters an atmosphere in which the principles of Theory Z are practiced.

Majority Rule Compared to Consensus

A comparative analysis between the majority rule and consensus, should further help the reader to understand why the latter is preferred over the former:

Majority Rule	Consensus
A decision is reached by selecting a solution which is acceptable to more than half the members of the team.	A decision is reached by selecting a solution which is acceptable to all members of the team.
Quality decisions are sometimes not made because every team member's decision may not be heard.	Quality decisions are a by-product of the process because every team member's ideas, reservations, and concerns are heard and responded to in a positive manner.
Assumes competition where "sides" are identified with one side attempting to win over the other.	Assumes cooperation where team members respect the rights of an individual to disagree with the team; individual's concerns and reservations are considered and everything is done to satisfy his or her needs. Thus, a win-win relationship is established.
Decisions are usually arrived at very rapidly.	Decisions are usually arrived at slowly by team members.
Implementation of a decision by team members is slow to be realized and sometimes is changed during the implementation process because every team member may not be committed to the decision of the other side.	Implementation of a decision by team members is realized very rapidly because all team members have agreed to support it.

The opinions of managers, supervisors, experts, specialists, and dominant team members, may influence the other members of the team to reach a decision.	The opinions of all team members, regardless of their power status, have no influence on the decision because egalitarianism is practiced throughout the process.
Acceptance of the decision is usually based on perceptions and judgements of facts.	Acceptance of the decision is based on facts and feelings of team members.

Procedural Steps for Achieving Consensus

Although there are only three major steps for implementing the consensus decision-making process, each is filled with essential points that must be mastered in order to produce united agreement on decisions:[2]

Step I.   Preparing for the discussion

There are two basic ways to introduce something to the team for discussion purposes in order to arrive at a consensus. Each is explained below:

1.   Construct a proposal to inform team members what must be achieved to fulfill their charge. Taking a cue from the book, *One-Minute Manager*, the proposal should have a goal and performance standards:[3]

Consensus Proposal

Goal:

To develop a competitive and easy to use microcomputer within one year.

Performance Standard: (This goal is satisfactorily achieved when . . .)

1.   the computer is built around a 16-bit microprocessor.
2.   the technical specifications are made available to other firms.
3.   the power of the computer is increased over standard models.
4.   the minimum capacity of the computer is 64K.
5.   the computer can be adapted to accommodate the software of our chief competitors with a minimum of expense.
6.   the parts of the computer already exist.

OR

2.   Establish an Agenda

The agenda can be established either prior to the discussion, or during the meeting. On-the-job situations will usually require the agenda to be developed during the meeting so that everyone will agree on what should be discussed and in what sequence. An example of an agenda is illustrated below:

AGENDA

Item	*Action*	*Presenter*
Backround data pertaining to the issue.	Report	Manager
How should the micro-computer be designed?	Consensus decision	Team
Background of competitive microcomputers.	Report	Specialists and Strategic Planners
What should be the performance standards?	Consensus decision	Team
Break		
Which managers and units should be involved in the initial design?	Consensus decision	Team
Date of next meeting.	Decision	Team

3.   Introduce the Item for Discussion

The supervisor or team leader introduces the goal or the item for the agenda. At times particularly where an impromptu meeting has been called to agree to a solution to a problem, the introduction should contain:

   a.   A precise definition of the goal or item to be discussed.

   b.   A clear statement of what has to be done to arrive at a consensus. This statement should focus on either what has to be accomplished, or what problem must be solved by the decision. When using a proposal for discussion purposes, the goal, if already given, should be considered in terms of identifying performance standards that need to be achieved to achieve the goal. Sometimes, the goal, as well as the performance standards, must be mutually agreed to by the team members. When using an agenda for discussion purposes, the team will need to mutually agree as to what the primary purpose of the meeting is, and should decide on how it should be done.

4. Present Background Information

The supervisor, team leader, or the team member introducing the goal or item for discussion should give the team as much background information as possible so that the team has a beginning base to make decisions. When the discussion progresses, other essential information will emerge from among team members.

Step II. Discussing the goal or item

The supervisor or team leader is responsible for helping the team build united judgement that will lead to consensus. The following represents the essential actions that will take place by the supervisor or team leader and team during the discussion phase for reaching a consensus.

1. Supervisor's Action

The supervisor or team leader introduces the goal or item to the team, defines the problems, provides background information, and recommends an approach to the problem.

Team Action

An individual team member may ask for clarification of the goal or an item, and more specific background information. The team member may use any or all of the clarifying material to supplement his or her original ideas.

2. Team Action

A team member responds to the idea of the supervisor, and includes his or her own ideas as it has been influenced by either the supervisor or team member.

Supervisor Action

As long as the ideas and opinions presented are relevant to the original goal or item, the supervisor encourages the team membership for more.

3. Team Action

Several team members begin to respond to the earlier goal or item, offering their own ideas and opinions. Each statement builds on those of other team members. As a result, each individual team member's comment is unique and has been influenced by the ideas and opinions of other team members.

Supervisor and Individual Team Member Action

During discussion, the supervisor and team members are responsible for conducting a smooth-operating meeting to reach a consensus by:

a) keeping team members from meandering.
b) probing for more ideas and opinions.
c) providing clarity; rephrasing unclear and complicated statements.
d) summarizing where agreements and disagreements exist.
e) citing new issues and problems when they occur.
f) making certain all viewpoints, reservations, impressions, feelings, and concerns, are heard and understood by the total team membership.
g) seeking process problems and working them through.

4. Team Action

Most viewpoints have been stated and team members begin to repeat themselves.

Supervisor Action

Team members are asked if anything new can be added to the discussion, and then test for a consensus by stating the position (solution) in which the team seems to be moving.

Step III. Arriving at a Decision

When all views have been heard, the supervisor orchestrates the activities necessary to aid the team to arrive at a decision:

1. Team Action

The team agrees or disagrees to the "consensus test" of the supervisor.

Supervisor Action

The supervisor makes certain that all concerns and objections have been addressed by going from one team member to another, observing nonverbal and verbal responses from team members.

2. Team Action

Team members listen and discuss each concern for the purpose of arriving at an agreement. At times, the decision which is arrived at may not entirely satisfy every team member, but it may be the best decision that can be agreed to at that time under the present circumstances. If one or more team members continue to have a problem with the decision, it must be "worked through" the process.

Supervisor Action

The supervisor continues to orchestrate the discussion of the team by encouraging each member to bring up and to reflect on all ideas and all concerns and reservations.

3. Team Action

It seems as though a consensus is reached.

Supervisor Action

The supervisor states the consensus decision to determine if every team member agrees, makes certain that certain responsibilities for carrying out the phases of the decision are assigned to a team member. If a proposal exists, every team member responsible for completing a function or activity which will have some impact on the decision, is required to sign the proposal as an indication of agreement. The signature is also used to indicate to the signees all of the persons who have in one way or another been involved in the decision-making process.

4. Team Action

A consensus cannot be reached.

Supervisor Action

The supervisor realizes that a consensus cannot be reached at the present time, a condition that usually means team members do not have enough information to render a good decision. The decision will have to be deferred until more information is given to team members, more discussion takes place, and the team members digest the information.

Sometimes the team may feel that a decision must be made, perhaps because of a time constraint. Therefore, it will be necessary to continue the discussion, and for members to "stretch" themselves to reach a decision that may not be the best, but one all team members can live with. The team should not be coerced or pressured into accepting a decision; vital by-products of consensus such as individual team member's commitment, improved coordination, etc. would be seriously missing from the result.

THREE CONSENSUS MODELS

Three of the most common consensus models can be useful on a unit or organizational basis:[4]

Panel Consensus

A variety of teams are set up in an inverted pyramid in order to winnow the various ideas offered as a solution to a given problem. There are five steps to this technique:

Step 1–Idea Generation

Organize multiple teams to generate a large number of ideas to a given problem, using the nominal group process. This generates improved quality of ideas and more variety than what is produced during a brainstorming session.

Step 2–Screening Process

Organize a variety of employees into 15 teams of 12-to-15 members. Charge each team with the responsibility for generating five best ideas presented.

Step 3–Select Action

Three teams of 5 experts with broad experience, selected from middle management meet with a facilitator to write a justification for the best ideas from the 75 ideas that have been presented.

Step 4–Refinement

Five top managers (with expertise in the problem) meet with a facilitator to select the best ideas from the 15 presented. They clarify, expand, and synthesize the ideas into five priority proposals without losing the unique character of the original ideas.

Step 5–Decision

In this final step, five top managers meet with a facilitator to select one or more of the ideas for implementation. If a consensus on an idea cannot be reached, the idea is sent to one of the preceeding teams to reactivate previous ideas.

Consensus is the basis for arriving at all decisions at each step. If a consensus cannot be reached, the idea may be discarded and the next item of priority activated.

Quaker Consensus Model (Quaker Process)

The Quaker Consensus Model is based on a number of principles which are used as a code of behavior employed at meetings scheduled to produce a consensus.

1. Avoid arguing for your own point of view.
2. Avoid the win-lose approach.

3. Avoid changing your mind to avoid conflict.
4. Avoid majority voting and other conflict-reducing techniques.
5. View differences of opinions as healthy.
6. View initial agreement with skepticism.

Filley's Consensus Model

Filley's Consensus Model is based on a set of prerequisites and prescriptions for arriving at the consensus. The prerequisites reinforce the prescriptions. These are:

1. Review and adjust the team in size, constraints, spatial arrangement, and communication.
2. Review and adjust the perception of the team members using reality testing to substantiate the facts.
3. Use reality testing to clarify and understand the attitudes and feelings of the team members to one another.
4. Depersonalize the problem.
5. Search for a solution by generating alternate solutions.

If these prerequisites exist, says the originator of this method, the probability of reaching a consensus is enhanced when the following prescriptions have been met:

1. Narrow the range of solutions.
2. Evaluate the solutions in terms of quality and acceptability.
3. Allow team members to justify preferences and feelings.
4. Agree on criteria of evaluation.
5. Use consensus when there is little expression of self-oriented need.
6. Review members evaluations of alternatives periodically.
7. Don't use techniques that avoid conflict.
8. Divide problems into parts for evaluation purposes.
9. Resolve conflict before continuing with the evaluation process.

ATTITUDES THAT SUPPORT CONSENSUS

The following attitudes will help the consensus decision-making process work well, encouraging a healthy psychological climate to arrive at a consensus and allowing each team member to improve his or her relationship with other team members:[5]

Engendering a Cooperative Spirit

Consensus decision making expects each team member to

cooperate. In a cooperative mood, team members will:
1. share information with others.
2. trust and care for each other.
3. accept individual differences as a value to the diversity of the team.
4. welcome viewpoints from other perspectives.
5. foster a win-win philosophy.
6. capitalize on their individual strengths and minimize their weaknesses for the benefit of the team.
7. recognize that there is not always a right solution, but one that may be a more appropriate solution.

Accepting the Criticism of Ideas

Ideas developed during the consensus decision-making process become the property of the team; when a team member brings forth an idea, it is usually because of his or her reservoir of knowledge, experience, etc., and the input of other team members. At another time and place with different team members, the idea may have been different. Once this is understood and accepted by all team members, each of them should feel at ease to criticize ideas, to change ideas, or to add a residual idea. No member should take any suggestions or changes as a personal affront.

Understanding the Positive Side of Conflict

Conflict is neither good nor bad. It can be handled on a win-lose basis or on a win-win basis. When it is handled on a win-lose basis, one side competes against the other and, although one side may win, neither side actually accomplishes much. However, when it is handled on a win-win basis there are no sides; everybody works cooperatively, exchanging ideas and opinions until a decision is reached that is satisfactory to all team members. Different points of view are catalysts. The strengths and weaknesses of each idea are examined in the crucible of interaction, through which a viable solution to issues emerges.

Valuing Human Feelings

If the consensus decision-making process is working effectively, each team member will value the feelings of the others; each member will approach an idea or decision in a healthy manner, caring for each other and considering the concerns of each team member, until a workable and acceptable solution is reached.

Equalizing Power

Information is power. Equalize power and you provide each team member an equal access to information; therefore, no one team member should have a monopoly on information, experience, skills, and ideas. When one member has information or anything else important to the team, all members should have access to that information. To determine if there is unequal power within the team, carefully consider the following questions:

1. Does one member talk more than any other and tend to dominate the team?
2. Does one member tend to show off how much more he has than others?
3. Does a member of the team think more highly of one member than any of the others?
4. Does one member contribute more to the discussion than the other members?
5. Does a member try to dominate the team?

If any of the above questions are answered in the affirmative, then make critical observation and review to determine the power overload and what steps should be taken to equalize it.

Respecting the Contributions of Team Members

Every human being can contribute something to a team. The contribution may be a person's analytical nature, the calm and relaxed manner in which a team member asks or responds to a question, the inexperienced manner of relating to ideas, or the sensitivity a person brings to the team. Consensus decision making means that every member can contribute to the team performance in unique and different ways. When team members feel that they are important, it is primarily because each person has demonstrated that he or she values the contribution of the other's. Each member fosters within the team a sense of responsibility, a sense of competency, a sense of dignity and worth, a sense of being useful and competent; all this helps to enhance their contribution to arriving at a decision.

Striving for Trust

Consensus decision-making means that team members must begin to trust each other. Trust can only result if group members are honest with each other.

1. Information will neither be destroyed nor concealed.

2. Members can depend on each other to abide by their agreements and to perform in a competent manner.
3. Members don't have to remind other members what they promised.
4. Members don't have to continuously defend their position or point of view.
5. Members will not become defensive when another member attempts to influence them.
6. Members do not have to conceal their feelings.
7. Members don't have to change their model to emulate another.

ATTITUDES THAT HAMPER CONSENSUS

Consensus is a powerful process for making decisions and getting people truly committed to their decisions. Certain attitudes can hamper the effect:

An Individualistic Philosophy

Consensus decision making encourages team competition as opposed to individual competition. When teams compete among themselves, the effectiveness of the team is based on how strong team members cooperate, get along together, care for each other, and demonstrate concern over different points of views. This kind of competition is healthy.

Individual competition is unhealthy and does not promote effective decision making. When a team member tries to achieve his or her own goal at the expense of the team goal, withholds information and manipulates other members to get acceptance of his or her own ideas, and pits one member against another to gain verbal approval—particularly within a team striving for consensus.

Selfishness

Some Americans have been taught the value of individualistic competition in ways which cause team members to exhibit selfishness. They may see their role in the team as one who merely contributes his or her own ideas, skills, talents, experience, and background to the discussion. Such an attitude prevents working out problems and arriving at solutions; it perpetuates an unhealthy relationship in a consensus making situation because team members think their personal goals and needs are superior to team goals.

Psychology of Owning Ideas

As a result of the individualistic orientation, team members often think of their ideas as personal property; they sometimes become annoyed when a team member is either critical or suggests changes. When this occurs, the defensive team member may argue for his or her idea rather than accepting improvements.

Not Dealing with Hidden Emotions

Team members may hide their true feelings about an issue because they have learned that the best way to deal with conflict and disagreement is to suppress it or to compromise in order to get rid of it. However, by compromising a position, they fail to fully deal with their hidden emotions and have given up a great opportunity to arrive at a creative approach to the solution.

Acquiescing to Authority

Sometimes team members will allow specialists, experts, or consultants to think for them and to arrive at decisions. By giving in to authority, these same team members surrender their power and defeat the purpose of consensus decision-making. When team members surrender their power and limit their participation in the discussion they, in essence, are denying the other team members a variety of viewpoints on an issue. Inactive team members also create other problems for the team as a whole:

1. They may fail to take responsibility for a poor decision.
2. They may not fully understand the decision, or may not be willing to implement the decision.
3. They dilute the effectiveness of the consensus-making process.

Team members will have social problems such as bias, prejudices, and assumptions that tend to influence their thinking. Team members who are not aware of these problems cannot deal effectively in the decision-making process; they will continue to exhibit these problems in one way or another during the discussion and when they arrive at solutions.

ALTERNATE FORMS OF CONSENSUS

Sometimes, a consensus may not be possible or may not be worth the time and effort to devote to the decision-making process. Alternative ways to deal with these situations are:

Consensus Decision with an Exception

Present a proposal to the team, which signifies an acceptance or rejection of the decision. The supervisor indicates those who favor the proposal, those who can live with the proposal, and those who are uncomfortable with it.

If no one is uncomfortable about the proposal, decision is implemented, but if some members are uncomfortable about it, they are requested to state their reasons and a discussion ensues. After the discussion, the supervisor will ask the team if the idea should be implemented over the objections of the minority. An affirmative vote means a majority rule. A negative vote means postponing the decision until a consensus is reached through a discussion.

Consensus by Committee

The team reaches a consensus on the proposal or item before discussing the solution. Sufficient time is allocated for interaction and clarification. If a major objection is raised over the solution, the team breaks up into miniteams for discussion and developing new proposals, amendments, etc. The mini-teams return to the larger team and see if a consensus can be reached. Those objecting to the proposal are asked to stay aside and let the majority rule on the solution. If those objecting to the proposal refuse to step aside, a committee is established representing an equal number of varied opinions. The charge of this committee is to meet and to reach a mutually acceptable proposal. The proposal is brought back to the team for a final decision. If a consensus is not realized, then the team will vote to accept a majority rule, which is usually three-fourths of the membership, then a three-fourth majority vote is conducted to accept the proposal.

COMMON TERMS RELATED TO CONSENSUS

Some terms associated with the consensus decision-making process are explained below:

1. **Blocking**–a consensus is considered blocked when one or more team members who have gone through the synthesizing process oppose the decision. Their action is termed blocking. Since the team is not ready to reach decision, more discussion must be held.

2. **Incubation Period**–the process of silencing the team

membership in order to give each member an opportunity to mediate the activity of the team, reduce anxiety, etc.

3. **Unanimity**—when every team member feels a particular solution is wanted most or is best. Consensus in not unanimity; it is the best solution that can be reached at a particular time and under the present circumstances.

4. **Compromise**—a situation in which each side gives up some demands or makes a concession to arrive at a decision. Compromise should never be mistaken as consensus.

SUMMARY

Consensus is a decision-making process where members of a team cooperatively arrive at a mutually acceptable decision which all members will agree to support; there are three major steps for implementing it: 1) Prepare for the discussion; 2) Discuss the goal or item; and 3) Arrive at a decision. Three common consensus models are: 1) Panel consensus; 2) Quaker consensus; and 3) Filley's consensus. Attitudes that support consensus are: 1) Engendering a cooperative spirit; 2) Accept criticism of ideas; 3) Understand the positive side of conflict; 4) Value human feelings; 5) Equalize power; 6) Respect the contribution of team members; and 7) Strive for trust. Attitudes that hamper consensus: 1) Individualistic philosophy; 2) Selfishness; 3) Psychology of owning ideas; 4) Not dealing with hidden emotions; and 5) Acquiescing to authority. Two alternative forms of consensus are: 1) Consensus decision with an exception; and 2) Consensus by committee. Terms related to the consensus-making process are blocking, incubation, unamity and compromise.

16

The Quality Circle Program

ONE OF THE most successful ways in which the Japanese have been able to establish a participatory decision-making process in the Type Z organization has been through the use of quality control circles, commonly referred to in the United States as quality circles.

More than 10 million people in Japan are circle members. Even though it will take years before the United States matches or exceeds this number, all the principles, practices, and problem-solving techniques were obtained from the United States. What is highly unusual about the Quality Circle Program is that the Japanese managers were practicing American-originated principles and practices while American managers were only giving them lip service. Many of the practices have been implemented in one way or another by some of the outstanding organizations identified by Peters and Waterman in their book, *In Search of Excellence*. Westinghouse alone has more than 15 thousand circle members.

A QUALITY CIRCLE DEFINED

A quality circle is a group of individuals (usually from three to eleven persons) who:

1. are employed in similar units.
2. are committed to improving organizational effectiveness.
3. voluntarily meet one day each week for about one hour to identify, select, analyze, and solve job-related problems in their area of responsibility.

4. verify the solution, recommend it to management, and implement the solution when possible.

The key term is commitment; far too many quality circles falter because their members lack the genuine commitment essential to success. Commitment comes only after circle members understand the value of the concept, are aware of its significance as a powerful process for organizational change, are fortified with knowledge and training in problem-solving techniques and group behavior, and are guided by a trained facilitator and circle leader.

OTHER NAMES USED TO DESCRIBE QUALITY CIRCLES

Since the advent of the quality circle concept, a host of names have been coined to describe quality circles:
- Employee participation circles
- Action teams
- Job enrichment teams
- Employee communication circles
- Participation action circles
- Professional development teams
- School improvement circles
- Working groups.

KINDS OF PROBLEMS QUALITY CIRCLES USUALLY SOLVE

Quality circles usually spend a large amount of their time solving problems that effect performance. After they have been in existence for a while and have matured, they have been known to tackle more complex and larger problems. Problems circle members identify usually fall into four categories:
1. those that have been neglected by management.
2. those that management are not aware of.
3. those to which management is too busy to give much attention.
4. those management thinks cannot be solved.

Depending on the organization, these problems may number in the hundreds, or even thousands.

Problems usually fall into three broad categories:

TYPE 1–those in which circle members have direct control over, and relate exclusively to, the individual unit of the quality circle.

TYPE 2–those circle members have limited indirect control over and which require the influence of upper level management. Although some of the problems involve job context, most deal with job content factors, such as policy and administration, supervision, working conditions, and interpersonal relations. Type 2 problems usually involve one or more units that have similar or common concerns.

TYPE 3–those which top management have direct control over, and usually involve job content factors such as achievement, recognition, work itself, respectability, advancement, and growth. Type 3 problems tend to be related to the organization as a whole. That is, problems that affect all units.

Initially, when the quality circle program is implemented, I highly recommend circle members to focus their attention on Type 1 problems. Once the program has had an opportunity to "thaw out," Type 2 problems can be tackled.

Initially, most of the problems that quality circles solve should take a minimal amount of time. As they begin to solve Type 2 problems, more time will be needed. However, most problems should be solved within three to six months.

Some organizations have been known to identify problems as projects or themes. Regardless of whatever identification that is given to the word, "problem," it should be consistently used throughout the organization.

PROBLEM AREAS THAT SHOULD BE AVOIDED BY QUALITY CIRCLES

In an effort not to encroach on the territory of unions the prerogatives of management, the steering committee that oversees the program will usually identify, via the quality circle charter, problems that the quality circle should avoid. Although these problems vary from one organization to another, the following appear to be the areas to avoid:

1. Wages and salaries
2. Fringe benefits
3. Disciplinary policies
4. Employment policies
5. Termination policies
6. Grievances
7. Collective bargaining items

8. Design of new products
9. Sales and marketing policies
10. Personalities

As a result of the quality circle program, a number of hybrids have been created that have, to some degree, strengthened its usefulness in solving, not only simple, but complex problems as well. Each hybrid is explained below,and a comparative analysis is shown in Fig. 18.

Joint Quality Circle

When the quality circle program begins to prove its worth, and many of the Type 1 problems have been solved, the facilitator should arrange to have two quality circles from different units come together, either on a temporary basis to solve a common Type 2 problem, or to meet on a permanent basis to share information on problem-solving activities. Usually, when a joint quality circle meets to solve a problem, it is disbanded until the facilitator or circle leader feels that another joint quality circle relationship is desirable because of a common concern.

Management Circles

Management circles consist of managers of similar units; they usually meet to share information on the activities of their quality circles, or to solve Type 2 problems. Although management circles are slow to emerge in most American organizations, there has been some recent interest generated by the International Association of Quality Circles.

Quality Teams

Quality teams are designed in a vertical manner and consist of managers from different units of the organization, who meet as a group to solve Type 3 problems, after which the teams are abandoned. When more organizations realize that basic and advanced problem-solving techniques are useful to solve major or complex organizational problems, more of them will adopt quality teams.

PURPOSES OF A QUALITY CIRCLE

The purposes of a quality circle will vary from organization to organization, depending on its unique needs. One method to assess the quality circle program is to evaluate the extent to which the purposes are being achieved. The following purposes relate to most quality circle programs:

1. To encourage a spirit of teamwork.
2. To tap the gold mine of unused skills, abilities and talents of employees.
3. To create an environment that is conducive to open communication and mutual trust among employees.
4. To enrich the job of employees by giving them the opportunity to share power and authority with managers.
5. To unleash the ideas of employees in solving job-related problems.
6. To create opportunities for employees to participate in and work together to improve their job situation.
7. To improve morale and job satisfaction.
8. To provide opportunities for professional and personal growth.
9. To foster an attitude of problem prevention and solving.
10. To provide opportunities for employees to become more motivated toward their job.
11. To increase and improve performance.
12. To provide employees with the opportunity to receive recognition from management for solving problems.
13. To reduce conflict between employees and managers.
14. To improve the quality of products and services.
15. To effect cost savings through on-the-job improvements.

MAKING THE QUALITY CIRCLE WORK

Several basic elements make the quality circle work, each of which has an essential function and serves a vital role:

MANAGEMENT

Top management support is essential if the quality circle program is to be successful. This support must demonstrate commitment to the quality circle concept; it must be shown through the acquisition of knowledge about the quality circle concept, the allocation of a budget for the quality circle program, visits to the various activities of quality circles, and the dissemination of written documents espousing the merits of the quality circle program. Middle management support is also important, and can occur only if the facilitator maintains a campaign to keep them informed by such activities as awareness sessions, publishing newsletters, and invitations to visit quality circle functions.

	Dissimilarities		Similarities
Quality Circles	**Management Circles**	**Quality Teams**	
• Homogenous	• Homogenous	• Heterogenous	• Utilizes facilitator and a leader
• Meet one hour per week.	• Meet one hour per week or more	• Meet as long as it takes to complete a given task	• Perpetuates a people-building philosophy
• Solve Type 1 problems and some Type 2 problems	• Solve Type 2 problems, sometimes acts as informative group	• Solve Type 3 problems	• Team-oriented
• Supervises the circle leader	• Senior manager is the leader	• Leader is appointed	• Performance monitored by steering committee
• Members decide own problems	• Top management and members decide the problem	• Top management decides the problem	
• Blue and white collar employees.	• White collar employees	• White collar employees	• Receive training in basic problem-solving techniques
• Solve numerous problems	• Solve some problems	• Solve a single problem	• Results-oriented
• Guided by a charter	• Guided by special policy	• Guided by a single problem	• May implement solution
• Problem-solving is continuous	• Problem-solving may be temporary or permanent	• Problem-solving is temporary	• Members are free to join or not to join
			• Conducts management presentation

Fig. 18: Circle-Team Analysis

STEERING COMMITTEE

The steering committee is usually composed of various managers from different levels of the organization; its membership is responsible for developing the charter governing the operations of quality circles, selecting a facilitator, establishing long- and short-range plans to guide the human efforts of the quality circle program, establishing a budget to accomodate the quality circle activities, determining the form of recognition to give to circle members, and doing whatever is necessary to effect a successful quality circle program. Steering committee members demonstrate support for the quality circle program by attending circle meetings, management presentations, and the annual quality circle conference.

FACILITATOR

The facilitator is a member of the steering committee, responsible for executing the activities of this governing body. Though not a member of the quality circle, the facilitator is responsible for the operations of the quality circle program and actively assists the circle leader to operate an effective and smooth meeting. The facilitator—the most knowledgeable person about the program—is actually a resource person, a trainer, a coordinator, a promoter, a problem-solver, and fills a host of other roles needed to ensure the success of the program.

CIRCLE LEADER

The circle leader is usually the immediate supervisor of circle members, although in some instances, other members have been known to assume this position. This person conducts the circle meetings and orchestrates all of the activities that make the quality circle work.

CIRCLE MEMBERS

The core of the quality circle is its members, who are usually volunteers performing basically the same type of work and who generally report to the same supervisor. They are trained in basic and advanced problem-solving techniques and in group dynamics.

MANAGEMENT PRESENTEES

Once a proposed solution has been arrived at by the quality circle, arrangements are made by the facilitator or circle leader for circle members to present their proposal to a group of managers for review and approval. This process is known as the management presentation. Those selected to sit in on this review are referred to as management presentees.

SPECIALISTS AND EXPERTS

Circle members do not have all of the answers to the problem of the organization; from time to time they need specialists and experts to assist them to define and analyze problems. So sometimes outside consultants may be necessary to assist in analyzing Type 2 and 3 problems.

NONCIRCLE MEMBERS

Although all employees of the organization are given opportunities to volunteer to serve on quality circles, some do not because of a host of reasons. Noncircle members should, however, be thought of as an important body in the organization and, therefore, should be involved in the quality circle activities as much as possible. From time to time they should be brought up to date as to the progress being made by the quality circle program through verbal presentations and written communiques. Circle members should also strive continuously to get noncircle members to join quality circles.

PHASES TO THE OPERATIONS OF A QUALITY CIRCLE

There are several phases to the operations of a quality circle, which must be viewed as a comprehensive and systematic process, as illustrated in Figure 19. If one or more phases are omitted or improperly executed, program results are likely to suffer.

Phase I—Identifying problems

Circle members use brainstorming to generate a large number and variety of problems from which the quality circle will consider in order to arrive at a single problem. Although circle members select their own problem, noncircle members should be encouraged to assist in the generation of problems.

Phase II—Selecting a problem

Circle members usually go through two to three rounds in order to select a specific problem to solve. During the initial brainstorming session, Type 1 problems should receive preference for two reasons: 1) to experience some quick successes, and 2) to gain some experience with the process.

Phase III—Analyzing the problem

Gather data and information about the problem; arrange it to depict peculiarities of the problem. Usually, data collection will involve the study:

1. reports
2. computer printouts
3. checklists
4. research data
5. information from specialists and experts
6. checklist or sheets
7. drawings.

Information collected during this phase should enable circle members to develop various displays to help illuminate the magnitude of the problem.

Phase IV—Analyzing the data

Organize the assembled data into histograms, scattergrams, graphs, pareto chart, control chart, etc. in an effort to analyze specific reasons for the problem.

Phase V—Solving the problem

Generate ideas as to how the problem can be solved, then select the most appropriate solution. Some techniques used during this phase are function analysis, force field analysis, and cause-and-effect diagrams. Use function analysis to determine an improved method for performing a task, process, etc. Force field analysis is used to determine whether to deal with a driving force or retraining force to solve the problem. The cause-and-effect diagram helps circle members identify the possible causes of the problem and to arrive at a solution.

Phase VI—Verifying the solution

Circle members verify the proposed solution by conferring with specialists and experts, or referring to some other source.

Phase VII—Presenting the proposed solution to management

The solution to the problem should be presented verbally and in writing to management as a prearranged meeting, known as the management presentation. One of the most exciting phases of the problem-solving process, it should be executed with care. An agenda is prepared to act as an instrument to guide the activities of the management presentation, which ideally, should be rehearsed as many times as possible until the circle members, as a group, are ready to give a command performance. Questions and answers, as well as a status report concerning the next project, are presented at the conclusion of the management presentation.

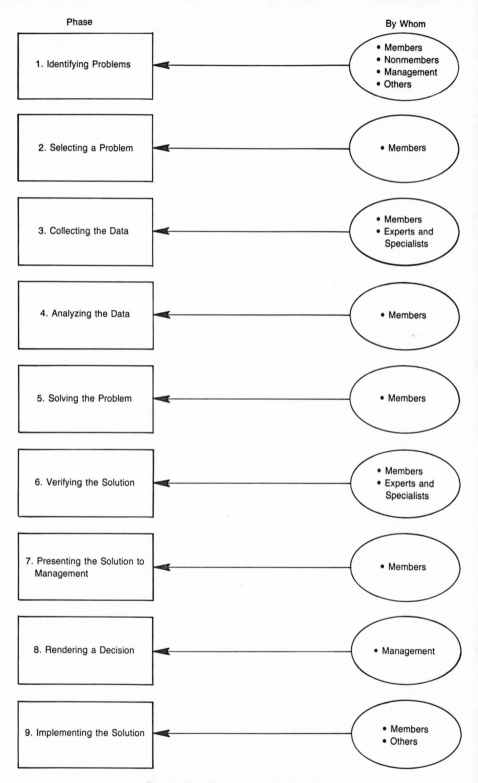

Fig. 19: The Phases of a Quality Circle

Usually, the presentation ends with management acknowledging the good work of the quality circle and recognizing them for their efforts.

Phase – VIII – Rendering a decision

Usually, management is ready to make a decision regarding the proposed solution at the conclusion of the presentation. This decision can be to approve the proposal, to reject it, or to withhold a decision until further information is forthcoming. My experience indicates that about 80 percent of the proposed solutions are approved by management at the presentation. Whenever a proposed solution is rejected, it is because either the facilitator or circle leader did not do his or her homework or receive prior approval for solution activities that cost large sums of money. At times, a quality circle may not get immediate approval because additional information is necessary, or the matter must be discussed with someone within or outside the organization. This is particularly true if another organization has implemented the solution proposed by the quality circle. Sometimes the quality circle must be prepared to come up with an alternative solution. At any event, management is expected to render a decision about the proposed solution within a reasonable period of time.

Phase IX – Implementing the solution

Whenever possible, the quality circle should develop an action plan to implement the solution to the problem. If this is not feasible, the quality circle should monitor the results of the individual or group responsible for implementing the solution. Periodically, program reports should be presented to management and employees in writing and/or verbally. Circle members must understand that it is not enough to solve the problem – the solution must also be implemented.

USING NONCIRCLE MEMBERS TO STRENGTHEN QUALITY CIRCLES

Neither the circle leaders nor the circle members have all the necessary expertise to analyze or solve problems. Consequently, all employees of the organization should be seen as a cadre of specialists in particular, identifiable areas which can be used to shed light on problems. The degree to which each employee may contribute to the analysis of a problem depends upon their uniqueness and individuality as far as their job is concerned. Circle members should not be reluctant to contact an expert from any area, as long as that person can be of service to them in the analysis and solution of a problem. One caution: sometimes, the individual called upon to assist in the analysis of a problem may want to take over the problem and to identify his or her perception of its real cause(s) with the problem. It will be the circle leader's responsibility to see to it that this doesn't take place; once the expert has related to his or her charge, then that person should leave the quality circle meeting.

Once a quality circle is given the opportunity to select a problem, the group should be provided with the time and resources to analyze the problem. There are three potential flies in the ointment:

1.   Managers may give lip service to the quality circle program, but remain reluctant to share power and authority with employees. Many human beings are addicted to power; once they assume it they are reluctant to surrender it to anyone, particularly to those below them in the organization. These same managers may either try to solve the problem themselves, or intentionally withhold information from circle members so that they fail in their attempt to do so.

2.   Employees, particularly the older ones, may be reluctant to analyze and to solve the problem, primarily because they are used to the subservient role they play within the organization. As a result, they don't feel right doing what managers have always done or were supposed to do. This traditional view of work either limits their acceptance of participatory management or the sharing of power and authority with managers.

3.   At times, circle leaders have been known to solve problems identified by the quality circle without properly involving circle members in the analysis of the problem. This attitude is a real threat to the quality circle concept:

   a.   the solution to the problem may not be what the circle members would have included.
   b.   the collective experience, skills, talents, and abilities, have not been used to analyze and solve the problem.
   c.   two powerful motivators—achievement and recognition—have not been fully realized by circle members.
   d.   circle members may have arrived at another cause of the problem and a solution which may be better and less expensive.

e. One of the most important rationales for the quality circle concept is people building or organizational development. When the analysis of a problem is assumed entirely by the circle leader without involving circle members, the real intent of the program is not being achieved. The circle leader must understand that he or she cannot ever have all of the answers to problems; an effective circle leader does not need to solve problems, rather to see to it that they are solved through appropriate leadership.

CRITERIA OF AN EFFECTIVE QUALITY CIRCLE PROGRAM

The quality circle program is a proven process for introducing change and effecting improved quality of services and products. Organizations that adhere to the established procedures for planning, implementing, maintaining, evaluating, and improving the quality circle program will reap high rewards in job satisfaction, cost savings, increased productivity, improved quality of work life, better morale, and a host of other benefits. When the quality circle program failed to produce the expected results, in all cases, the human variable was solely responsible for the failure. To reduce the probability of failure, the following criteria or indicators should be followed to implement the quality circle program:

1. top and middle management demonstrate strong support through their attendance at training sessions, steering committee meetings, circle meetings, and management presentations.
2. management provides guidance and control by establishing a steering committee.
3. membership in a quality circle is limited to eleven members.
4. participation in the program is voluntary.
5. circle members are able to choose their own problems, analyze them, propose a solution and, if possible, implement the solution.
6. quality circle meetings are held on a workday or circle members are paid overtime when meeting takes place after the workday.
7. a philosophy emphasizing people building exists.
8. circle members are committed and function as a team.
9. power and authority of management is shared with em-

ployees. Top management provides support through personnel appointments, budget, long-range plans, and attendance at quality circle activities.

10. facilitator is carefully selected.
11. facilitators and circle leaders receive training in problem-
solving techniques, communication, group dynamics and
motivation; all employees and managers receive awareness
training in the quality circle concept.
12. the facilitator attends quality circle meetings until circle
members are able to function effectively by themselves
and then is phased out of the meetings.
13. management responds to proposed solutions in a timely
manner.
14. circle members are recognized by management for their
problem-solving efforts.
15. the quality circle program is assessed and improved
periodically.
16. the quality circle program is initiated on a pilot basis first,
and then expanded throughout the organization after adjusting for minimizing problems.

SUMMARY

A quality circle is a group of three to eleven persons, employed
in similar units, who are committed to improving organizational
effectiveness by voluntarily meeting one day per week for about
an hour to identify, select, analyze, and solve job-related problems
in their area of responsibility. Some other names used to depict
quality circles are: employee participation circle, action teams, job
enrichment teams, and working groups.

There are three types of problems: Type 1 problems are those
in which circle members have direct control; Type 2 problems
are those in which circle members have limited control, but require the influence of another person; and Type 3 problems are
those over which top management have complete control. Some
problems should be avoided by quality circles. These usually encroach on the job territory of units. The elements of a quality circle are: 1) management; 2) steering committee; 3) facilitator;
4) circle leader; 5) circle members; 6) specialists and experts;

and 7) nonmembers. There are several phases to the operation of a quality circle: 1) identifying problems; 2) selecting a problem; 3) collecting data; 4) analyzing the data; 5) solving the problem; 6) verifying the solution; 7) presenting the proposed solution to management; 8) rendering a decision; and 9) implementing the solution. Noncircle members should be used to strengthen the quality circle concept.

17

How Quality Circles Solve Organizational Problems

THE QUALITY CIRCLE concept is utilized by thousands of profit and non profit organizations in the United States to solve unit problems that once inconvenienced employees and employers. The time is appropriate to use the quality circle concept on a broad organizational level to solve organizational problems.[1]

DIFFERENCES BETWEEN UNIT AND ORGANIZATIONAL QUALITY CIRCLE PROGRAMS

There are distinct differences between the unit and organizational quality circle programs which those practicing the quality circle concept should understand and use to strengthen both programs.

UNIT QUALITY CIRCLE PROGRAM

A unit quality circle program is a participatory decision-making process that involves a homogeneous group of employees in solving unit problems. The preceeding chapter dealt with the unit quality circle program.

ORGANIZATIONAL QUALITY CIRCLE PROGRAM

An organizational quality circle program is a participatory decision-making process involving a large, heterogenous number of employees and others in the solution of complex organizational problems. The differences between unit and organizational quality circles are:

Unit Quality Circle	Organizational Quality Circle
Solves Type 1 and 2 problems only.	Solves Type 3 problems only.
Uses brainstorming to identify problems.	Uses nominal group process to identify and/or solve problems.
Usually involves 3-to-11 members in the problem-solving process.	Can involve as many as 110 people in the problem-solving process.
Solutions are presented to management for approval.	Solutions are presented to an executive circle consisting of top managers for the purpose of reaching a consensus.
Experts and specialists are brought in on the problem-solving process on a need basis.	Experts and specialists are brought in on the problem-solving process as a requirement to convert the resource circle to a quality team of management circle.
A management presentation is conducted to present the solution to management for approval.	An executive presentation is conducted to present the solution to top management for the purpose of reaching a consensus.
Meets one hour per week to solve problems	Meets days or weeks to solve problems.
Homogeneous group.	Heterogenous group.
Less interpersonal problems.	Prone to have more interpersonal problems because of the number of members.

Impact on the organization is dependent on types and number of problems solved.	Impact on the organization usually is major.
Minimum involvement of a cross-section of people.	Maximum involvement of a cross-section of people.

PROGRAM PLANNING PROCESS

The program planning process is a planning sequence that provides for a systematic process of decision making at various levels of the organization to maximize input.[2] It is particularly useful for identifying organizational and strategic problems, and for arriving at appropriate creative programs to solve them. There are basically five phases to the program planning process, as illustrated in Figure 20.

Phase I—Exploration of problems

There are two stages to this phase, the first of which begins with the selection and convening of a large cross-section of persons (known as the resource group) of the organization involving one or more of the following:

1. Stockholders/Stakeholders
2. Customers/Clients
3. Employees
4. Front-line Supervisors

A resource group is a carefully selected group of employees, usually consisting of 55 to 110 people, who have volunteered to solve organizational problems. This group should provide a cross-fertilization of ideas on problems confronting the organization. Resource group members may be selected by the following criteria:

Position	Ethnicity
Function	Location
Age	Stakeholders
Sex	Others

The CEO, in conjunction with other personnel or executive circle, usually makes the decision as to the size and make-up of the resource group. The composition or mix of people in the resource group is determined by the type of organizational problems to be solved. Unlike the unit quality circle program, the major problem category is decided by top management. If the CEO desires to solve a problem pertaining to improving the quality of working life in the organization and is interested in getting maximum input from employees, the resource group may be composed chiefly of a cross-section of employees throughout the organization. On the other hand, if the problem is why a new product has failed to generate the projected income, a group of consumers, managers, and employees may have to be organized into a resource group to obtain combined creative judgment. Determining the proper mix of people to be on the resource group is a very delicate task and should not be seen as an easy chore since different resource group compositions often will generate different ideas and may not produce the best solutions to problems.

The resource group should strive to use the consensus decision-making process. When this is not possible, it should revert to a majority rule. Even in a large group of 100 members, an effective facilitator can often obtain a consensus concerning problems and their solutions.

The purposes of a resource group are as follows:
1. maximize the amount of conflict inherent with change.
2. provide more creative ideas for solving problems.
3. ensure that the initial decisions concerning either problems or solutions have been addressed as intended.
4. provide for a comprehensive attack on organizational problems and solutions.
5. arrive at a consensus regarding the most appropriate solution to a problem.
6. tap the gold mine of untapped talents, skills, etc. of a cross-section of employees to solve organizational problems.

When established and used successfully, the resource group can be a powerful basis for exploring and selecting organizational problems involving a large number of people from a variety of areas and for solving problems which hitherto management thought were not possible.

Members may or may not be requested to examine problems on a personal level. Here, the need is to determine the extent to which organizational problems may have adversely affected the attitudes (feelings) of employees. Finally, the coordinating facilitator will spend the rest of the time explaining the format of the

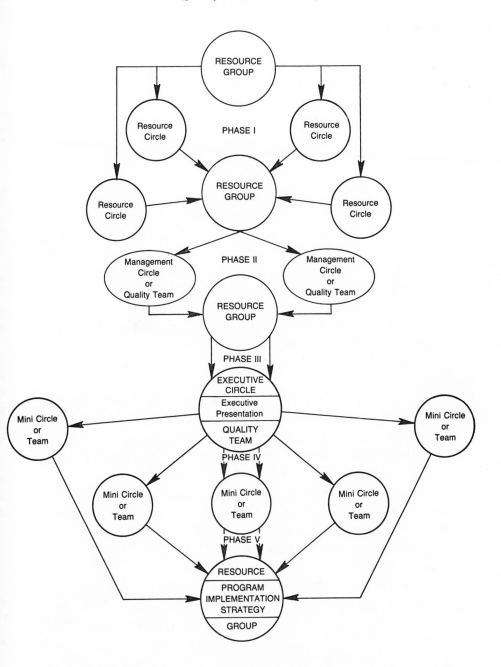

Fig. 20: The Program Planning Process

nominal group process which will be the guidance system for exploring problems. Some time is devoted to questions and answers. The members of the resource group are then requested to go to the rooms designated on their respective cards.

The second stage of this exploratory phase involves dividing the resource group into resource circles, groups of three-to-eleven members of the same composition as resource group. These resource circles are convened to use the nominal group process or other appropriate problem identification techniques to identify and select organizational problems. Resource circles are an important component to solving organizational problems because they are used to divide the resource group into more manageable parts to identify and select organizational problems, to present the problems to the resource group, to help the resource group arrive at a consensus, and to make certain that the agreed-upon problem has been properly addressed.

Outside of normal training received in the unit quality circle program, no special training is required of resource circle members other than the techniques for using the consensus decision-making process.

Each resource circle, headed by a leader, uses the nominal group process to structure the activities for exploring problems.

1. Upon arriving in a resource circle, each member is provided with a nominal group process problem worksheet and a ranking card similar to the ones illustrated in Chapter 6.

2. When the members are seated, the circle leader explains the nominal group process to them and requests them to spend 30 minutes in silence, listing all organizational (and sometimes personal) problems on their nominal group process problem worksheet.

3. A recorder, nominated by the membership or selected by the leader, lists the individual responses of the resource circle members on a flipchart. Proceeding around the circle, each member has one response per turn until all of the responses have been given. When a flipchart sheet is full, it should be taped to the wall where everyone can view it. Any member having the same idea as another raises his or her hand. The recorder counts the number of similar responses and indicates the number next to the item.

4. After all ideas have been posted, members are given a coffee break.

5.   After the coffee break, each resource circle should spend about thirty minutes clarifying, defining, and/or elaborating on any item. No attempt should be made to combine items.

6.   When the discussion period has ended, each member is requested to indicate on the ranking cards five organizational problems which he or she feels are the most important. When this cycle has been completed, the recorder collects the nominal group process ranking cards and records the results (the count) next to each item on the flipchart sheet.

7.   The individual resource circles reconvene in the general meeting room where the individual leaders will report the results of their circle. After the reports, members of the resource group discuss the results to clarify them. After the discussion, additional ranking cards are distributed to each group member, who is asked to silently rank the five most important items. If a consensus is to be reached over the five most important problems, the resource group should select either ten or fifteen problems, and use them to reach a consensus. The process can also pertain to other aspects of this process. After a reasonable period, the leader asks the members to indicate their vote for each item. The five highest ranked items are announced. A brief discussion may be held to clarify any opaque points.

8.   At the conclusion of this general session, the coordinating facilitator thanks the group for their assistance and explains the remaining phases of the problem-solving process.

The resource circle is requested to select representatives for the next phase.

RATIONALE FOR THE RESOURCE GROUP AND RESOURCE CIRCLES
Phase I of the program planning process is functional because:
1.   those closest to the problems should be involved in exploring the dimensions of the problem.
2.   research seems to indicate that the nominal group process is superior to the interacting group (brainstorming) because it produces a higher number of problem dimensions, higher variety of ideas, and higher quality ideas.
3.   organizational and personal problems should be explored using a variety of human sources within and outside the organization.
4.   those experiencing the problems should have the opportu-

nity to assign priorities in which problems should be solved.

5. management should be forced to deal with organizational and personal problems of employees in order to improve total performance.

6. a minority of individuals should not be permitted to explore the problems of an entire group.

CONDUCT OF RESOURCE GROUP AND CIRCLE MEETINGS
Preparatory Stage

1. Decide on the composition of the resource group.
2. Assign participants to small groups by indicating name and room number on cards.
3. Prepare nominal group process solution worksheets and ranking cards.
4. Construct the agenda.
5. Obtain flipchart, magic markers, and pencils.
6. Secure large meeting room and several small meeting rooms.
7. Select resource circle leaders.

Execution Stage
Meeting of the Resource Group

1. Introduction
   A. Registration and Coffee.
   B. a CEO presents welcome address.
   C. Indicate keen interest in getting input from the group.
   D. Indicate that the emphasis will be on exploring problems only.
   E. Explain the need for organizational dimension problems and/or personal dimension problems.
2. Familiarize group with nominal group process
3. Request participants to break up into resource circles
   A. Select a recorder.
   B. Refamiliarize participants with nominal group process.
   C. Distribute nominal group process problem worksheet, ranking cards, and pencils.
   D. Initiate the process.
      i) Generate organizational dimension problems.
      ii) Generate personal dimension problems.
      iii) List alternative ideas.

      iv) Indicate additional alternative ideas.

      v) Rank ideas.

      vi) Elect resource circle representatives.

4. Reconvene the resource group

    A. Review individual ranking of ideas.

    B. Select best five ideas.

    C. Briefly discuss five best ideas and make adjustments, if necessary.

    D. Ask for representatives for the next phase.

Phase II–Exploration of Knowledge

This phase is similar to Phase I, the essential difference being that a quality team or management circle is organized to solve the problem.

A quality team is composed of three to eleven members comprised of heterogeneous members of the resource circle, appropriate specialists and experts, and other members, as determined by the coordinating facilitator, to solve organizational problems.

Although unit quality circles are established on a permanent basis by the people of similar units, quality teams are established by employees of dissimilar units or engaged in different functions. Quality teams are usually established to work on a specific problem and, when solved, they are sometimes dissolved.

Members on the quality team are usually a heterogeneous group of managers and employees who will enhance the make up of quality teams and actually solve the problems determined by the resource group. This provides for some creative problem solving and reduces the conflict usually associated with change.

The quality team is formed simply by adding a number of volunteers from various levels of the organization to each resource circle in order to produce a better spread of representatives on each team. If the resource circles are comprised chiefly of employees from one particular unit, the CEO or coordinating facilitator may find it desirable to select a person from two other units, a frontline supervisor or a middle manager, and a top manager and assign to each quality team.

The mix of people on the quality team is just as important as the mix on the resource group and should be accomplished after a great deal of thought.

A designated number and mix of volunteers are requested to

serve on quality teams. Three quality teams are generally adequate to solve organizational problems at one problem-solving session. The teams:
1. solve problems identified by the resource group.
2. present solutions to the resource group, then assist it in reaching a consensus.
3. receive the ideas of experts and specialists, then use the ideas as the basis for solving problems.

MANAGEMENT CIRCLES

A management circle consists of employees drawn from similar work units; all have managerial or supervisory responsibilities. A typical management circle will consist of either first-line supervisors, middle managers, or top managers. Each of these circles may work on independent or similar problems. Some organizations have been known to establish management circles solely on an informational basis.

Management circles will not generally be used to solve organizational problems, but there are some instances when they can be instrumental in solving problems which involve identifying purposes of the organization, developing values, preparing management philosophy, developing organizational properties and objectives, and preparing strategic plans. There are also some instances in which top managers may be organized into management circles to solve a problem peculiar to this level within the organization, such as addressing the issue of incentive pay or bonuses for top managers. If management circles are used, they serve the same functions as quality teams.

Prior to convening Phase II, the coordinating facilitator, assisted by some resource circle leaders, divides the five highest ranked problems in both problem dimensions into major and minor categories. These categories with their designated ranking are indicated on flipchart sheets and taped on the front wall, where they are visible to all members.

The coordinating facilitator, assisted by the steering committee or top management, identifies internal and external consultants, specialists, and experts, to enrich the make up of the quality teams or management circles. Experts and specialists provide ideas and other information to help quality teams or management circles to arrive at best solutions to problems. They are also often used to help verify solutions. Usually, the quality teams or management circles will determine the kind of experts or specialists they will need to focus on solutions. It is the responsibility of the coordinating facilitator to acquire the knowledgeable people.

The experts and specialists are given the brief charge to saturate the quality team members with ideas. Some techniques can be employed to do this effectively:

1. show audio-visual aids relevant to the problems.
2. cite research.
3. describe ideas that have worked for other organizations.
4. indicate why others failed to solve a given problem.
5. show the latest trends and developments.

During the problem-solving meeting, the expert and/or specialist will not attempt to solve the problem, but will generate ideas, question members as to why a certain solution was chosen, provide alternatives, get members to assess the pros and cons for selecting a particular solution, and verify whether a particular solution will work.

Each internal and external consultant, specialist, and expert are given a card with a number designating the particular location of their assignment. The coordinating facilitator should arrange to have a similar mixture of resource persons for the management circles or quality teams. In addition, each person is provided with sufficient nominal group process solution worksheets and ranking cards to respond to the ranked problems.

It is often profitable for the group when knowledgeable persons are invited to present ideas for solving the problems. Sometimes existing solutions are discussed by the members prior to each presentation in order to set the right tone or atmosphere for critiquing existing and new solution components and resources. After the solutions to the problems have been identified, the resource group reconvenes to decide which of the alternatives should be implemented.

During the meeting of the resource group, it would be appropriate for the CEO to make a brief presentation similar to Phase I. After the CEO's presentation, the coordinating facilitator:

1. explains problem dimension arrived at by the resource circle in Phase I. Usually the resource circle leaders are called upon to elaborate on what was decided in Phase I.
2. discusses the charge given the quality teams or manage-

ment circles to deal with the problems identified in Phase I. More specifically, they are requested to identify existing and new solution components and new and required resources.

Let's say the identified problem is reducing employee absenteeism. An example of an existing solution component could be the present use of a control chart to monitor employee absenteeism. An existing resource could be the availability of an attendance improvement coordinator. A new solution component would be to establish a computerized employee attendance profile program. A new or required resource could involve the proposing of a microcomputer to computerize an employee attendance profile program. A form is illustrated under Figure 21-21a for this purpose. Each team or circle is asked to generate ideas for solving the problems, and not merely to represent their individual unit or function.

3.   reviews the nominal group process that will be used in this phase.

4.   responds to questions and answers posed by any member of the resource group.

5.   requests members to go to the designated rooms indicated on their individual cards, then organize in quality teams or management circles.

During the second stage:

1.   each person is requested to use the nominal group process solution worksheets to list existing solution components and resources for organizational and personal problems and, when completed, new solution components and new resources that are required.

2.   after about 30 to 45 minutes of listing existing and new solution components and resources, the recorder collects the nominal group process solution worksheets, lists the information on flipchart sheets, and tapes them on the wall.

3.   after a coffee break, each management circle or quality team discusses the various existing components, new-solution components, and resources to determine the most appropriate combination of solution components and resources for each problem.

4.   at the conclusion of the discussion, the entire group meets and receives a report from each team or circle regarding its solution components and resources. Each report is recorded and num-

bered on a flipchart sheet, then posted on the wall. Each list can be discussed for elaboration and clarification.

5. when the discussion has ended, each team member or circle uses the nominal group process ranking card to rank choices of solution components and resources.

6. the coordinating facilitator thanks the group for their assistance, explains the remaining phases of the problem-solving process, and asks the group to select representatives for the next phase.

QUALITY TEAM OR MANAGEMENT CIRCLE MEETING
Preparatory Stage

1. Select knowledge consultants, specialists and experts.
    A. identify external consultants
    B. identify internal specialists and experts
2. Meet with knowledge consultants, specialists, and experts to discuss their charge and inquire about their needs.
    A. welcome address
    B. request them to focus on resource circles' ranked ideas
    C. request resource circle reresentatives to be available to elaborate on ranked ideas
3. Assign outside consultants, internal specialists, and experts to quality teams or management circles.

Execution Stage

1. Convene individual meetings with quality teams or management circles.
    A. review nominal group process with participants
    B. introduce and ask consultants, experts, and specialists to focus on the generation of alternative ideas
    C. clarify alternate solutions through interaction between team or circle members and knowledge persons
    D. initiate nominal group process by having members list exsisting and new solution components and resources on the nominal group process solution worksheet. (Refer to Figure 4)
    E. list all solution components and resources on flipchart
    F. discuss the list
    G. rank the solution components and resources
2. Reconvene meeting with resource group.

    A. present and discuss the ranked solutions
    B. reach an agreement on the acceptable solutions
3. Explain the remaining phase of the process.
4. Ask for representatives for Phase III.
5. Give appreciation comments.

Keep the focus on existing and new solution components and resources to solve problems. Professionals provide a legitimate endorsement of solution components and resources to solve problems. The process activates different types of creative insight

NOMINAL GROUP PROCESS SOLUTION WORKSHEET

Name _____   Date _____

☐ PROBLEM DESCRIPTION

EXISTING SOLUTION COMPONENTS:

1. _____

2. _____

3. _____

4. _____

5. _____

6. _____

EXISTING RESOURCES:

1. _____

2. _____

3. _____

4. _____

5. _____

6. _____

Fig. 21a: The Nominal Group Process Worksheet

by the comingling and interaction among various disciplines within the groups.

Phase III—Convene the Executive Presentation

During this phase, a designated quality team or management circle meets with the executive circle to review the priority problems and solution components and resource needs.

The executive circle, a group of four to six top managers, is organized by the CEO for assistance in reaching a decision which affects the total organization. Although the executive circle is com-

NOMINAL GROUP PROCESS SOLUTION WORKSHEET

Name _____   Date _____

□ PROBLEM DESCRIPTION

NEW SOLUTION COMPONENTS:

1._____

2._____

3._____

4._____

5._____

6._____

NEW RESOURCES REQUIRED:

1._____

2._____

3._____

4._____

5._____

6._____

Fig. 21: The Nominal Group Process Solution Worksheet

posed of top managers, the composition can vary depending on the organization and the problem. Here are some typical variations:

Model A	Model B
CEO	CEO
Vice-presidents of divisions	Board members (2)
Outside experts and	Vice-presidents of divisions (2)
specialists	Major stock/stakeholders (2)

Model C	Model D
	CEO
CEO	Vice-presidents (2)
Vice-presidents (2)	Middle managers (2)
President of union (1)	President of Union (1)
Board member (1)	

The main responsibilities of the executive circle are:

1. to assist the CEO investigate all the alternatives in arriving at a decision.
2. to prepare organizational policies and procedures statements.
3. to receive recommendations from quality teams and management circles and subsequently render a decision.
4. to provide guidance and directions for involving multiple levels of the organization in problem-solving.
5. to approve program strategies.

Although the training of members of the executives circle is not intensive, some training requirements will help strengthen the decision-making process:

1. basic understanding of the quality circle concept.
2. competence in brainstorming and the nominal group process.
3. proficiency in consensus decision-making.
4. proficiency in team building, conflict resolution, etc.

The primary reason for this phase is to reach a consensus with the executive circle on the solutions and resources regarding the five problems that were previously identified by the resource circle, or solved by the quality teams or management circles, and given priority by the resource group. Each problem is discussed separately and a decision is reached before proceeding to the next one. The steps for conducting the executive presentation are:

1. Selected members of the quality team or management cir-

cle provide background information on each problem. Questions may be asked of team or circle members if necessary to clarify the presented problem.

2.   For each problem presented, existing and new solution components and resources are identified and discussed. Minor changes may occur. A consensus is reached on all solutions and resources. If a consensus cannot be reached, it is sent back to the quality team or management circle for further work.

3.   The executive circle has made a decision on acceptable and unacceptable solutions and resources, the CEO and other members of the executive circle extended their appreciation for a job well done, and the meeting is adjourned.

IMPORTANT POINT:

Some quality teams or management circles may prefer to base all discussion on each problem on the program implementation of strategy plans. If this is desirable, then Phase IV should precede Phase III.

This phase is an excellent opportunity to present top management with the overall needs of the organization based on the identified needs of the resource group. It provides an ideal time to review with top management the developmental process and actions that took place during the problem-solving process. It provides top management with an opportunity to receive an in-depth analysis of problems and solutions; it becomes a basis for quality team members or management circles to interact with top managers, thereby gaining an improved organizational perspective of why certain actions can and cannot be initiated.

Phase III is a great opportunity to work out problems and reach a consensus of the best course of action to implement the solution to a problem; it provides top management with a much broader view of the organization because of details discussed throughout the presentation.

EXECUTIVE PRESENTATION
Preparatory Stage

1.   Determine who should be present in the executive presentation.
2.   Prepare an agenda.
3.   Rehearse presentation.

4. Post and cover all charts until their contents are presented.
5. Pass out proposed solution worksheet.

Execution Stage

1. Present information on the nominal group process.
2. Explain the intent of the executive presentation.
3. Present information of resource group and quality teams or management circles.
4. Identify existing and new solution components and resources.
5. List all reservations and concerns regarding the program implementation strategy.
6. Render a decision by top management.

Phase IV—Preparation of Program Implementation Strategy Plans

Two to four individuals from the quality team or management circles are organized into miniteams to prepare a program implementation strategy plan for each prioritized problem. The number of problems will dictate the number of miniteams to be organized.

Miniteam

Miniteams are sub-groups of a quality team or management circle, consisting of from two to four members who have volunteered:

1. to conduct investigations and reviews in order to report their findings to the team membership.
2. to work on sub-projects—activities necessary to complete projects—as determined by team members.
3. to prepare action plans to implement solutions arrived at by team membership.
4. to arrive at a consensus of the best course of action to take in order to solve a problem.
5. to present the substance of the action plan to their own quality team members or executive circle.
6. to assist in resolving problems that have occured during the decision-making process.

In addition to the training members of miniteams have acquired through the unit quality circle program, each person should also receive some training in operational planning, consisting of:

1. preparation of short-range objectives
2. development and use of performance standards
3. construction of action plans

4. assessment of alternatives
5. preparation of controls
6. presentation of plans
7. development of reports

To complete the program implementation strategy plan:

1. Cite each problem as illustrated on the flipchart sheet. Its ranking is also indicated.

2. Show proposed solution components with ranks as indicated on the flipchart sheets.

3. Indicate the existing and new solution components and resources in the appropriate space.

4. Identify the party who is responsible for completing the strategy, when the strategy will be launched, what support services will be needed to implement the strategy, how the strategy is to be evaluated, and what will signal an exception to each plan.

When each program implementation strategy has been completed, ample copies should be duplicated for each resource group member so that a brief presentation can be conducted by each miniteam to determine if any errors, omissions, or problems exist. At this time, the miniteam members should be extremely alert for complete and accurate details concerning each program implementation strategy. Copies should go to the group in Phase II so that if there are any discrepancies or problems, they can be accommodated prior to Phase V. The coordinating facilitator will usually forward the program implementation plan to the group in Phase III and request an acceptance of each strategy. By preparing the program implementation strategy, team or circle members get an opportunity to review all of the particulars before presenting them in Phase V.

A final review of all of the activities that lead to this phase is automatic, providing a final check by which quality team or management circle members remain sensitive to all of the critical elements reported in Phases I, II, and III.

Preparatory Stage

1. Secure adequate program implementation strategy forms.
2. Devise a list of miniteam or circle members.

Execution Stage

1. Organize into miniteams to prepare a program strategy implementation plan for each problem.

2. Critically review each plan.

3. Forward copies of completed plans to the executive circle.

4. Present copies of completed plans to coordinator.

Phase V–Program Strategy Presentation

The purpose of this meeting–the convening of the resource group–is to review all of the steps leading to this phase, to discuss individual program strategy implementation plans, to receive suggestions and comments from group members, and to reach an agreement over plans.

1. Upon arriving at the final general meeting, each participant is provided with a name tag and a packet.

2. The CEO should make some complimentary remarks indicating the value of the meeting and cite how the results are expected to improve conditions for employees and the organization.

3. The coordinating facilitator reviews the activities and outcomes achieved in Phases I, II, III and IV using visual aids prepared in each phase.

4. Miniteam leaders using either transparencies or flipchart sheets describe the prioritized problems, solution components and resources, and program implementation strategies.

5. Group members are requested to refer to their packets for copies of the program implementation plans; led by the coordinating facilitator, they are invited to question any of the contents presented. If a serious discrepancy exists between the intent of the resource group members, an attempt is made to resolve the problem during the resource group meeting. If the coordinating facilitator feels that a solution cannot be worked out, that problem is to be further dealt with in a meeting between or among the parties involved. All recommendations, changes, additions, and modifications are to be voted by the general assembly. Unless a consensus or majority vote is reached, the exception is not acted upon.

6. The coordinating facilitator closes the general meeting with comments of appreciation to the participants and indicates that there will be other problem-solving sessions to achieve maximum involvement in the decision-making process.

7. Immediately after the general meeting, the coordinating facilitator and miniteam leaders meet to adjust program strategy implementation plans.

8. All minor changes are forwarded to executive circle members. Major changes are presented to the executive circle by the coordinating facilitator and team leaders during a special executive presentation. The results of this meeting are forwarded to each participant and acted upon accordingly.

Phase V:

1. gives each level of the organization an opportunity to be involved in the decision-making process.

2. allows participants the last word on the program strategy implementation plans.

3. provides each representative an opportunity to experience each phase of the process.

PROGRAM STRATEGY PRESENTATION
Preparatory Stage

1. name tags
2. prepare packet (include program implementation strategy)
3. prepare an agenda
4. secure all presentation aids.

Execution Stage

1. convene resource group meeting
2. CEO address group indicating his or her appreciation for their participation
3. present prioritized problems, solution components, resource needs, and implementation plans
4. resolve discrepencies
5. close the meeting
6. make adjustments in plans
7. forward adjustments to appropriate persons

This comprehensive problem-solving process will not be an easy task; time and patience are needed to let the interaction process work. Interpersonal problems must be anticipated and dealt with before they become severe. Everyone must have an equal voice in the decision-making process regardless of position. The goal is a majority vote or concensus on all decisions during all phases.

This process requires the careful coordination of each phase, stage, and activity by the coordinating facilitator and leaders; and it requires understanding that maximum input from all levels of the organization will lessen problems and conflicts and will enhance the total performance of the organization.

MODIFYING THE PROGRAM PLANNING PROCESS

Some CEO's have found it convenient to modify the program planning process by eliminating the resource group; they use instead one quality team or management circle to work on a problem decided by the CEO or identify their own problems and solve them. When the resource group is absent from the process, the decision-making should be by consensus. Sometimes, the CEO is a member of the quality team or management circle. If this is the case, there will be no need to present the solution to an executive circle.

An advanced form of the quality circle concept that has lead to the solution of organizational problems, as opposed to unit problems, was created at the McCormack & Company. During his first year as president, Mr. Charles McCormack established a multitude management system using management teams chiefly composed of middle managers to identify, analyze, and solve organizational problems involving packaging, product development, distribution, sales, quality, etc. Today, more than thirteen management teams consisting of 7 to 20 managers have been etablished. Although top mangers select the initial management team members, subsequent members are voted in by management team members. As an incentive, each team member receives cash as well as extra vacation time for serving on the team. Semiannually, each member's performance in the team is evaluated and ranked by the other members based on creativity, judgment, achievement, and human relations. The top ranked 30 percent receive automatic reappointment and elect other members. The program is seen not only as a vehicle for solving organizational problems, but as a training program.

THE NEED FOR FACILITATORS

To become a certified quality circle facilitator, an individual must complete a minimum of five days or forty hours of comprehensive training conducted by a certified facilitator in the various phases of the quality circle concept, then pass an extensive examination. The International Association of Quality Circles in St. Louis, Mo., and a number of private organizations, such as Quality Circle Institute in Red Bluff, Calif., provide training for facilitators, circle leaders, and members.

When solving organizational problems, two certified quality circle facilitators are used. Since the group is too large to be managed by one person, two facilitators can back each other up by picking up something the other may have missed; better coverage is provided groups, and the multitude of activities involved with complex organizational problems requires that two persons do the orchestrating. If one facilitator becomes personally involved in the process, it is easy to turn the job over to the other; and, in general, the process becomes less exhausting and demanding.

TRAINING REQUIREMENTS

The following groups are associated with the organizational quality circle program and training requirements:

Group	Training Particulars
Resource group	Minimum quality circle training
	Consensus decision making
	Team building
Resource circle	Brainstorming
	Nominal group process
	Data collection
Quality team and management circle	Basic unit quality circle training (for leader) and organizational quality circle training
Executive circle	Minimum quality circle training
	Consensus decision making
	Team building, group dynamics
	Theory Z

Miniteam	Same as quality team and management circle. In addition, some training in the preparation of reports and plans
Experts, consultants, and specialists	Presentation of information
Facilitator	Basic unit quality circle training (for facilitators) Organizational quality circle

Because it will take time to master the program planning process, some coordinating facilitators insist on using rank instead of consensus to arrive at problems and solutions.

THE RANKING PROCESS

Ranking either problems or solution components can be executed with ease if the following steps are carried out:

1.   Have participants identify their most important problem or solution components and give it a value of 5, then have participants select their next most important problem or solution component and give it a value of 4. Continue this process until all five problems have received a value.

2.   Start with "1" as the highest value and proceed until all items have received a rank.

3.   Have all participants give their ranking cards to the recorder.

4.   Prepare a tally sheet. Indicate along the horizontal axis the number of votes. Along the vertical axis indicate the number of items being voted.

5.   Record the value of each vote for each item in the space provided.

6.   Add the sum of each item. Identify the higher sum, the next, etc., and rank accordingly.

7.   Announce the five items with the highest sum.

SUMMARY

The program planning process is a planning sequence that provides for a systematic process of decision making at various levels of the organization to maximize input. There are five phases to this process: 1) exploration of problems; 2) exploration of knowledge; 3) convene the executive presentation; 4) preparation of program implementation strategy plans; and 5) program strategy presentation.

18

Team Building: A Synergistic Process for Change

A GLANCE AT the organizational chart of many American companies, corporations, and organizations gives the immediate impression of power, responsibility, and authority. Closer inspection of the chart makes room for reasonable doubts, and interviewing persons who work for these companies, corporations, and organizations opens a Pandora's box of contrary impressions.

The Japanese management specialists give little weight to the accuracy with which the average organizational chart in this country reflects the realities of management in a given organization. And small wonder. In every organization there are sub-systems and informal groups where decisions are made and power is exchanged. These groups are subtle and often are not even reflected on the organizational chart. Ironically, they are where organizational dysfunction usually occur.

To create a more functional organization, managers should look to their sub-systems and informal groups to effect change by consciously recognizing, continuing, and developing (building) these groups into teams, which are a means to improve the larger organizations.

A TEAM DEFINED

A functional team is a task-oriented combination of personnel who have in common:

1. they are representatives of important sub-systems of the organization.
2. they have some degree of reciprocal influence over each other.

3. they interact through a formal sub-structure.

4. they seek to achieve common organizational goals.

SOME BENEFITS OF TEAM PARTICIPATION

There are many benefits associated with team participation, however, the following are the most important ones:

1. Team members are able to deal more effectively with authority and leadership; they know where decisions come from, which in turn enhances their acceptance of them.

2. Multiple heads are better than one. When teaming is accomplished effectively there is synergy. The wisdom, knowledge, talents, interests, and information of the team is greater than the sum of their parts. The task of managing an organization is very complex; no one person has such a wide range of skill or knowledge to perform this task successfully.

3. By participating in team synergy, it is possible to experience a new kind of satisfaction that extends beyond the satisfaction of individual effort, the achievement of group goals as well as individual goals.

4. Decisions arrived at on a consensus basis by teams are more likely to be carried out without being sabotaged or changed much.

5. Teaming provides a basis for individual members to support each other through acquiring trust, caring relationships, intimacy, and sharing power as problems and issues are being worked through.

PREREQUISITES FOR TEAM BUILDING

Team building, a crucial aspect of Theory Z, focuses on a small number of employees who participate in making decisions on how a job, function, or task should be completed. It is based on premises that teams reach more creative decisions than individual employees do, and that team members are more motivated to carry out team decisions than decisions made by individuals. Before team building can be implemented with a high degree of success, certain prerequisites must be in evidence:

1. The group must have emerged into a team; individual members must be working together, ironing out difficulties, resolving conflicts, and maintaining an effective internal communication network.

2.   Team members must believe there are areas where significant changes may be needed. The supervisor can help team members to discover this need.

3.   The need for improvement must come from within; outside or external change imposed on the team will, to a large degree, be limited.

4.   The team must have the power and authority to act. It is fruitless to identify improvement areas if one is not able to do something about it.

5.   Team members are finding new ways of doing things; they must be willing to try out new processes, new procedures, and new practices; they must be willing to accept the consensus decision-making process and problem solving. This may necessitate changing behavior as well as attitudes.

Goals: A team . . .
. . . is aware of the purposes and mission of the organization.
. . . agrees to work together to determine what solution is acceptable to all of its members.
Values: A team . . .
. . . values equalized dispersion of power among all of its members.
. . . values team competition as opposed to individualistic competition.
. . . values consensus decision making.
. . . values the opportunity to solve unit problems.
. . . values individual differences among its members.
. . . values conflict as neither good nor bad.
. . . values participation on the part of all of its members.
. . . values knowledge, cooperation, and the well-being of all of its members.
. . . values the discussion of attitudinal and cognitive issues.
Decision making: A team . . .
. . . realizes that there is no single "right" solution.
. . . realizes that a decision by the group is one that all members are expected to abide by.
. . . realizes that if consensus decision making cannot be reached, more information and discussion is necessary.
Decide: A team . . .

. . . will indicate when something is said or done where members cannot agree.

. . . will always strive to negotiate differences among its members.

. . . can assume a statement is acceptable unless a member indicates direct disagreement.

Skills: A team . . .

. . . shares information with its members.

. . . strives for caring relationship, trust, and intimacy among its members.

. . . knows how to work together for the purpose of discovering which idea or solution is more acceptable to all of its members.

. . . understands how to prepare operational plans.

Operation: A team . . .

. . . expects every member to participate in the meeting.

. . . recognizes that any member can block a decision if he or she finds it unacceptable; however, blocking should be used with prudence.

. . . supports all other units within the organization.

. . . provides a basis for improving performance through training.

. . . acts responsibly in meeting the individual needs of its members.

. . . taps the strengths and talents of individual members.

6. Team must attain concrete results on the short-term and then on a long-term basis. Immediate success motivates the team, and encourages the members toward long-range goals.

7. Team members must be willing to conduct a self-assessment of their efforts in order to determine strengths, as well as weaknesses with the idea of capitalizing on strengths and minimizing weaknesses.

8. Team members must be open with each other and understand that the feelings, attitudes, and emotions of each person are important and must be critically reviewed in order to raise hidden problems to the surface.

THE STAGES OF TEAM BUILDING

For a collection of individuals to become a functional team, they must be team building; members must devote time to activities which improve and nurture individual and group awareness. In the process, they must become more sensitive to the needs and functions of each other. Team building will take time, patience, and a great deal of hard work. The time necesary to effect a functional team will vary with the time offered to different tasks and actions, and how the human experiences are spread over a certain period of time. In effect, the time it takes will depend on the number of individuals involved and the quality of the relationship. In some cases, a team does not become actualized for at least a year.

Teams go through stages which vary with each team and do not necessarily follow a particular sequence.

Stage One. Individual Self—Awareness

Individual team members should experience a number of activities that will enable them to become more aware of themselves on any individual basis, and understand how their behavior and attitudes affect other team members. Individuals should learn to assess their feelings about others by listening to what their team mates think and feel; this will enhance sensitivity to others when functioning as a team.

A highly specialized consultant should be retained to provide this complex and specialized professional knowledge over a span of time. This will help each team member to find himself or herself in the team, and to develop a high level of sincerity and awareness of others. For most team members, this stage will bring:

1. a strong desire to support others
2. a capacity to accept each person's human model as being important
3. opportunities to see others as individuals rather than some preconceived role-players.

The following questions can be useful for consultants to use in demonstrating to individual team members how to become more aware of themselves, and how to understand the impact of their behavior and the attitudes of others in the teaming process.

What are my strengths and weaknesses? How can I use my strengths to assist individuals of the team? How can I avoid or minimize my weaknesses to strengthen my relationships with others?

What addictions tend to get me into more trouble with others of the team? Do I strive for power? Do I crave for sensation? Do I have a high need for security?

Am I a maintenance seeker? (A person who is inclined to be satisfied with the status quo and reluctant to risk his or her job.) Am I a goal seeker? (A person who is always looking to improve conditions and who is willing to risk almost anything to have a goal.) Am I uncomfortable with individuals who are not like me? Do I mistrust individuals who are always trying to meet some deadline? Do I know the value of both maintenance and goal seekers? Am I capable of learning from both? Am I content to be a goal seeker or maintenance seeker?

Do I strive to love others? Do I really love myself? Do I know what love is or isn't? Do I practice love? If not, why not? Am I afraid to love? Do I love excessively?

What motivates me the most and the least? Do I understand the team motivation? Do I know how to motivate?

Am I a right- or left-sided dominant thinker or am I a balanced thinker? Do I understand the difference? Do I tolerate those who think differently than myself? Do I try to be a balanced thinker?

What are my biases, prejudices, and assumptions about others? Can I detach them when I relate to others? Am I really honest with my feelings about others? Do I make myself gain a better appreciation of others?

The main thrust of any kind of activity or training that is offered to enhance self-awareness is not to change either individuals or the team as a whole, but to enable each person to accept what is human and personal about individual team members.

Stage 2—Team Awareness

The team becomes aware of itself as an entity. Within this framework, members begin to acquire knowledge and skill in the process of building teamwork. This awareness is brought to the forefront by the team leader, the supervisor, who, in a Theory Z organization, should be the leader of the team initially. The supervisor must not only direct, administer, oversee, survey, but must be able to lead the team to induce motivation within each individual, so that the team becomes a powerful vehicle for constructive change.

Similar to the team realizing itself, the supervisor must be able to recognize his or her own strengths, weaknesses, and limitations. Once they are recognized by the person, they will be more readily recognized by individual team members. The degree to which the supervisor receives input from the team will not only strengthen his or her own ability to lead, but will move the team in a forward motion. Today, during these contemporary times, team members are too sophisticated and educated and will not bend to dictatorship and in some instances democracy. Perhaps the ideal process for getting maximum involvement and commitment to change is through the consensus decision-making process. When the supervisor uses this decision-making mode, more responsibility and accountability are accepted by the team. As a result, the ability of the supervisor to lead through a participatory decision-making process will demand a great deal of knowledge and skill by all parties involved.

Jerry Sanders, president of Advanced Micro Devices, Inc. has established what is one of the nation's finest management structures, composed chiefly of teams. All employees are identified as team members. Teams are led by a managing director and are organized around specific responsibilities, such as "The Quality Central Reviewing Inspection Team" and "The Mail and Literature Distribution Team."

The following are some assumptions about leadership which, if realized, will help the team become more aware and grow into the next stage:

1.   A supervisor must earn the right to lead and must continue to grow in the process.

2.   No one kind of leadership is appropriate in all situations. The experiences and expectations of team members should, to a large degree, decide leadership style.

3.   Race and sex do affect or alter leadership.

4.   It is not the quantity of decisions the team has made that determine its freedom to act; it is the quality or significance of those decisions.

Stage 3 — Team Organization

The team begins to organize itself in order to deliver its charge. Information is shared, discussed, and reviewed with the members. This information should include:

1. specific charge of the team
2. team leadership
3. power and authority of the team
4. goals and objectives
5. decision-making process
6. parameters
7. team roles and responsibilities

In addition to processing information in this stage, the team will need to use a variety of tools and instruments as it makes progress. In a real sense, tools and instruments will enable the team to study itself and keep itself growing at the same time it is functioning. Sometimes, team specialists should be brought in to give the members assistance, and more insight about itself. As the team is building, it should begin to function consistently and in a smooth manner to carry out its sub-charges. Therefore, it should have decided on the following alternatives to operate on a daily basis:

1. type of meetings
2. communication channels
3. allocation of time for training
4. use of space

Some tools and instruments useful for the team to learn more about itself are:

1. a video taping of the team's meetings
2. taping of members' perceptions of the strengths and weaknesses of the team
3. a critique of the team's meetings
4. administration to the team of an attitudinal survey.

Both the supervisor and the team members should decide which of the above tools and instruments will be used to conduct a self study.

Step 4 — Team Operations

Individuals will begin to see their efforts pay dividends as the team functions on an improved level. They will see their learning and experience expand to the world of work; they will see the value of sharing their individual skills, talents, and knowledge with their team members; they will begin to turn to the support of certain team members when they run into difficulties; they will use the individuals in the team to assess their own progress; and they will begin to depend more on team members for psychological comfort when undergoing duress or other problems. During the operation of the team, synergy should become evident. The team will emerge as a greater workforce to solve problems. It will begin to exert its influence and test its power. As a result, team performance will continue to increase and members will become happy over their share of the efforts of the team. Some of the areas where team building will be experienced, are:

1.   Monitoring of individual team member's performance, done by the supervisor or members, or both.

2.   Team cohesiveness through teamwork and inter self-development.

3.   Training and growth changes occur as a result of needs required to be satisfied in order to achieve a given end.

4.   Responding to crises in a highly acceptable psychological manner.

Stage 5 — Team Success

A functional team operates with a great deal of cohesiveness: its members share responsibility, the supervisor knows when to be directive and nondirective; trust, intimacy, and caring among team members are quite evident in its daily operations, and decisions are made using consensus. A team operating in this manner should make a meaningful impact on the organization, although sometimes a successful team can become a threat to others within the culture. How can the team use its new power and influence to produce acceptance of itself and what it is setting out to achieve? How can it avoid or minimize conflicts inherent with success? Successful teams can often address these questions effectively. effectively.

Stage 6 — Team Maturation

If a team is performing in a satisfactory manner, then it has grown to the mature stage. There is a tendency to perpetuate a team if it is successful, although I feel that a team in its original form should not extend beyond three years and less than two. Team building is never really ever completed. It must be constantly worked at and continually redeveloped when new members are added. There are three courses of action for a team once it has matured: 1) it can be disbanded; 2) it can be replicated; and 3) it can change direction.

Disbanding a Team

Once a team has completed its project or mission, it can be disbanded. Team members are customarily told in advance that the group will have a limited life and in many cases even have a voice in determining the span of existence.

When a number of computer firms made their initial entrance into the microcomputer market, IBM waited to see how the market would develop. In addition, this giant firm waited to examine the characteristics and specifications of each of its competitor's computers. Finally the chairman, team of specialists, experts, and top managers, were organized into a team and charged with the responsibility of planning and developing a microcomputer within a period of one year. Today, IBM is fast becoming the leader in microcomputers in the United States.

In the IBM situation, a team of selected employees, some coming from different divisions and units, were organized to complete a particular charge. Once its mission had been accomplished, the team was abandoned.

Replicating a Team

The best way to replicate a team is by having one of the members of a successful team leave it to organize another team. This process is sometimes referred to as nucleation.

Changing a Team's Direction

While completing one project, a team can recognize the need to pursue an entirely new one. To do this, team members should move systematically through the stages that took them this far.

Team building is a process. As such, it involves becoming and growing. When it becomes a being by perpetuating itself, it becomes a system.

The Major Components of Team Effectiveness

It is important for the supervisor to understand the two major components of effectiveness. Fortified with this information, he or she should be able to determine if the rewards under each component are being experienced by team members and, if not, take appropriate action.

1. Communication Effectiveness

The first component of team effectiveness, as illustrated in Figure 21, is communication effectiveness. When team members are communicating effectively, they fulfill a personal need to socialize and interact. The more meaningfully they interact, the higher the level of communication and the higher the probability of team effectiveness.

Communication effectiveness refers to the quantity and quality of interaction operating among team members. It involves morale, communication, harmony, absence of conflict, etc., all of which depend upon team cohesiveness, which is facilitated by three variables, each having the potential to increase interaction between and among team members:

a. Similar characteristics and traits

Teams whose members come from similar work areas have similar interests and similar training; they have a higher potential for interaction. Employees who have common work sentiments–in terms of philosophy, goals and objectives–usually are more attuned to each other, and are prone to communicate more freely and openly.

b. Contact frequency

Because employees with similar characteristics and traits are more prone to interact, interaction is heightened with the frequency of scheduled and unscheduled meetings.

c. Behavior expectancy

Team members with similar traits and characteristics are each able to predict with a fair degree of reliability what the others would do under a given set of conditions. This enhances interaction effectiveness. The more team members come from similar areas and interests, the more they are able to predict behavior and attitudes.

The rewards usually associated with effective communication are security and social acceptance. These rewards are associated with personal goals and are not directly related to organizational goals.

2. Problem-solving effectiveness

The second component of team effectiveness, as illustrated in Figure 21, is problem-solving effectiveness, which is realized by actualizing (promoting, identifying, selecting, pursuing, and achiev-

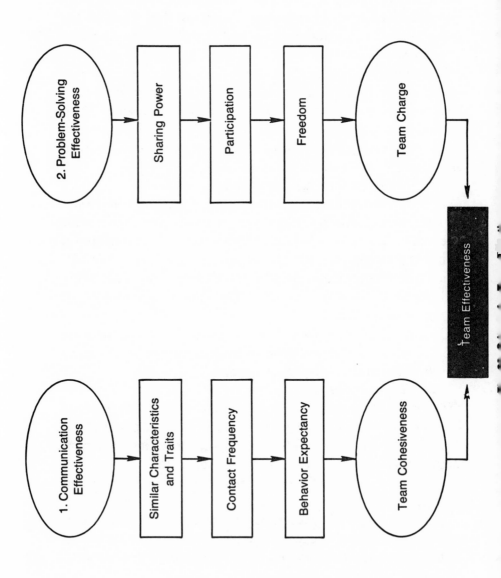

ing organizational objectives) goals of the team. The more satisfaction the team members achieve through performing their charge or purpose, the higher the problem-solving effectiveness. As a result of the team members' efforts in problem-solving opportunities, they receive intrinsic rewards for fulfilling their charge.

Problem-solving activities primarily result from three variables, each having the potential for increasing problem-solving effectiveness:

1. *Shared Power*

When employees are seen as managers and are given the opportunity to plan and control their work, they are more prone to solve job-related problems.

2. *Participation*

The involvement of members in change goes a long way in improving organizational effectiveness. When team members participate in change, they develop an ownership in the change process. The greater the participation, the higher the level of problem-solving.

3. *Freedom*

The more freedom given to team members, the more likely problems are to be resolved.

The key component of problem-solving effectiveness is team assignment. As team members identify with assignment or change, the greater the level of problem-solving effectiveness. The greater the amount of shared power, freedom, and participation, the greater the problem-solving effectiveness of the team.

Rewards received through problem-solving effectiveness are motivational in nature, involving self-esteem and self-actualization. As a result, personal, as well as organization objectives, are achieved.

Initially, team effectiveness is achieved through a dependent relationship between communication effectiveness and problem-solving effectiveness. Once achieved, however, the relationship gradually transcends from dependence to interdependence. With time, problem-solving effectiveness depends upon genuine and lasting communication effectiveness. Continued communication effectiveness is heavily dependent upon problem-solving effectiveness.

Influencing Positive Team Behavior

The supervisor is undoubtedly the most important factor in determining team effectiveness. Some basic principles of group dynamics the supervisor should know in order to influence positive team behavior:

- Encourage every team member to become involved in the team process.

- Refrain from dominating and don't permit team members to dominate team discussions.

- Enable team members to satisfy their personal goals while achieving team goals.

- Maximize strengths and minimize weaknesses of all team members.

- Work to obtain synergy.

- Avoid minimizing the importance of a person or reducing a person's value to the team.

- Remain alert and open to new ideas and suggestions and be willing to learn from individual team members.

- Recognize and reward team members for their participation.

- Create an advice-seeking attitude by probing and making certain the team member understands what will accrue to him or her for the advice.

- Face up to resistance by verbalizing it, avoid blaming someone, and identify why the opposition exists.

- Tell the whole truth.

- Reassure tense or nervous team members by having them vent and explore their true feelings.

- Establish high standards and expectations and act as a model to be emulated.

- Don't rush into solutions, probe instead of giving answers, and summarize team decisions.

TEAM BUILDING ACTIVITIES

The most desirable activities to help build an effective team are those that can be conducted as part of the routine process of teaming. The following represent some improvement activities that should be used by the supervisor to best meet the needs of the team:

Prepare a mission statement

Some interaction action and interplay during the process of developing a mission statement gives direction to the team and is an excellent way to begin to build effective teamwork. Have each member write his or her own version of a mission statement. Discuss each version, and then apply the consensus decision-making process to arrive at the team's mission statement.

Develop a code of conduct

A code of conduct is a list of behaviors and attitudes covering the actions, words, and deeds to which a team agrees. A Theory Z organization may define a set of behavior–or code of conduct–it expects from all its employees; it may identify their behavior as its organizational character, as operational guidelines, or policies and procedures. One of the first activities of a Quality Circle (see Chapter 16) is to define its code of conduct.

The same technique used to develop a mission statement can also be used to develop a code of conduct. Instead of using the common brainstorming method of producing a code, it may be better to use the nominal group process and to reach a consensus on the final mission.

Set goals

The mission statement should provide a basis for team members to interact for the purpose of influencing joint action and for arriving at a set of goals to accomplish its purposes. Each activity should afford the team members an opportunity to learn more about themselves and to understand each other better.

Receive and discuss job responsibility

Another activity that has provided team members a better understanding of other members and their job functions is the review and discussion of each person's job responsibilities. Each member should write a paragraph outlining his or her responsibilities and be prepared to discuss the salient features.

FACTORS THAT MAY AID OR IMPEDE TEAM BUILDING

For a team to become effective within the building process, team members must be aware of factors that can aid or impede their performance; each team member can then minimize the factors that impede performance and maximize those that will aid performance. Such factors are:

1.   Organizational Structure

The structure of the organization – its policies, procedures, systems, and program – will have either a positive or negative impact on team performance. If the procedure for communicating to team members is closed, team members' performance will suffer. If an adequate reward system is installed in the organization, teamwork will most likely be enhanced. Within the organizational environment there are other factors that may either aid or impede teamwork such as facilities, employees, services, materials, climate, managerial performance, etc. If a structure that is conducive to teamwork does not exist, it must be established to foster improved teamwork and for the overall improvement of the total organization.

2.   Team Charge

A team must have a purpose; without one there is no need to establish a team. It is critically important for the team to have goals and activities which are directed to achieve a given end. A general charge should be given to team members in writing and verbally, in order to clarify any misunderstandings. In addition, the psychology of ownership principle demands that members set their own goals and control how they are to be achieved. Finally, individual personal goals must take a back seat to group goals; only then will there be legitimate teamwork.

3.   Team Roles

When roles are clear within the team, less conflict will occur, issues can be solved more easily, and team meetings will operate more smoothly.

Maintenance needs are prerequisites for motivation. Without them, people become dissatisfied. Role definition is one such maintenance need that must be met if a team is to perform in an effective manner. Some questions related to team roles are:

1. Do we know the role of the supervisor, its members, and others?
2. How much power do we have to make a decision?
3. What issues or situations are we not allowed to address?
4. Does any role conflict?
5. What limitations are imposed on the team?
6. How are issues resolved when there is a conflict?

4. Teamwork Processes

Team members must know how to operate as a team, and must be trained in the ways of working together. If team members are expected to solve all problems via consensus, the full membership must be trained in the consensus process.

If the process is to operate effectively, team communication must be at its optimum level; team members must know what is to be communicated within the team, to whom, by whom, and how often. The work process must be achieved in a functional meeting which will hold the attention of its members. Dysfunctional meetings will lose the membership. To some degree, the team leader will be responsible for bringing this off. The leadership style of the supervisor will affect the team's communication, decision making, work processes, morale, and overall effectiveness.

5. Team Relationships

The quality of interaction among team members will, to a large degree, determine the degree to which the team will be effective in achieving its charge. Unless problems are brought out into the open and developed to a satisfactory resolution, the team will begin to experience diminished effectiveness. Improper behavior will affect attitudes, emotions, and feelings, and will eventually doom the team to prevent poor relationships from destroying a heavy communication network with each team always striving to improve interpersonal relationships between and among team members.

TRAINING REQUIREMENTS FOR TEAM BUILDING

The following chart depicts a minimum training program for building teamwork:

Subject Areas	*Rationale*
Conflict resolution Group dynamics	To enable participants to develop skills in resolving conflicts with individuals and groups to enable participants to communicate with others; confronting issues and working out difficulties.
Motivation	To provide participants with the skills and techniques for motivating others.
Time management Management by objectives (MBO)	To train participants how to make the best use of time; to teach them to plan and control activities to improve performance.
Consensus Decision making	To enable participants to resolve issues and difficulties in order to reach an agreement to solve problems; to assist participants to nurture a caring, intimate, and trusting relationship with others.
Unit Quality Circle Program	To train participants to effectively use a proven problem-solving process to solve job-related problems.

Assessing the Team Building Process

Whenever a team meets, the latter part of the meeting should be devoted to a self-assessment of the meeting. Questions that should be responded to are as follows:

1. What should the team member continue to do to perform well?
2. What should the team membership stop doing to perform well?

3. What should the team membership do differently to perform well?

Self-assessment helps foster conscious team building because it: 1) gives team members an opportunity to indicate what they like and dislike about individual members, and the group as a whole; 2) provides opportunities for team members who may disapprove a particular segment of the process an opportunity to be heard; 3) provides an opportunity to clarify issues and misunderstandings; 4) provides time for the team to suggest ways to improve the process; and 5) indicates to the membership that the process for working on individual group behavior to solve problems is a serious business.

ENSURING BALANCED PARTICIPATION

No team member should be left out of the meeting. In addition, no team member should be allowed to monopolize or dominate the meeting. The following represent some techniques for ensuring balance in meetings:
1. Rotate various tasks among the full team membership.
2. Use a circular table or desk to convene the meeting. In this way, there will appear to be no specific head at the team.
3. Use the round-robin process for obtaining input as indicated in the brain storming and the nominal group process.
4. Limit the time a team member can speak on an issue.

SOCIAL INTERACTION

Social interaction can occur during and after meetings. Some ways to provide for social interaction during the meeting:
1. Start the meeting about a half-hour early. Schedule the meeting for 7:00, but start official business at 7:30.
2. Introduce each new member to the entire team.
3. Have each member say something about himself or herself that would be of interest to the team.

BREAKS DURING THE MEETING

Allow time for breaks, tell a joke or an amusing incident, or enforce a rule that requires every member who says a certain word to put a certain sum, a dime or quarter, in a "kitty."

RECOGNIZING NEW MEMBERS

Although the membership of a team should not turn over with any degree of frequency, new members should be acknowledged. It is best to do this by following a set of formal procedures for making new members feel welcome and accepted by the membership. This is also an excellent opportunity to clarify what is expected of each team member. A member who leaves the team for one reason or another should also be acknowledged by the leader. When a member announces his or her departure, it is thoughtful for the leader to recognize what the member has provided to the team and to indicate some kind words if they are genuine.

SUMMARY

A team is a task-oriented combination of personnel who has the following in common: 1)   representatives of important sub-units of the organization; 2)   possess some degree of influence over each other; 3)   interact through a formal sub-structure; 4)   seek to achieve common goals. Team building is any planned activity and/or experience that helps to enhance the operational effectiveness of a functional team and improves its ability to resolve issues and conflicts as team members work toward the solution to a problem. The stages of team building are: 1)   individual awareness; 2)   team awareness; 3)   team organization; 4)   team operations; 5)   team success; and 6)   team maturation. The major components of team effectiveness are: 1)   communication effectiveness; and 2)   problem-solving effectiveness. Some activities that will aid team building include: 1)   preparing a mission statement; 2)   developing a code of conduct; 3)   setting goals; and 4)   receiving and discussing responsibility. Factors that may aid or impede team building consist of: 1)   organizational structure; 2)   team charge; 3)   team rules; 4)   team procedures; and 5)   team relationships.

19

Employee Inspirational Activities

BONUS INCENTIVES HAVE become very important to the success of Theory Z organizations. Japanese offer their employees a bonus of nearly half the annual salary. Excellent organizations implementing aspects of the Theory Z concept also offer their employees a wide variety of bonus incentives, but these are not the only means to inspire or motivate employees. Rewards, status, routine inspirational activities, recognition, celebrations, inspirational gatherings, management discussion sessions, and suggestion programs have all been used to good effect. Each of these activities and programs, properly implemented, can play an important part in demonstrating to employees that the organization cares for them, wants them to feel good about themselves, and wants them to like the organization as they perform their responsibilities and functions.

EMPLOYEE INSPIRATIONAL ACTIVITIES

Employee inspirational activities are actions initiated by management in an effort to recognize, stimulate, motivate, or reward the work force for any one or more of the following:
- to maintain or enhance loyalty
- to communicate its true feelings to top management
- to engage in social and recreational affairs
- to improve morale
- to get a sense of belonging
- to improve performance

Some readers may feel that inspirational activities are not too important for improving productivity or quality, but almost without exception, all Theory Z organizations think differently; they have initiated a host of actions designed to show to employees that they are important and are cared for by the company. In some organizations, these activities have become so important that millions of dollars have been spent to initiate them. Inspirational activities fall into some basic categories:[1]

Reward Inspirational Activities – when an employee's performance reaches or exceeds a given standard.

(a)   **Million Dollar Club**: when a salesperson's sales reaches one million dollars within a year, he or she is admitted to the Million Dollar Club.

(b)   **Golden Circle**: A person's sales is within the top ten percent of the salespersons. A quality circle saves one million dollars for the organization through its problem-solving efforts.

(c)   **One Hundred Percent Club**: A person is admitted to this club when his or her performance plan has been achieved at a one-hundred percent level.

Doyle Dane Bernback International, Inc. features a unique inspirational program which seems to want employees to remain with the organization. Annually, employees who have been with the company for ten years or more attend a luncheon and are awarded stocks. Those who have been with the company for ten years are given $100 in stock; 15 years, $150; 20 years, $200; and 25 years, $250.

When Reward Inspirational Activities are initiated, the employee usually gets his or her name listed among others, may receive a certificate, get his or her name printed with an appropriate designation or a plaque.

Status Inspirational Activities – are actions designed to upgrade the status of employees. The intent here is to improve egalitarianism by reducing the number of positions in the organization, thus reducing the various levels of power. It is not uncommon for a Theory Z organization to have only two position classifications such as technician and administrative. Here are some examples of position titles used to improve employee status:

1.   Technician
2.   Crew members

3. Support staff
4. Administrative
5. Partner
6. Associate.

Some Theory Z organizations refer to their employees as "the extended family" to emphasize the holistic relationship they have with its members.

Routine Inspirational Activities – are actions that involve all employees and occur on a daily basis.

(a) **Recitation of Credo**: All employees join in daily recitation of the organization credo.

(b) **Song**: All employees join for a daily session to sing the organization's song.

(c) **Physical Fitness Exercise**: All employees participate daily in performing certain exercises to keep them physically fit.

(d) **Breakfast Meeting**: All employees meet over breakfast together and discuss job-related matters.

Recognition Inspirational Acitvities – are actions that involve recognizing employees for participating in a social or recreational activity.

(a) **Intramural Sports.** All employees who participate in intramural sports receive a jacket, shirt, cap, or some other item denoting their membership. Usually, the best team or individual receives an award (medal, plaque or cup) that may or may not include a dinner. Activities are often tennis, racquetball, softball, track, bowling, etc.

(b) **Group activity.** All employees who participate in a group activity such as a quality circle, receive some title change, are awarded pens, buttons or badges; design their own logo, establish their own code of conduct, and have their own printed stationery.

(c) **Honor roll.**   Units that excel in performance are admitted to the honor roll or club. Individual employees usually receive either a pen or certificate.

Celebration Inspirational Activities – are actions initiated to honor employees.

(a) **Quality Circle Annual Conference.** Once a year, each quality circle gets an opportunity to present its most outstanding solution to a problem to its peers and their family members at an annual conference of quality circles. Each presentation lasts about five minutes.

(b) **Performance Outcome Conference.** At a designated day or time during the year, an annual conference is held, either for all managers and supervisors or all employees. Each unit head gives a brief description of his or her unit's performance, and indicates why performance was either on, below or above plan.

Inspirational Gathering Activities. Each year, all employees attend a family picnic, enjoying refreshments and a show given by employees. At times, these gatherings consist of superior-performing employees making motivational speeches to employees. These gatherings tend to be highly motivational and to some degree inspire employees to perform better.

Management Discussion Sessions – are informal meetings between employees and top management. Some activities are:

(a) **Ask Me Any Questions.** Meetings are usually attended by the chief executive officer and one or two of his or her senior staff. Employees are requested to ask any questions that are on their minds. Prior to the interaction, the chief executive officer requests employees not to criticize or laugh at any questions asked by an employee. If the chief executive officer is unable to answer the question, it is written down, the name of the person asking it, and the date. Each question is responded to, if not immediately, within a few days.

(b) **Talk Back to Boss.** These discussions tend to be gripe sessions; they are intended to give employees an opportunity to give the chief executive officer information on what they dislike about management or policies and procedures of the organization. Prior to the meeting the chief executive officer explains to management the rationale for the meeting. It is important for each manager to feel that they will not be punished or reprimanded for performing or not performing an act that is not in tune with its principles and practices. Managers are also told that they will get immediate feedback from the chief ex-

ecutive officer, that they will be requested to look into
the matter, and that they will be expected to remedy the
situation, if necessary.

Other titles used to describe these meetings between top
management and employees are "soul-searching meeting," "open
forum," and "bitching session."

Suggestion Program—A suggestion program is a formalized
procedure, established by management to solicit from employees
ideas for improving performance, productivity, or quality, and to
reward all suggestions accepted. These programs improve employee relations, provide suggestions from those closest to the
problem, provide an effective system for generating numerous ideas
for improving the organization, and ensure reward for those who
have ideas for improving the organization.

Some necessary factors to make certain the suggestion program
is successfully implemented:

(a) Top management must understand the advantages of a sug-
     gestion program and feel that there is a real need for it.
     The suggestion program must not be implemented in iso-
     lation, but must be an outgrowth of the philosophy and
     purpose of the organization.

(b) The expectations of the suggestion program should be
     delineated in a policy statement, and must be made clear
     to all employees. A committee should be organized con-
     sisting of a cross-section of employees to prepare the policy
     statement.

(c) There should be a clear distinction between the sugges-
     tion program and quality circle and bonus programs.

(d) Someone should be designated to oversee the program.

(e) The union should have endorsed the program, and should
     be represented on the policy committee.

(f) The immediate supervisor should be totally committed to
     the program through actions, words, and deeds.

TECHNIQUES FOR IMPLEMENTING A SUGGESTION PROGRAM

Although a suggestion program should be planned according to
the needs and requirements of a particular organization, some techniques will mean the difference between the success or failure of
the program:

1. Develop a comprehensive plan for implementing the suggestion program.
   a. Describe the person in charge of the program; cite all functions and responsibilities.
   b. Describe the composition and function of a policy committee.
   c. Give the contents of the policy statement.
   d. Show how the policy statement will be presented to employees.
   e. Show how the program will be launched and promoted.
   f. Show how suggestions will be accepted and rejected.

2. Identify how eligibility for rewards will be determined. This activity should answer who is eligible and ineligible for participating in the suggestion program.

3. Determine the procedure for entering suggestions; show how an individual or committee will accept and reject suggestions. Another related item that must be considered here involves deciding to use a suggestion box, suggestion committees, inspectors, suggestion secretaries, etc.

4. Determine the reward. Rewards for accepted suggestions usually start at ten percent of the savings from labor and materials that resulted from the suggestion. If suggestion "x" saved $20,000 in labor and $5,000 in materials, the total savings is $25,000; this would produce an incentive reward of $2,500 for the individual.

Kodak started its suggestion plan back in 1898; any employee whose suggestion saves the organization money is rewarded with a percentage of the savings. If the suggestion results in a new product, the employee receives the equal of 3 percent of the first-year sales of the product.

It is usual for an individual employee to receive a reward for an accepted suggestion. I suggest that organizations aspiring to implement Theory Z should offer individual and team rewards for accepted suggestions; this reinforces teamwork, and individuality. Although the reward for individuals is usually cash, this is not necessarily true for teams. Team reward may be a party, dinner, or some other benefit.

5. Devise a technique for handling rejected suggestions in a

humane manner. In some organizations, a policy exists for indicating the reason for each rejection.

6. Prepare a marketing strategy to promote the suggestion program on a continuous basis and to keep employees informed as to what suggestions were accepted, and what teams and individual received them.

7. Determine types of suggestions that will be considered for an award. Typical standards for rewards for suggestions which earn awards involve:

   a. improvement in quality of product.
   b. improvement of service to customers.
   c. improved storage, packing, or shipping.
   d. improvement in working conditions.
   e. increased cooperation.
   f. improvement in methods, techniques, and procedures.
   g. improvement in productivity.
   h. reduction or prevention of waste.
   i. reduction in defects and rejections.
   j. improvement of tools, machines or equipment.
   k. improvement in handling methods.
   l. reduction in time.
   m. reduction or elimination of unnecessary procedures, paperwork, materials, equipment, etc.

Bonus Incentive Program—is a sum of money, determined by formula or by some other method, awarded to an employee or group of employees after they have excelled in the conduct of their work. It is a reward for past effort and a motivation to future effort.

There are some secondary purposes:

1. Demonstrates a caring relationship between employees and management.
2. Helps improve morale.
3. Gives employees a feeling that they are important.
4. Gives employees a piece of the "action."
5. Helps foster egalitarianism.

Procedural Steps for Establishing a Bonus Incentive Program— Some steps that must be initiated by all programs:

1. Select someone to head a committee. Usually someone from top management is designated to be in charge of a committee to

oversee the development of the bonus incentive program. This person should be given a charge and deadline for inaugurating the plan. Certain other features of the program—size, composition, etc.—can also be given to the overseer.

2. Discuss the proposal with the union. If the organization has a collective bargaining agreement, the union must be brought in on the embryonic development of the program. Management and union officials should organize a committee to formulate the policy and procedural steps.

3. Organize a Committee. If a union is not affiliated with the organization, a committee of employees and management should be organized to work out the bonus incentive program.

4. Conduct Meetings to Formulate Policy and Plan. The chairperson should convene frequent meetings with the committee to develop an action plan for fulfilling its charge. At the initial meeting, the CEO should address the committee, cite its charge, and identify other particulars about the proposed bonus incentive program. Subsequent meetings should consider:

A. Formulation of a policy statement, which should contain a grand policy statement, the purpose of the program, and the procedural steps for determining and rewarding the bonus.

B. Construction of the Bonus Incentive Program, which is based on the policy statement, and should consist of:

i)   An analysis and background, where the reason for the program should be delineated, along with what the program is projected to do for the organization. Obviously, the purpose and philosophy of the organization should be the foundation for establishing a bonus incentive program. Some organizations present in this section the evaluation of the program by presenting an introduction and underlying facts and assumptions.

ii)   A determination of the type of bonus incentive plan. The commmittee will have to consider:

- —Growth in earnings
- —Top management discretion
- —Growth in sales
- —Straight profits
- —Return on equity
- —Return on sales

–Return on assets
–Return on investments
–Profit sharing (percentage)
–Gain sharing

When the committee has made a decision on the bonus factor, it should give some serious consideration to the following:

a) standards for judging performance
b) a starting or base point for matching performance or achievement (against goals, objectives, standards, plans, budget, or competition)
iii) a determination of the period for distributing bonus. The bonus can be rewarded either on a weekly, monthly, semi-annual, or annual basis. Consult with the employees; before the decision is made, one should discuss the advantages and disadvantages of each rewarding period. Consider the extent of the workload on those calculating and disbursing the bonus. A plan that dispenses bonuses on a weekly basis will require more work than one that is disbursed on a semi-annual or annual basis.

C. Preparation of an implementation plan, which details how to install the program:

i.) present proposed bonus incentive program to chief executive officer
ii.) receive approval for program from chief executive officer, with or without changes
iii.) distribute program to employee
iv.) clarify particulars about the program to employee
v.) discuss recommended changes; make as necessary
vi.) report changes to employees
vii.) distribute revised bonus incentive program to employee

D. Prepare a promotion program, which should include the printing and distribution of a booklet on the promotion, bonus awards, etc.

E. Develop an evaluation plan, which allows employees to determine their feelings about the program and how the program should be approved. Once the results of the evaluation have been assessed, they should be studied, a plan should be devised to improve it, and these improvements should be reported to the employees.

ADVANTAGES AND DISADVANTAGES
OF A BONUS INCENTIVE PROGRAM

The following appears to be the most important advantages and disadvantages of a bonus incentive program:

Advantages:

1. Employees have an opportunity to share in the profits of the organization.
2. Employees are actively involved, from the beginning to the evaluation.
3. Morale is enhanced.
4. Increased productivity and quality are more likely.

Disadvantages:

1. Sometimes its short range effects will have devastating impact on long-range results.
2. Sometimes the percentage of bonuses involves management only.
3. Individual bonus may impair morale in a Theory Z organization.
4. Bonus plans tend to be abandoned during hard times.

FACTORS THAT WILL IMPEDE THE
BONUS INCENTIVE PROGRAM

Some factors may impede the success of such a bonus program unless serious attention is given them:

1. The short range effect of awarding a bonus may establish a certain mind set in employees that may have some adverse effect on long-range bonuses.

2. In some organizations, only top-level management are offered bonuses.

3. The formula for determining the bonus must be easily grasped by employees or they will be participating in a process they don't understand and could quickly learn to resent.

4. Every employee should be told the starting point for determining bonus. Failure to do so will reduce the trust that should exist between employees and managers.

SUMMARY

Employee inspirational activities are actions initiated by management to stimulate, motivate, or reward employees. Reward inspirational activities occur when an employee's performance reach or exceed a given standard. Status inspirational activities are actions designed to upgrade the status of employees. Routine inspirational activities are actions that involve all employees; they occur daily. Recognition inspirational activities recognize employees for participating in a social or recreational activity. Celebration inspirational activities are initiated to honor employees. Management discussion sessions are activities that involve an informal meeting between employees and top management. Suggestion program is a formal procedure, established by management to solicit from employees ideas for improving performance, productivity or quality, and to reward those, if the suggestion is accepted. A bonus incentive is a sum of money that is determined by formula in a gain or profit-sharing plan that is rewarded to employees or group of employees as a means to motivate them to excell in the conduct of their work.

Notes

I have used short-form notations for all references in this section; a complete citation for each source appears in the bibliography. J.L. Jr.

Introduction
1. Mink, Shultz, and Mink, pp 9 - 13

Section One
1. Peters and Waterman, Jr.; Ouchi; and Pascale and Athos

Chapter 1
1. Ouchi, p. 10
2. Krathwohl, Bloom, and Masia, pp 63 - 175

Chapter 2
1. Mayeroff, pp 13 - 28
2. Mayeroff, pp 29 - 40

Chapter 3
1. Mink, pp 46 - 47
2. Rotter, pp 1 - 7

Chapter 5
1. Blakeslee, pp 3 - 19
2. Blakeslee, pp 49 - 51

Section Two

Chapter 6
1. Steiner, pp 153 - 155
2. Mink, pp 23 - 44
3. Van de Ven and Delbecq, pp 203 - 212

Chapter 7
1. Steiner, pp 155 - 161
2. Mink, pp 96 - 100
3. Ohmae, pp 42 - 49

Chapter 9
1. Ohmae, pp 100 - 109

Chapter 10
1. The substance of this chapter was based in part on Simon, Howe, and Kirschenbaum.

Section Three
Chapter 11
1. Nadler, pp 60 - 110

Chapter 12
1. Ouchi, pp 17 - 25

Chapter 13
1. Blanchard and Johnson, pp 25 - 35

Chapter 14
1. Terrs, p. 30
2. Avery, Aurine, Streibel, and Weiss, pp 11 - 14
3. Blanchard and Johnson, pp 25 - 35
4. Hopkins, pp –
5. Hopkins, pp 19 - 22

Chapter 16
1. "Problem-Solving Techniques for Management Circle and Quality Teams," AQC 1983 Annual Conference Transactions, International Association of Quality Circles, Memphis, Tennessee, pp 563 - 582
2. Delbecq and Van de Ven, pp 466 - 492

Chapter 18
1. Peters and Waterman, Jr., pp 235 - 278

Theory Z Glossary

CAREER PATH PROGRAM. A succession of preidentified on-the-job learning experiences involving a variety of multiple functions scheduled on a long-term basis that are geared to improve the employee's skills and worth to the organization.

CARING. A process of nurturing a social relationship between a manager and employee whereby either party is willing to share and/or sacrifice time, money, energy, and other resources so that both or either parties may grow and develop.

CERTIFIED QUALITY CIRCLE FACILITATOR. A person who has completed a minimum of five days or 40 hours of comprehensive training by a certified facilitator in the various phases of the quality circle concept and has passed an extensive examination.

CIRCLE LEADERS. Usually the immediate supervisor of a unit, trained in the quality circle concept to provide leadership for circle members to solve unit problems.

CIRCLE MEMBERS. Volunteers who perform basically the same type of work and generally report to the same supervisor, who are trained in the quality circle concept to solve job-related problems.

CODE OF CONDUCT. A list of behaviors to which all members of a team subscribe as a guide to thoughts, actions, words and deeds.

CONCENSUS. A decision-making process whereby members of a team (group) cooperatively arrive at a mutually acceptable decision which all participants agree to support.

CRITICAL ANALYSIS. An examination of the strengths/opportunities and weaknesses/problems of an organization accomplished to improve its performance.

CULTURE. An integrated pattern of human behavior that includes thought, speech, action, and artifacts that depend on managers and employees capacity for learning and transmitting acceptable on-the-job behavioral attitudes to succeeding generations of employees.

DIALOGUE SESSIONS. A discussion between two or more persons involving multiple topics.

EGALITARIANISM. A process that provides security, economic and social equality for all employees.

EXECUTIVE CIRCLE. A group of top managers (usually from four to six) organized by the CEO to help reach a decision which affects the total organization.

FILLEY'S CONSENSUS MODEL. A set of prerequisites and prescriptions for arriving at a consensus. The prerequisites provide reinforcement for the prescriptions.

FUNCTION STATEMENT. A broad descriptive statement indicating what a unit has to accomplish to meet its responsibilities.

GOAL SEEKER. A person who is always looking to improve conditions and is willing to risk almost anything to reach a goal. (See Maintenance seeker.)

HEAVY CONTACT ACTIVITIES. Any activity involving two or more persons requiring the consumption of a large amount of time and energy. (See Light contact activities.)

HUMANISTIC. Any program, process, system, thought, or action based on the nature, dignity, interests, welfare, and ideals of human beings in the work force.

HUMANISTIC COMPETENCIES. Behavioral and attitudinal skills that relate to the positive feelings of human beings.

INCULCATING THE PHILOSOPHY. The process of impressing upon employees the importance of certain macro-principle guidelines or expected behavior, attitudes, and parameters for the successful operation of the organization.

INTIMACY. The process by which managers establish a personal and earnest relationship with employees through the initiation of frequent social contacts, the nurturing of mutual trust, and the maintenance of security and good will.

INTUITION. The process of making a decision about people for some purpose relating to either ideas, work solutions, methods, materials, etc. that involve the evaluation of both quantitative and qualitative information, with more emphasis given to introspective and judgmental data concerning human beings.

JOB ROTATION. A formal plan for assigning employees to different functions in a variety of training activities across functions.

JOINT QUALITY CIRCLE. A temporary joining of two quality circles from different units to solve a problem peculiar to both circles.

LIGHT CONTACT ACTIVITIES. Any activity involving two or more persons that does not require a great deal of human energy, which usually lasts only for a few moments. (See Heavy contact activities.)

MAINTENANCE SEEKER. A person who is inclined to be satisfied with the status quo and is reluctant to risk his or her job. (See Goal seeker.)

MANAGEMENT. The process of getting things done through and with people.

MANAGEMENT CIRCLE. A circle consisting of managers of similar units that usually meet either to share information on the activities of quality circles or to solve Type 2 problems (which see).

MANAGEMENT PHILOSOPHY. A statement describing desirable and expected behavior and attitudes of managers in the pursuit of their job as builders of people.

MANAGEMENT PRESENTATION. The process by which a quality circle presents information pertaining to a problem and a recommended solution to one or more managers.

MANAGEMENT PRESENTEES. One or more managers who meet to receive a presentation on a problem and to render a decision on the solution.

MINITEAMS. Sub-groups of a quality team or management circle.

MISSION. A statement delineating the general purposes of an organization; it is designed to fulfill certain economic and social desires of people the organization serves and employs.

NO LAYOFF. A policy by which an organization hires permanent employees and guarantees them a job for life or until the age of retirement.

NOMINAL GROUP PROCESS. A structural method that allows maximum management involvement in making decisions through a controlled interaction process.

ORGANIZATIONAL AUDIT. A process by which a critical analysis of an organization is conducted by assessing its resources, identifying strengths, opportunities, weaknesses, and problems; recommendations follow.

ORGANIZATIONAL OBJECTIVES. A statement used to define broad, general, and long-term descriptive purposes of an organization, it provides definitive direction for management and employees, and serves as an instrument for interpreting human efforts.

ORGANIZATIONAL QUALITY CIRCLE. A participatory decision-making process that involves a large, heterogeneous number of employees and others in solving complex organizational problems.

PERFORMANCE EVALUATION. A critical assessment of work performed by a person, conducted formally or informally by an individual or group.

PROGRAM PLANNING PROCESS. A planning sequence that provides a systematic process of decision making at various levels of the organization to maximize input.

QUAKER CONSENSUS MODEL. A code of behavior governing the manner in which meetings should be conducted to provide a consensus on a major issue.

QUALITY CIRCLE UNIT. A group of three to eleven persons who are employed in similar units, committed to improving organizational effectiveness, voluntarily meet one day each week for about one hour to identify, analyze, and solve job-related problems in their area of responsibility; verify the solution, recommend it to management, and implement the solution when possible.

RESOURCE CIRCLE. A group of three to eleven members of the same composition as the resource group that is convened for the purpose of using the nominal group process.

RESOURCE GROUP. A carefully selected group of employees usually consisting of 55 to 110 people who volunteer to solve organizational problems.

RESPONSIBILITY CHART. A chart indicating the various units and sub-units within an organization, and a description of what each has to do to accomplish its purpose.

SERIOUS CONVERSATION. A discussion between two or more persons that covers one specific topic.

SHARED VALUES STATEMENT. A statement that identifies the basic and common beliefs top management and employees feel are desirable throughout the organization and in private life.

THEORY Z ORGANIZATIONAL PROPERTIES. A statement describing a set of features characterized as being Theory Z that are formulated in order to provide parameters, and to give direction and guidance to management in the operation of the organization.

TOP MANAGEMENT VALUES STATEMENT. The collective beliefs, feelings, and attitudes of top managers of the organization.

TRAINING. An organized activity designed to improve an employee's job performance and worth to the organization.

TRAINING STRAND. A continuum of training activities that are designed to prepare an employee to perform one or more specific functions.

TRUST. The anticipation that the behavior of a manager and employee will always be responsive and supportive to the benefit of both parties.

TYPE 1 PROBLEMS. Problems over which circle members have direct control and which relate exclusively to the individual unit of the quality circle.

TYPE 2 PROBLEMS. Problems over which circle members have limited or indirect control, and which require the influence of upper level management.

TYPE 3 PROBLEMS. Problems over which top management have direct control and which usually involve job content factors such as achievement, recognition, work, responsibility, advancement, and growth.

Bibliography

Auvine, Brian; Betsy Densmore; Mary Extron; Scott Paole; and Michel Shanklin. *A Manual for Group Facilitators*. Madison, Wisconsin: The Center for Conflict Resolution, 1978.
This rather inexpensive book will be found quite useful for first-line managers who work with teams. It provides almost everything necessary to facilitate the management of people in such areas as group dynamics, crisis intervention, and problem solving.

Avery, Michel; Brian Auvine, Barbara Streibel; and Lennie Weiss. *Building United Judgment: A Handbook for Consensus Decision Making*. Madison, Wisconsin: The Center for Conflict Resolution, 1981.
This is perhaps the most comprehensive book ever written on consensus decision making. Its thirteen chapters cover such topics as step-by-step process for arriving at a consensus, what to do if a consensus cannot be reached, what is the role of the facilitator and how to adapt the process for special situations.

Bartov, Glenn. *Decisions by Consensus*. Chicago: Progressive Publisher, 1978.
This small package of a book does an outstanding job explaining how the Mormons used consensus more than 300 years ago. It does a more-than-adequate job explaining the step-by-step process for arriving at decisions using consensus.

Bennett, Dudley. *TA and the Manager*. New York: AMACOM, 1976.
Explains how to apply transactional analysis to management. Emphasis is given to a systematic approach to understanding human behavior so that managers can improve their skill in dealing with employees.

Blakeslee, Thomas R. *The Right Brain: A New Understanding of the Unconscious Mind and its Creative Powers*. Garden City, N.Y.: Anchor Press/Doubleday, 1980.
The author, an engineer, explains how one section of the brain has gone neglected for years. Experiments are discussed to substantiate the author's claims. Suggestions are offered showing ways in which managers can learn to be better managers by becoming integrated thinkers.

Blanchard, Kenneth and Spencer Johnson. *The One Minute Manager*. New York: William Morrow and Co., Inc., 1982.
For years, too many managers have been maintaining that their tight schedule does not permit them to meet with their employees on a frequent basis. This obviously has had some negative consequences. The authors of this best seller suggest how managers can become more productive by applying the technique of one minute or more visitations, one minute of direction and guidance, and one minute of feedback.

Christopher, William F. *Management for the 1980's*. New York: AMACOM, 1980.
The author identifies principles and practices that will be expected of the managers during the 1980's. Although some obvious topics have been omitted, most readers should find it interesting to read and practice.

Cummings, Paul W. *Open Management: Guides to Successful Practice*. New York: AMACOM, 1980.
The author shows how managers can improve their management style using a non-manipulative approach. Conflicts, problem solving, performance approval, power and politics, self-development are only a few of the topics discussed.

Deal, Terrence E. and Allan A. Kennedy. *Corporate Cultures: The Rites and Rituals of Corporate Life*. Reading, Mass.: Addison-Wesley Publishing Co., 1982.
The author does an outstanding job explaining how values affect everything in an organization. Considerable attention is given to the ingredients that affect the culture and how they can be reworked to strengthen it. Some attention is also given to how the organizational culture of the future will be vastly different from the present.

Delbecq, Andre L., Andrew Van de Ven, and David H. Gustafson. *Group Techniques for Program Planning: A Guide to Nominal Group and Delphi Processes*. Glenview, Ill.: Scott Foresman and Co., 1975.
The authors of this book explained a modified brainstorming process that will enable managers to engage a large number of employees in solving complex organizational problems. Research is cited indicating that the nominal group process tends to be superior to brainstorming in several ways.

Drefack, Raymond. *Making It in Management: The Japanese Way*. Rockville Center, New York: Farnsworth Publishing Co., Inc., 1982.
An excellent sequel to Ouchi's book, Theory Z, this book illuminates the philosophy and various practices of Japanese management and shows what Americans can do to improve and surpass the success of the Japanese. Some of the points not covered by Ouchi are explained in this excellent book.

Feinberg, Mortimer R., Robert Tanofsky, and John J. Tarrant. *The New Psychology for Managing People*. Englewood Cliffs, N.J.: Prentice-Hall, Inc., 1978.
Although this book was written several years ago, its findings in behavioral psychology are applicable today. The research is analyzed and used as the basis for providing useful techniques for dealing with employees.

Gardner, James E. *Training the New Supervisor*. New York: AMACOM, 1980.
Offers managers suggestions for establishing an effective training program that will help improve quality and productivity.

Goldberg, Philip. *Intuitive Edge: Understanding and Developing Intuition*. Los Angeles: J.P. Tarcher, Inc., 1983.
Finally, an entire book on intuitive thinking. The author does an excellent job showing the reader how to recognize and take full advantage of the power of intuitive thinking. Not only are six major functions of intuition identified and explained, but the latest brain research findings and laboratory work illuminated.

Hughes, Charles L. *Goal Setting: Key to Individual and Organizational Effectiveness*. New York: American Management Association, 1965.
A classic book that covers the entire spectrum of goal setting. This author emphasized the human perspective of goal setting when it was not fashionable.

Ingle, Sud. *Quality Codes Master Guide*. Englewood Cliffs, N.J.: Prentice-Hall, Inc., 1982.
One of the first commercially produced books on the quality circle concept. The author covered most of the important points in order to establish a quality circle program, although additional reading is suggested, particularly in problem solving.

Iwata, Ryushi. *Japanese-Style Management: Its Foundations and Prospects*. Tokyo: Asian Productivity Oraganization, 1982.
The author presents a plethora of management techniques, some new, some old, to increase quality and productivity. Nine lessons are cited and explained to help American managers catch up and exceed the rate of quality and productivity being experienced by the Japanese.

Kelsey, Morton T. *Caring—How can We Love One Another*. New York: Pauleat Press, 1981.
This is an excellent source for readers who are interested in improving their capacity to care more. Some of the interesting chapters are on loving oneself, loving the enemy, and loving and listening.

Keyes, Ken, Jr. *Handbook to Higher Consciousness.* Marina del Rey, Cal.: De Vorss & Company, 1975.
This best selling book should be read by every manager who desires to improve his or her human experiences when dealing with people. The author identifies the three human addictions of security, sensation, and power, and identifies a systematic process for rising above them.

Knowles, Malcolm and Hulda. *Introduction to Group Dynamics.* Chicago: Association Press, 1972.
Basically a primer on the forces operating within human groups. It describes why people act in groups, what the research indicates, and how groups can be improved.

Krathwohl, David R., Benjamin S. Bloom, and Bertram B. Masia. *Toxonomy of Educational Objectives. The Classification of Educational Goals. Handbook II: Affective Domain.* New York: David McKay Co., Inc., 1956.
This book is a classic and is used in education circles to classify and explain the various levels of attitudes, known as the affective domain. It is useful for measuring attitudinal growth of a person before and after a training activity.

Leavitt, Harold J. *Managerial Psychology.* Chicago: The University of Chicago Press, 1964.
This book is heavy with the psychology of management. The author explains how managers can become more effective with employees by applying what has been learned through research.

Lee, Sang, M. *Management by Multiple Objectives: A Modern Management Approach.* New York: Petrocelli Books, Inc., 1981.
This book is an advancement of the MBO process. It should be read by those who have a working knowledge of MBO; the author demonstrates how mutually exclusive objections can be integrated with the goals of the organization.

Mayeroff, Milton. *On Caring.* New York: Harper & Row, 1971.
Probably one of the best little books on the subject of caring. The author presents several dimensions of caring which deserve special attention by the contemporary manager.

Mink, Oscar G., James M. Shultz, and Barbara P. Mink. *Developing and Managing Open Organizations.* Austin, TX: Learning Concepts, 1979.
This book could well have been entitled Theory Z Organizations. The authors describe the essential elements of an open organization, cite how to develop and manage one, and elaborate on the action steps for evaluating the "openess" of an organization.

Myers, M. Scott. *Every Employee a Manager*. New York: McGraw-Hill, 1981.
M. Scott Myers wrote the first edition of this book in the 1960's, well
before Theory Z was created. The reader will find that many of the principles detailed in 185 pages are connected with what was found in both
Theory Z and excellent organizations. It would be worth the efforts of
managers to capture the principles expounded by the author and to integrate them into a management philosophy and style.

Nadler, Leonard. *Developing Human Resources*. Austin, TX: Learning Concepts,
1970.
This book should be read by every trainer. Although Section I acts as
a background to trace the progress of training in organization, Section
II and III get more to the point and explain methodologies and the role
of the trainer.

Ohmae, Kerrichi. *The Mind of the Strategist*. New York: McGraw-Hill, 1982.
One of the best books on strategic thinking available today; Ohmae
presents creative techniques for making strategic decisions, describes various step-by-step techniques for using strategic thinking in the work environment, and provides concrete examples to illustrate his points. At
the close of the book, the author dispels some myths about Japanese
management.

Ouchi, William. *Theory Z: How American Businesses Can Meet the Japanese
Challenge*. Reading, Mass.: Addison-Wesley Publishing Co., 1981.
The author of this best seller actually invented the Theory Z management approaches. He compares Japanese and American management
styles. The similarity between excellent organizations in the United States
and Theory Z organizations in Japan are also discussed.

Pascale, Richard T. and Anthony G. Athos. *The Art of Japanese Management:
Applications for American Executives*. New York: Simon and Schuster, 1981.
The authors of this best seller explain the hard S's of management as
being structure, systems, strategy, and make a case for blending them
with the soft S's of style, staff; skills and superordinate goals in order
to produce a more productive organization.

QC Circle Headquarters, *QC Circle Koryo — General Principles of the QC Circle*.
San Jose, CA: QC Circle Headquarters, 1980.
Considered by many to be the bible, this was written by the father of
quality control circles. It has a wealth of essential information that is
designed to assist any organization to establish a quality circle process.

Quick, Thomas L. *Person-to-Person Management*. New York: St. Martin's Press,
1977.
Gives some practical day-to-day advice on how a manager can manage
more effectively. It is highly informative and offers some invaluable hints
that many managers will find useful.

Randolph, Robert M. *Planagement — Moving Concept into Reality*. New York: AMACO, 1974.
In this interesting book, the author creates a new management approach that describes how to integrate planning with managing. Emphasis is directed to the individual manager as a planning/management center.

Schonberger, Richard J. *Japanese Manufacturers Techniques: Nine Hidden Lessons in Simplicity*. N.Y.: The Free Press, 1982.
The author identifies what American managers can learn from the Japanese to surpass them in quality and productivity. It should be read if only to reinforce the reader's knowledge about the Japanese way of managing the work environment.

Short, James H. *Working in Teams: Practical Manual for Improving Work Groups*. New York: AMACOM, 1981.
This book is an excellent source for improving managers' ability to work with teams. It is practical and provides a wealth of how to apply the knowledge gained through research to improve teams effectiveness.

Steiner, George A. *Strategies Planning: What Every Manager Must Know*. New York: The Free Press, 1979.
An excellent introduction to the major elements of strategic thinking and planning. Particular attention should be given the chapter on the mission of an organization, which will help the reader formulate a complete statement of philosophy. (Quite often many organizations define its mission only to omit an essential item.)

Peters, Thomas J. and Robert H. Waterman. *In Search of Excellence: Lessons from America's Best Run Companies*. New York: Harper & Row, 1982.
Once the reader gets through the theory section of this classic, he or she will be introduced to eight characteristics that separate excellent from not-so-excellent organizations. Many of these characteristics were found in highly successful Theory Z organizations. A key observation in this book is that many not-so-excellent organizations in America do not have a support system to encourage employees to take risk and create.

Index